no DEPRESSION

no DEPRESSION

AN INTRODUCTION TO ALTERNATIVE COUNTRY MUSIC.
WHATEVER THAT IS.

edited by Grant Alden and Peter Blackstock

 DOWLING PRESS NASHVILLE, TENNESSEE

Contents

Preface

Alternative country, whatever that is. No matter how we've tinkered with the slogan that appears below the logo on the cover of *No Depression* magazine, the gentle sarcasm with which the phrase "alternative country" was first chosen seems rarely to have translated.

We started the magazine in our Seattle homes, at the trailing edge of the grunge years. From this distance it is hard to imagine what we were thinking, what we expected, why exactly we started *No Depression*—except, perhaps, that our instincts and love of the music got ahead of the native caution that stifles most such dreams.

Yet there we were, way too late one night in August, 1995, in the studio of legendary graphic designer Art Chantry, pasting down columns of text run out on a word processing program at Kinko's. We stopped work just long enough to see the Bottle Rockets play down the road at the Tractor Tavern. Juggling work and play has been a constant state of affairs ever since, frequently during the rush to deadline.

Anyway, we printed 2,000 copies of that first, 32-page issue with Son Volt on the cover, promised to come out quarterly, and were astonished when the thing sold out. As 1998 begins, we're a bimonthly with 96 pages or more, printing 13,000 copies. And Vol. 1, No. 1 is a collector's item.

We don't visit Kinko's much anymore, but the magazine still comes out of our homes (one now in Nashville and one still in Seattle, plus a third front in the Seattle basement of our business partner Kyla Fairchild, without whom this growth would have been unimaginable). It's an ongoing parade of electrons via phone, e-mail and computer screen, the stereo going pretty much constantly.

The stereo's the important part there. Past the "alternative country" tag (a phrase Grant first heard from Bev Chinn, who was then managing the San Francisco band Tarnation), we have fought hard not to define the music we write about six times each year. And it really is about the music.

Both the music and the magazine have received attention disproportionate to their commercial impact. We like to think that's because the music we're writing about truly is compelling, and the magazine's not half-bad. In any event, it's that national attention which prompts this anthology and not, we hope, an advanced case of hubris. The phrase "No Depression" is now tossed around by many of the same hands that dealt "grunge" when we started the magazine. This book, and the magazine we still lovingly labor to produce, are as much definition as we're prepared to offer.

The book is intended as a primer, as an introduction to permutations of traditional American music for which there is no radio format (Americana comes closest), almost no television coverage and modest distribution. And yet the musicians persevere, writing amazing songs and touring clubs across the country to slowly increasing crowds.

We have tried to select a cross-section of articles, mindful of space limitations. The frustration, of course, is that there are dozens of articles not yet written (and at least a dozen more already written that just wouldn't fit), so any such anthology is inevitably incomplete. Nevertheless, our intent was to strike a balance that is representative both of the music and of the magazine. The book begins with a conversation between Waylon Jennings and Billy Joe Shaver and concludes with a Charlie Louvin interview. In between, you will discover an assortment of artists who are either too old, too loud or too eccentric for country radio. Out there in the margins, that's where some of the most rewarding music is to be found.

Authors have been encouraged to correct the odd error of fact or grammar, and we have added a selected discography to each article (excluding greatest hits, titles out of print, and random promotional collector-geek releases), but otherwise the essays are pretty much as they first appeared.

That's our story.

It wouldn't have been possible without the musicians and our many talented contributors. It also wouldn't have been possible without the help of early supporters, including Art Chantry, Debbie Dodd, Rick Gershon, Mary Schuh, and Jenni Sperandeo. Finally, this book wouldn't be possible but for the enormous patience and understanding of Susan Thomas and Maryglenn Jordan from Dowling Press.

—Grant Alden and Peter Blackstock

P.S. Oh, yeah. About that magazine. We're delighted that you bought this book, or at least picked it up off the shelf. *No Depression* is available in its bimonthly magazine form on newsstands everywhere. However, for a mere $18 a year we are able to induce an official United States Postal Service employee to deliver it to your door. Assuming you live in the U.S. Rates are higher abroad. Sample copies (again, within the U.S.) are $5. Make checks payable to *No Depression*, and send 'em to P.O. Box 31332, Seattle, WA 98103. Thanks.

Waylon Jennings and Billy Joe Shaver

by Grant Alden

Billy Joe Shaver is trying to keep to the shade, but there isn't much, just a patch of trees, some trucks, and a big red sun. He's shoulder to ankle in worn blue denim, and his face is sun-scarlet under a well-bent white hat. Every once in a while he runs out of words to pass the time and reaches into the cab of his dusty van for another slug of Gatorade. And he's tired, though he's too proud to show it and too polite to say anything. He's been working since 8 A.M., starting the day shooting a video and taking the stage again in mid-afternoon for a fast four-song set.

And, yes, we are in Luckenbach, Texas, with Willie and Waylon and the boys.

On this windless, 100-degree day, Willie Nelson is a gracious host to 11,000 fans (and several hundred more backstage) for his annual Fourth of July picnic. He sits in with his guests off and on all day long, as always, then closes the show in the not-quite-cool evening air with a largely impromptu set including his old friend, Waylon Jennings.

The party is also an annual reunion of sorts for veterans of the storied '70s outlaw country movement, a lingering reminder that the life of that party came from Austin, which rests about an hour and a half east of here. And Luckenbach—with a population of twenty-five, the smallest of several Central Texas towns that has hosted Willie's Picnic over the years—isn't the only place the outlaws have been reunited lately. Houston-based Justice Records recently released Shaver's new album, *Highway of Life*, as well as Waylon's latest, *Right For the Time* (not to mention a new Kris Kristofferson disc). And Willie himself only just left the Justice stable to release the beautifully pacific *Spirit* on Island.

That, at fifty-five, Shaver is working to promote only his ninth long player says much for the unfairness of things. So does the fact that his first six LPs were then out of print, recently anthologized in a one-disc set by Razor & Tie, and in a two-disc set by German label Bear Family.

Maybe Billy Joe wouldn't be here without Waylon; maybe he'd be just another idiosyncratic songwriter who got a few cuts in Nashville. Just another idiosyncratic songwriter? No, that's not quite right. He was and is that rarest of talents, an utterly distinctive, impeccably honest writer of songs. It was Bobby Bare who first gave Shaver a songwriting contract, and Kristofferson and Tom T. Hall both had hits with his songs (hell, even Elvis recorded one). But it was Waylon's almost-all-Shaver-penned *Honky Tonk Heroes* that solidified his reputation.

Now that last is a bad sentence, because the grammar leaves open the question as to whose reputation was solidified. But we'll leave it like that, because there are those who argue *Honky Tonk Heroes* was the first outlaw country record, and it's hard to imagine Willie and Waylon and the boys wouldn't need last names without it.

Not that Waylon was an unknown in the early '70s. He'd come out of Lubbock as one of Buddy Holly's Crickets (the second incarnation), and gave up his seat on that ill-fated plane to the Big Bopper. Though he strung together a series of Top-10 hits in Nashville in the '60s, Waylon and the Music Row establishment ultimately didn't get along, and the rest is a pile of gold records.

When Waylon's tour bus materializes, it is blissfully air-conditioned. Shaver takes a welcome seat and, despite their years together, is bashful. By any useful artistic measure, the two men are equals, but you can't eat those measuring cups, so his deference is, perhaps, understandable. Besides, despite all the stories, Shaver is a shy fellow. And so for twenty-five minutes, with Waylon's grandson watching from the floor, two old friends got to play catch-up.

Waylon Jennings: What are you interested in, then? We don't really like each other.
Billy Joe Shaver: That's true.
No Depression: Well, you almost came to blows…

Billy Joe: We've done that a lot (*laughs*). I've heard things cocked behind my head.

ND: But you never pulled it.

Waylon: Nah. Tell you about that. You know what? I was strung out, and I was finishing one album, but I done told him, "Don't let nobody else get them songs." Well, hell, you know, when you first come to town and somebody tells you something like that, anybody that does, they should explain everything to you. After you've been there a while, you understand how those things work. Hell, here I am in the studio, singing songs but they ain't his. So he decided to tell me, he says, "If you're going t' do an album," he says, "You told me you was gonna do m' goddamn songs, now are you goin' do 'em or am I gonna have to whip your ass?" (*laughs*) Then later…

Billy Joe: I didn't know no better.

Waylon: Well, that's the way you do it, you know. You got my attention. (*laughs*) And so it still was a while, but when you did get in the studio, I'm recording there and I've got laryngitis right in the middle of it. Well, I've got coke-itis. You know. So Billy Joe comes in there, and I have this deal that I figured out on this one song.

Billy Joe: This is the trick.

Waylon: What I had done was, he had a song that was the same tempo all the way through, and I had it where I did it halfway through, I put it into gear, and did it real fast. And that was "Honky Tonk Heroes."

Billy Joe: That was true, yeah.

Waylon: Well, he didn't write it that way.

Billy Joe: Uh-uh.

Waylon: And I didn't have enough sense to ask him, before I did the track. So Billy come in, he said, "Whatcha doin' to my goddamn song?" (*laughs*) Now, here's a guy, you know, I was pretty hot then.

Billy Joe: You know what? I can't believe I did that, 'cause if I'd'a known, it scares me to death. Everybody in town was givin' me such an honor, to be in the position I was in, and I just got out there and I was raisin' hell about it. (*laughs*)

Waylon: I was wrong, 'cause I had not asked him, first. Because you know what? They're like your little babies, when you write songs. And to this day…the other day somebody sent me a new demo with a song of mine, it took me a couple of times listening to it before I didn't want to go over and whup his butt. So I understand. I couldn't show him what I was going to do 'cause of the laryngitis. I said, "When I get through with it, if you listen to it and you don't like it, I'll do it the other way." That's where all that came down.

Billy Joe: I liked it, though. I liked it. I acted like I didn't, but I liked it better that way. But I couldn't do it that way. I didn't know how to do that, back then.

Waylon: Actually, the way that happened is, we'd been doing it so long the other way and it wasn't coming together, and I tell you who give me the idea. What was the guitar player on there? Randy Scruggs.

Billy Joe: Randy Scruggs, yeah.

Waylon: Randy got to doing it t'other way, and he stopped and started just doodling.

Billy Joe: Yeah.

Waylon: And I thought, hmm. Maybe that's what I need to do. Because I was losing it on the second half.

Billy Joe: Oh it made it, it made the song, yeah.

Waylon: For me, yeah.

Billy Joe: I've gotta admit one thing, too. On "Ain't No God in Mexico," there was some stuff—you were real high, man—and you wrote some of that and I didn't give it to you.

Waylon: I don't remember that. (*chuckles*) OK, we're even.

Billy Joe: Well, that's all right, ain't never been a hit, so what the hell was the difference? (*laughs*)

Waylon: (*sings*) "Me and Louise Higenbothem." That was great.

Billy Joe: You know where I came up with that?

Waylon: No, that's what knocked me out. 'Cause I knew a girl named Higenbothem, they were neighbors of mine. They had the Higenbothem Lumber Company.

Billy Joe: Oh, yeah? Her father was a policeman of some sort.

Waylon: (*disappointed*) Uhhh. Oh, was he?

ND: Which would have been why her name stuck in your mind?

Billy Joe: Yeah, yeah. Well.

Waylon: Mighta been.

Billy Joe: Might have been.

Waylon: We get along good.

Billy Joe: Yeah, we wrote one song Elvis recorded.

Waylon: In the dark.

Billy Joe: Yeah, it was in the dark. In about five minutes. "Just Because You Asked Me To."

Waylon: Me and him, you know, the reason I treat him so polite is because we're the same kind. And if I do something he don't like, he'll come get me, get mad as hell at me, and I'm the same way with him. Ah, but that's the way it's supposed to be, anyway.

Billy Joe: That's the way it oughta be. (*Stands up to shake hands.*) Love ya.

Waylon: Love ya, too.

ND: Have you two toured together?

Waylon: Oh, yeah. Australia, you know…

Billy Joe: (*laughs*) And you know how Waylon is about airplanes? There was that little prop job come up 'side the building, and Waylon said, "Oh, no, we're not going on that," and they shuttled us over to the big plane. Of course, he was upset already. We're going up the stairs, and I'm right behind him, and I started singing (*sings*) "Chantilly Lace…" (*laughs*) And he starts, "I'm going to kill you, I'm going to kill you."

Waylon: (*laughing*) You did that. The tour before—actually, the tour ran through New Zealand—and we was goin' to fly on down to Christchurch, there in New Zealand.

Billy Joe: I didn't go on that deal, no.

Waylon: Well, we're out on the runway, fixin' to take off in this big plane, 747. Take off down the runway, and Montovani's playing. And they pull down there and then stopped. Just shut that sumbitch down. And they backed up, turned it around this way and come back up there, and then they turned it around like they was goin' go up again, and Buddy Holly started singing "Peggy Sue." And so Kris Kristofferson, and John Cash, and all of 'em looked at me. And I says, "We ain't goin' on this sumbitch." So we made 'em take us back to the gate and got us another airplane.

Billy Joe: That's smart.

Waylon: It's crazy, go from Montovani to Buddy Holly. Not a chance. I still don't like airplanes.

Billy Joe: Yeah, it does put you plumb out of control.

Waylon: And I'm a control freak, really, about my family, and the people around me.

Billy Joe: You know what you get to do? You get to say "Tha-tha-tha that's all, folks." (*laughter*) That's on your new album.

Waylon: Oh that's that new one, yeah.

Billy Joe: I love that. Of course I still love that song about the guy who said, "If I'd'a killed her I'd be out by now."

Waylon: "I coulda killed her and I'd'a been out of jail by now." You know what? That was about a guy, he was playing golf, really. But Tony Joe White, Tony come home and told me about it.

Billy Joe: You mean that's for real, then?

Waylon: Yeah. And then I got thinkin' about it, and he's right, man. (*laughter*) Kill somebody and in eight years your butt's free.

Billy Joe: Yeah, yeah.

ND: You've both made, to my ear, comparatively peaceful records.

Billy Joe: (*reluctantly*) Yeah.

Waylon: (*puzzled*) What…

Billy Joe: This last record I made, I made one just recently, it's pretty peaceful, yeah. His is, too. Yours is laid back, pretty much. A lot of acoustic stuff. Mine is, too.

ND: Well, I meant more that you sounded more peaceful as people.

Waylon: If you really believe that, it's your first mistake. (*laughs*) I think we are, hell.

Billy Joe: Yeah, I do, too.

Waylon: 'Cause, you know…we had little reasons to not be very peaceful. Record companies…

Billy Joe: Yeah, that's true.

ND: Has that changed that much over the years? The mythology to my generation is that you two changed not just country music, but the whole business in some ways, by taking things under your control.

Billy Joe: I didn't do anything. I just met this man and he did the songs I wrote, and then that did it for me. I wrote some songs, that's it. Waylon's the man. I remember when RCA and them guys would come down there, just giving you hell. Saying "This ain't goin' sell, this ain't goin' sell," and going through all that crap. I remember that. Jeez, I stayed out of the way but it was a tough time.

Waylon: It was, you know. But you know what happened to 'em, is they actually beat themselves. They tried to destroy what we were doing, and that music was the big part. There wasn't no way they could destroy it, and they didn't know that. When we came to town, you had to use their studios, you had to use their songs, you had to record four songs in three hours, and, if you had a great song and it wasn't happening, you didn't say, "Well, let's just do three." No, whatever you got in that little length of time was what you had to live with. And that was no good. That was like cuttin' cookies. Me singing with the Nashville sound was like putting honey on chocolate cake. It was just syrupy; it just didn't work. And I didn't want to cause no trouble, because when you get there you think they ain't goin' let you sing.

Billy Joe: That's true. That is true.

Waylon: They did. The thing about it, it was people who had gone to college and got a four-year degree in marketing, and they wanted to come and tell you they knew more about your music than you did. Now the bad part is, we didn't know what the hell we were doing! (*laughs*) And they thought they knew more about it. They really did.

Billy Joe: They honestly did.

Waylon: And you know what? And I never realized what they was up to. Even when I started selling millions of records, they would still stop my album somewhere and say, "We don't like it." And of course I would say "Blow it out your…somethin' and I don't care; I don't have to please you." But what they did is, it became a matter of record that they had something to do with that album by stopping it. That's job security. "What albums was he involved in?" You know? We had a big meeting one time in New York, and I said, "You know what your problem is? I know your problems. You know what you can't do, but you ain't got a clue about what you can do." And that's the way it was. I got the best story on Billy Joe.

Billy Joe: What's that?

Waylon: Well, Billy Joe had written one of the greatest songs I've ever heard in my life, called "Oklahoma Wind." Well, there's a line in there, about this Indian guy, and it says, "He lay dying in a woman's wing." And I thought, man, a woman holding this man while he's dying. What a great deal. And so, I told Billy Joe, I said, "My favorite lines in the world is 'The Oklahoma Kid lay dying/In the woman's wing.'" And he says, "Yeah, it is good." But he says, "But you know, we went over to see him, and that place was so damn filled up and had so many people in it, they had to put him over in this woman's wing in the hospital." (*Slaps his forehead to general laughter.*) I said, "I hate you!"

Billy Joe: Waylon did "Old Five and Dimers," and he said, "Yeah, Billy, I feel bad about owning this Cadillac." I said, "Well Waylon, give it to me!" (*laughter*) That cleared it up real good. (*laughs*)

Waylon: That old thing. That old lead-lookin' thing.

Billy Joe: Remember that old Cadillac you had?

Waylon: The orange one?

Billy Joe: Yeah, that orange lookin' thing.

Waylon: Yeah, I painted all of it black. Including the license plates. I've still got that.

Billy Joe: Do you really?

Waylon: Yeah, in the warehouse. I need to get it out. That's the best car I ever had. I used to jump curbs...

Billy Joe: I know, I've seen you. Whiskey bumps all over it.

Waylon: (*snorts*) Ha! Whiskey bumps?

Billy Joe: All over the damn thing.

Waylon: Now, you may hear that again, but you won't get no credit.

Billy Joe: That'd be all right. You can get me back for...

Waylon: Whiskey bumps, I love that.

Billy Joe: Oh, go right ahead. Naw, I done stole a buncha shit from him he don't know about.

ND: Do you think you changed Nashville in the end, or has it gone back to exactly the way it was before?

Waylon: It's almost back to the same. It is for people who let it be. One thing about it now, you can get all the freedom that you demand. But these new guys, I feel sorry for 'em, because they're even told what hat to wear. One of them guys, a pretty tough kid—looked like he might be a little scrapper—I said, "Where'd you get that goddamn hat?" He said, "Well, my manager and the record company made me get this one." I said, "They made you do that?" I said, "I don't think I'd let 'em do that."

Billy Joe: I tell you, whoever's selling them hats is making a *killing*.

Waylon: Yeah, ain't that the truth.

ND: Is country music now just going to be another form of pop music, or is this just a phase?

Waylon: You can't kill something that's right, that's good. You know what I mean? But I have said it, and I'll say it again, I don't want to be remembered from this era. The way they choose things now, is they go up there and say, "Can you dance to it?" And then they say, "Can you make a video about it?" And down here about third place they say, "Is it a good song?" The song always made what we did. And we knew. I wrote things that people didn't understand 'til I did it. But now, they'll record anything. And they're told what to do. And some things, they get a good hook line.

Every song he ever wrote, and I tried to have it in every one I wrote, had the title and the melody and equally important was that hook line.

Billy Joe: Throw-away line. We called it the throw-away line.

Waylon: Yup, yeah.

Billy Joe: "Too much ain't enough" or something like that. We used to actually call it a throw-away line.

Waylon: (*laughing*) I used that twice in my new album.

Billy Joe: Did you?

Waylon: I said, "Billy goin' kill me."

Billy Joe: You know, I thought I heard something familiar there.

Waylon: Oh, yeah. Both times. And, hey, I didn't realize I put 'em both in that damn thing.

Billy Joe: I went to sleep on it a couple times, but I'm not real sure… (*laughs*) I'm just kidding you.

Waylon: Life ain't easy around him.

Billy Joe: I know it ain't. It sure ain't.

ND: Do you regret the wild days at all?

Waylon: Shit no. I wouldn't want to try to live through 'em again.

Billy Joe: Oh, I tell you what.

Waylon: But I wouldn't take for a minute of it. You know what? They were dead wrong in Nashville, in the music business. They were robbing us, and they still do. They're thieves.

Billy Joe: Well, the art is really suffering now. I feel that. Over in Europe they seem to hang in there with the artists.

Waylon: They know all about it. They know who wrote it.

Billy Joe: The machine they got goin' now's got different kind of cogs in it. And if we come back around, with this simple stuff—it's not really simple—simplicities don't need to be greased, I think. And it just don't fit in what they're doing, and that's why it's a little bit hard for 'em to accept. I understand all of it, but it don't change the way I write songs. And I probably won't get very many recorded today (*laughs*), especially after you saying all those bad things you did about me. (*laughs*)

Waylon: I don't care, because, you know I don't want to do that kind of song; I won't do that kind of record, and I feel sorry for the artists. But there's two or three of 'em can't sing, and they have to use these little note-benders to bring their voice up. They do a thing called "comping," where you do five different versions, and they'll take one word outta here, and a half-word out here and all this stuff. It's pitiful.

Billy Joe: But the live performance, you get to really see how that is. (*laughs*)

Waylon: You've got to face the music, yeah.

Billy Joe: They don't let 'em lip-sync much anymore. I was out here doing that this morning. Out here doing a video, lip-syncing.

Waylon: Was you? That never ceases to embarrass me.

Billy Joe: I did lip-sync, and I done it good, too.

ND: Was that your first time?

Billy Joe: Yeah. I was singing. I was trying to get over that monitor. I was singing louder than the thing.

Waylon: Well you've gotta sing it. Or it ain't goin' work.

Billy Joe: Yeah, it's different for me. It's new for me.

Waylon: I've never liked that. I keep thinking of Lawrence Welk.

Billy Joe: (*laughing*) And the little bubbles?

ND: Does it aggravate both of you that, after all the songs you've written and sung, all the records you've sold, that it's now a lot harder to get played on country radio?

Billy Joe: You know, I never had it. So I don't miss it. But Waylon…

Waylon: I don't see what age has to do with it.

Billy Joe: …it just kind of upsets me. It seems like it's against the law to do stuff like that.

Waylon: If they said to me, said, "Waylon, you could be big, selling millions of records, or you could be the biggest star in country music," I'd say no. I'd say no, really. I wouldn't want to mess with it anymore. You know what I like? I like 2,000 people. When they listen, they listen to my songs. I'm really not crazy about this [Willie's picnic]. I just did Lollapalooza, and I'll tell you what: that's one of the best audiences I've ever played to. Even all the wild stuff that goes on with it. Because you know what? You can look in their faces. And see. And I never saw a mean-lookin' face there. (*Someone enters the bus to remind Waylon he has a show to do.*) I'm going to have to figure out what I'm going to do here.

Billy Joe: Man, I really want to thank you for letting me come in here and talk with you.

Waylon: What are you talking about? Sit down. Just give me your money, don't be giving me your goddamn thanks.

Billy Joe: I got no damn money. I ain't got no money.

Waylon: (*mimics*) "Ain't got no money." (*leans into the mike, quiet*) Some of us has got a hit. [Patti Loveless is running Shaver's "When the Fallen Angels Fly" up the charts.]

Billy Joe: No, I hasn't either. IRS got it.

Waylon: Oh, IRS. Yeah, that's what Willie said, too. He kept whining about that, till here come all these people, bought all that shit and give it back to him. (*laughs*) I tell you what happened. I tell you how he got out of it. He told on all of us.

Billy Joe: (*serious*) He *did*?

Waylon: Yes. You wanta kill him first, or you want me to? I'll kill him and you can break his legs.

Billy Joe: I can't kill him, didn't bring any silver bullets. And I ain't even real sure I might even have to have some stakes. (*laughs*)

"Tall Tales, Tiny Towns, and Texans" first appeared in *No Depression* #5 (September–October 1996).

Selected Discography

Billy Joe Shaver, *Old Five and Dimers Like Me* (Monument) 1973, reissued (Koch International) 1996.

Shaver, *Tramp On Your Street* (Praxis/Zoo) 1993.

Waylon Jennings, *Clovis to Phoenix: The Early Years* (Zu Zazz) 1995.

Waylon Jennings, *Hangin' Tough* (MCA Special Projects) 1995.

Shaver, *Unshaven: Shaver Live at Smith's Olde Bar* (Zoo/Praxis/BMG) 1995.

Shaver, *Highway of Life* (Justice) 1996.

Waylon Jennings, *Right for the Time* (Justice) 1996.

Mickey Newbury

by Kurt Wolff

It's a cloudy January afternoon when I first get Mickey Newbury on the phone. "How's the weather down there?" he asks. I'm in San Francisco, he's in Oregon, and we're both patiently awaiting what excitable weather reporters have predicted to be another massive rainstorm.

It's ironic, though, that the first thing we talk about is rain, because it's something that anyone who spends time with Newbury's music quickly becomes familiar with. Sometimes drizzling, other times pouring, and occasionally crackling with thunder, several of Newbury's early albums are accented with the sound of rain, usually falling in the empty spaces between songs.

"The reason why I put rain on those albums," he explains, "aside from the fact that I liked the mood, was because there was so much hiss on the damn tape."

Along with the rain sounds, Newbury's albums from the late 1960s and early '70s (*Looks Like Rain, Frisco Mabel Joy,* and *Heaven Help the Child* are three of his best) are full of soaring vocals, echoing drumbeats and complex arrangements—sometimes full and lush (with steel guitars, Newbury says, playing the string parts), other times delicate and minimalist. Surprisingly, though, these albums were not made in Music Row recording palaces, but in a four-track studio in a converted garage. The studio was run by a Nashville session man named Wayne Moss, who was also a member of the group Area Code 615. While not exactly "garage" recordings in the rock 'n' roll sense, the operation was ground-level enough that white noise became a problem from so much "ping ponging"—the process of transferring vocal and instrumental parts from one track to another.

"I would go back to my boat [at the time, Newbury was living on a houseboat outside of Nashville] and listen to the album [*Looks Like Rain*], and it would never bother me. I was cutting it during the winter, and most of the time it was raining. I was laying in bed one night, and I had some wind chimes outside my boat, and they were dingling along, and I got to thinking: I come back here and listen to my tracks, and like them, and go back to the studio and the hiss drives me crazy. And the reason why is because rain sounds exactly like static. So when I put the rain in, it blended into the static, and it sounded like there was continuous rain. Your mind actually was fooled into believing there was rain in places there were no sound effects at all."

Everytime it rains, Lord, I run to my window
All I do is just wring my hands and moan
Listen to that thunder, Lord, can't you hear that lonesome wind moan?
Tell me baby, now, why you been gone so long
   — "Why You Been Gone So Long"

Mickey Newbury has a strong, versatile tenor voice that has to be one of the most beautiful to pass through Nashville—full of dusty melancholy, sad longing, and a piercing, haunting glow. Since his debut album, *Harlequin Melodies*—released in 1968 by RCA Victor (an album he says he detests)—Newbury has made fifteen albums, up to and including 1996's *Lulled By the Moonlight*. Even during his heyday in the 1960s and '70s, however, Newbury was better known for writing songs than for singing them.

From today's perspective, though, it's clear Newbury was a major player in a musical revolution of sorts that swept through Nashville during that period—revitalizing country music with fresh ideas; acknowledging a broader range of influences (psychedelic rock, folk, blues, R&B); and ultimately winning the industry a much larger fan base in the process. Artists such as Newbury, Willie Nelson, Bobby Bare, Kris Kristofferson, Tom T. Hall and Waylon Jennings not only had sincere respect for country icons such as Hank Williams and Roy Acuff, but were fans of the music of "outside" artists like Bob Dylan, the Beatles, Lightnin' Hopkins and Ray

Charles. These influences couldn't help but seep through the pores of their songs.

"Yeah, there was just a handful of people who really did it, and they opened the doors for everybody else," says Newbury. Radical changes took place in Nashville, including breaking away from the studio system (the Nashville Sound), writing songs that defied formalistic conventions, and adopting a more open-minded attitude toward music that spoke clearly to young and old, folk fans and farmers alike.

When Newbury chose to record his second album, *Looks Like Rain,* in Moss's converted garage studio, for instance, it was a defiant move—and this was several years before the term "outlaw" (and the names Willie and Waylon) became chic.

"The president of Mercury told me he hated the album. And I told him to kiss my ass, I'd buy it back. Which I did. And I turned around and sold it to Elektra Records for $20,000 more than what I bought it for."

Originally released in 1969, Elektra re-released it in 1973 as a double-album package with *Live at Montezuma Hall.*

"Elektra Records was a great label when I signed [in 1970]. That's when Jac Holzman was running it. It was like a family."

Born in 1940 and raised in Houston, Newbury has been writing songs professionally since 1963, when he pulled into Nashville and began working for the publishing company Acuff-Rose. Over the next ten or fifteen years, he saw some of the nation's top artists (Eddy Arnold, Ray Charles, Tom Jones, Andy Williams, Elvis Presley, Joan Baez, Kenny Rogers, B.B. King) record his songs. "San Francisco Mabel Joy," "She Even Woke Me Up to Say Goodbye," "Funny Familiar Forgotten Feelings," "An American Trilogy," "Poison Red Berries" and "33rd of August" are just a handful of his better-known tracks. More than a few of these renditions topped the charts, making Newbury one of Nashville's hottest properties at the time.

"I had a hit every year just about from 1965," he says. "By 1970 I had had enough success to retire."

In addition, Newbury landed tracks on several popular albums, including Kenny Rogers' *The Gambler,* Joan Baez's *Diamonds and Rust,* and more than one Elvis Presley release. (Presley even turned Newbury's "An American Trilogy"—an inventive, fused arrangement of the traditional tunes "Dixie," "Battle Hymn of the Republic" and "All My Trials"—into one of his signature songs.)

"You get a catalog like that, and it's like having an oil well," he said. "Because every time the technology changes, all of those albums re-sell."

And these weren't formula songs. "I know one of the biggest hits I ever had, 'She Even Woke Me Up to Say Goodbye,' the title was only in the song one time," says Newbury. "Everybody in the world said you've got to take the title and bang it in people's ears over and over again. And I never agreed with that."

Instead, the song focuses on a single moment—a man waking up alone after a breakup—and allows the subject to unfold gently. An emotionally complex mixture of sadness and spiritual strength, the words speak of his broken heart, but at the same time show that he knows she did all she could to make things work. "She didn't mean to be unkind," Newbury sings, "Why, she even woke me up to say goodbye."

"Somebody that can get up and write a song that says 'the sun is shining today,' when it's raining like hell outside, I don't understand that process," says Newbury. "I wish to hell I could do it. Be worth a hell of a lot more money, but I wouldn't get any satisfaction out of writing like that."

"San Francisco Mabel Joy," probably Newbury's best-known and most-recorded song, is another heart-wrenching tale. This time the protagonist is a "Waycross, Georgia, farm boy" who aches to see the world, hops a freight train to L.A., and meets "a girl known on the strip as San Francisco's Mabel Joy." It's about the collision of country innocence with the bitter, hard reality of city life—a profoundly sad song that sends chills up my spine with every single listen.

"Everybody assumed that country people were ignorant," he says, getting onto a topic that has always irked him—how country musicians and fans have typically been perceived by the rest of the world. "I'm country, and I'm educated. I grew up in the city, but when I visited all my kinfolks in Kountze, ninety miles from Houston, we're talking outhouse time and no electricity. So I was exposed to two different worlds. But I wasn't ignorant. I was also reading Ferlinghetti and Shakespeare, and listening to all kinds of music, from classical music to blues."

Hints of rural Texas country seep into almost everything Newbury has written and recorded—trains are a recurring image—but over the years he's dabbled in a wide range of styles. He says he was always more of a folksinger than a country troubadour (he never toured with a band). He cut his teeth in the 1950s singing in a vocal group called the Embers in black R&B and blues clubs across Texas (where he was known to people like Gatemouth Brown and B.B. King as "the little white wolf"). And he notes that two of his favorite albums are *Pet Sounds* and *Rubber Soul.* In addition, he's a huge fan—and a friend—of Ray Charles.

You can hear these and other influences mingling together in Newbury's songs: the silly, psychedelic rambler "Just Dropped In (To See What Condition My Condition Was In)," a hit for Kenny Rogers & the First Edition in 1968; "Cortelia Clark," a paean to a blind street singer who won a Grammy but died alone; and the upbeat, folksy "How I Love Them Old Songs." In one corner of his catalog is the painfully sad "Frisco Depot" and the spiritually exhausting "The Future's Not What It Used to Be." Newbury has also written out-and-out rockers ("Dizzy Lizzy," "Mobile Blue"), recorded gospel material ("His Eye Is On The Sparrow"), and says he's currently writing in "kind of an uptown blues, downtown jazz, whatever you want to call it mood. Songs like from the '40s." His current album, *Lulled By the Moonlight*, is dedicated to both Stephen Foster and Don Gant, a good friend who worked at Acuff-Rose ("a lot of songwriters you'd never have heard of if it wasn't for Don Gant").

The core of Newbury's style, though, is probably best represented by sweeping, near-epic songs like "Heaven Help the Child" (which references bohemian culture, Fitzgerald, and Paris in the '20s) and "San Francisco Mabel Joy." Shifting slowly from a quiet beginning to a grandiose finale, they're steeped in melancholy, and are musically and emotionally complex.

"People have referred to me as a poet a number of times," says Newbury. Considering his subject matter and his approach, it's not surprising—yet he doesn't like it. "I'm a songwriter. I'm very satisfied with just being known as a songwriter."

Yes, Frisco's a mighty rich town, now that ain't no lie
Why they got some buildings that reach a mile into the sky
Yet no one can even afford the time just to tell me why
Here's this world full of people and so many people alone
     — "Frisco Depot"

It's partly a result of the unfortunate sway of time and circumstance that Newbury's songs are not well-known these days among newer generations of country fans. A big part of his obscurity, however, can be explained by the fact that he gave up performing twenty-three years ago. "I've got a bunch of kids, and it was hard staying away from them," he says. He also moved to Oregon—where his wife is from—which made traveling to gigs much more complicated. "It just got to be more of a hassle than it was worth." Plus, he says, by the mid-1970s, "the folk scene had gone away, and there was no place to play."

"Basically," he says, summing up the experience, "I'm a writer who sings as opposed to a singer-songwriter. I can sing four or five times a year and be contented. And that's what I've been doing."

Currently, Newbury lives in an old farmhouse in Oregon's Willamette Valley with his wife and three of his children. He doesn't have a record label at the moment; in 1994, he helped found Winter Harvest, which released *Nights When I Am Sane*, a live acoustic album and Newbury's first in six years. (The label later also released albums by Steve Earle and Mark Germino.)

Newbury's newest collection, *Lulled By the Moonlight*, is a limited-release, eighty-minute CD available only by mail order. He recorded the album in Nashville at a place called the Record Club, and released it under the label name Mountain Retreat.

"I'm having to poor-boy it. I mixed it in one night, and did the graphics and the cover in two hours. Working like that is pretty hard, but when it's coming out of your own pocket, it's the only way you can do it. It costs so much money to cut these days it's unbelievable.

"I'm still old fashioned in the way I cut. If I go in the studio, and we don't get it in the first or second take, I pass it up." It's a method, he says, that he's pretty much always followed. "I can't go back and sing something over and over again. I don't know how in the hell anybody does it."

For people today who are proud fans of Kris Kristofferson, Willie Nelson, Guy Clark and Townes Van Zandt, it's almost ironic that Newbury's name often draws a blank stare. Because not only were these artists more or less contemporaries of his, but in some cases it was Newbury—already an established songwriter by the mid-1960s—who got them their start in Nashville.

For starters, he turned Roger Miller onto a brand new song called "Me and Bobby McGee," written by Newbury's good friend Kristofferson. ("I had to grab

Roger Miller by the ears just to make him listen to it," Newbury recounts.) Though Janis Joplin's version is the most widely known, Miller's 1969 recording of the song was the first major turning point in Kristofferson's career.

He also helped win a break in Nashville for the late Van Zandt, an artist for whom Newbury has the highest regard. Newbury says he met Townes at Jones Recording Studio in Houston, a business in which Newbury was a silent partner.

"Anybody who can't recognize the genius of Townes Van Zandt, I don't want to spend more than five minutes talking to them about music," says Newbury firmly. "How could it get much better than 'If I had No Place to Fall' or 'Our Mother the Mountain' or 'Quicksilver Daydreams of Maria' or 'St. John the Gambler'?"

He speaks the titles of these Van Zandt songs as if they were Biblical psalms.

"'The brown of her skin made her hair a soft golden rainfall, that spills from the mountains to the bottomless depths of her eyes,'" he says, reciting the line from "Quicksilver Daydreams of Maria" off the top of his head, slowly and with obvious reverence. "That's some of the most beautiful imagery I've ever heard in my life.

"So then you wonder why he was not successful. And the only reason why is because he didn't have the break—the right people around him doing his deal. Because there's no doubt he worked; he was a road warrior. I got very frustrated trying to get his songs cut. I beat my brains out trying to get Johnny Cash to cut 'St. John the Gambler.' It would have been a smash by him."

"Mickey brought me up here," Townes told me during a 1994 interview. "He came and visited a gig I did in Houston, and he said, 'Man, you got to come to Nashville.' I said 'Sure, I'll go anywhere. I'll go to Wyoming, or Seattle…'"

The outcome of that trip was Townes' debut album, *For the Sake of the Song*, co-produced by Jack Clement and featuring liner notes by Newbury. "I didn't have to go through back doors," Townes went on. "I just came straight down the freeway. And it was because of Mickey."

Just as Newbury speaks of Townes' songs with the highest regard, Townes expressed an intense respect and admiration for his friend's music as well. "It was really funny trying to explain—I can't call it '*explain*'—but I'd tried to tell Jeanene [Townes' wife] about the sound of Mickey's voice and the guitar on a good night at the same time. It's hard; you can't do it. It's like from outer space. I've heard about people trying to explain a color to a blind person. Like Helen Keller. There's no way to do it."

He picked his guitar up, shuffled down the walk
The cars uptown wound round the buildings at his feet.
Looking mighty proud, that old man, with his battered hat in his hand
Lord he sung a song that made me weep.
— "Cortelia Clark"

During our long phone conversation, it quickly becomes apparent that Newbury's musical knowledge is vzst. He speaks authoritatively of George Jones' voice ("the greatest chops I've ever heard in my life"), Lefty Frizzell's influence ("every kid that's singing right now is either mimicking Lefty Frizzell or George Jones"), George Strait's music ("You know what I hear in his voice? Sincerity"), and the once immense power of DJ Ralph Emery.

And then Newbury gets on the subject of Ray Charles, who, he says, "did more for contemporary music than anybody alive. You remember 'Born to Lose' and 'I Can't Stop Loving You'? That was first time that that kind of blues treatment had been given to country songs."

He's speaking of Charles' groundbreaking *Modern Sounds in Country and Western Music* album from 1962, which skillfully blended blues, country, pop and R&B into a whole that was vibrant and genuine.

"One of the greatest thrills in my life was having Ray Charles cut my songs. But I've never lost my awe of him even when I got to know him. He is just such a…soulful person. I can't explain it. You'd have to be around him. Talk about charisma. He is the only person I've been around that I ever got that feeling from. When he walks in the room, you know he's there."

"It's been an interesting life," he says, pausing the conversation for a moment of reflection. "I've had the great fortune to be around people who have made the changes in music, who have really been the pioneers. Joan Baez was a pioneer, Waylon Jennings and Willie Nelson were pioneers, Ray Charles was a pioneer. I've been really lucky."

Today, Newbury continues to plan his future. For one thing, he wants to expand *Lulled By the Moonlight* into a much larger project, and get into a proper mixing studio—which he hopes to do with the help of some friends in Hollywood. He still writes plenty of new songs as well.

"I never start with any preconceived ideas about what the song is going to say. I just sit down at the piano or with a guitar, and write what I happen to be feeling that day. You want to hear a couple of new songs?"

The cordless phone crackles as he walks down a hall, opening and closing doors. He sits at a piano and punches a few chords. "Can you hear that OK?" And then he proceeds to sing two brand new compositions that are no less beautiful for being carried through hundreds of miles of telephone cable.

Do you ever have a longing for a pure and simple time
When all we had between us was a dream and one thin dime
And we were flat out on the highway with no place to be but gone
Some memories are better left alone

"Okay, that's a three o'clock in the morning song," he says of the tune, immediately jumping out of his singing voice and back into the conversation. "I bought this old farmhouse, and am in the process of rebuilding it. It leans, and it's old…and I know exactly what every word in the song is talking about. I didn't sit down just to write lines; they all have a meaning to me. If I ever had to write where it didn't have, I wouldn't write."

"Nashville Heydays and Rainy Houseboat Nights" first appeared in *No Depression* #8 (March–April 1997).

Selected Discography:

Mickey Newbury, *Nights When I Am Sane* (Winter Harvest) 1994.

Mickey Newbury, *Lulled By The Moonlight* (Mountain Retreat) 1996.

Guy Clark

by Bill Friskics-Warren

If the late Townes Van Zandt's vivid, impressionistic lyrics make him the James Joyce of Texas songwriters, then Guy Clark is the Lone Star State's Ernest Hemingway. Clark's economical use of language and gripping way with a narrative, whether portraying moments of great intimacy ("Desperados Waiting For A Train," "Like A Coat From The Cold") or epic grandeur ("Texas–1947," "The Last Gunfighter Ballad"), are among the qualities that his songs share with Hemingway's work. Another is Clark's gift for getting at the heart of an event or experience – what the writer James Agee calls "the cruel radiance of what is."

Which is why it's such a shame that the only recorded versions of Clark performing his most enduring songs are those available on the formulaic Nashville-produced albums he made for RCA and Warner Brothers during the late '70s and early '80s. None of these are bad records, but not one does justice to Clark's singular storytelling genius; *Old No. 1*, his 1975 debut, transcends indifferent production often enough to achieve near-classic status. Even there, however, Clark's vocals rarely evince the unhurried, conversational authority of the records he's made since 1988's *Old Friends*.

"If I'd'a had any sense I'd'a done something different, but I didn't," said Clark during a recent interview at his Nashville home. "When you record those first records, they are what they are. You can't go change 'em."

Maybe not, but aware that his best songs have gained resonance over the years, Clark decided to present them in a more sympathetic live setting, much as folk-blues singer Chris Smither did with his long out-of-print Poppy material on 1991's *Another Way To Find You.* "I've been wanting to do a live album for probably ten years," said Clark, "mainly to go back and record some of those songs that I do every night—'LA Freeway,' 'Desperados Waiting For A Train,' 'Texas – 1947'—because every time I play 'em I play 'em better than I ever did."

Clark and his band certainly proved as much in November, 1996. For three consecutive nights, they took up residence at Nashville's Douglas Corner Cafe to record the aptly titled *Keepers.* Clark says he picked Douglas Corner, an intimate neighborhood tavern in the city's Melrose District, as the site for the project after hearing an album that friends and frequent collaborators Verlon Thompson and Suzi Ragsdale had recorded there. "It just knocked me out," said Clark, referring to Thompson and Ragsdale's *Out Of Our Hands.* "I was just like, man, this is what I wanted to sound like. The idea of just sittin' in a circle in the middle of the room with the band and playin' live seemed to me a really good way to jump into live recording."

Clark and a handful of pickers sat amid the snug confines of Douglas Corner, surrounded by parlor lamps and a hundred or so people each night, and played their sets in what most closely resembled a living room. Clark's band included his son, Travis, on bass, Verlon Thompson on acoustic guitar and harmony vocals, Kenny Malone on drums, Darrell Scott on acoustic guitar, mandolin and dobro, and Suzi Ragsdale on accordion and harmony vocals.

Although Clark is happy with the material included on the CD, he nonetheless observed that there are plenty of "warts" on it, adding that he was apprehensive the first night, especially since he'd never done a live recording before. "I mean, it's loose," he went on to say, "but they're such great players—and we had three nights to pick fifteen tunes from."

Judging from the way the Douglas Corner audiences hung onto Clark's every word—there's not a cough or tinkling glass on the tape—he needn't be apologetic. The fifteen warm, inspired performances documented on *Keepers* not only stand with Clark's best recorded work, they'll likely become the definitive statement of the Texas native's songwriting and storytelling artistry.

Song selection alone would be enough to guarantee the record's popularity. In addition to seven of the ten songs that comprised *Old No. 1*, it features one or two numbers from each of Clark's subsequent major-label records up through *Better Days*. But what sets the thirteen previously recorded songs on *Keepers* apart from their studio predecessors is the red-hot picking of Clark's largely acoustic band. The earthy, homespun quality of his last three records is still evident, but the imagination and abandon that his band displays in the live context is amazing, as Clark's enthusiasm attests. "The second night was just smokin'," he said of the ensemble's Friday evening performance at Douglas Corner. "We seem to get better every time we do it. I love playin' with those guys. You don't have to tell 'em anything. All they've gotta do is know the song."

Indeed, like accomplished jazz improvisers, Clark's *Keepers* band puts on a clinic. The blazing yet soulful mandolin and guitar breakdowns on "Texas–1947" and "Texas Cookin'" are perhaps obvious examples. More revealing, however, are those moments when the group introduces musical elements not typically associated with Clark's country and blues-based arrangements. There's the gypsy swing of "Heartbroke," for instance, or the lilting accordion and mandolin conjunto of "South Coast of Texas." "Homegrown Tomatoes" has a loose, jug band feel, especially Travis Clark's fluid bass lines, while undercurrents of Irish music run throughout the proceedings, most notably on such heart-rending numbers as "She Ain't Goin' Nowhere" and "That Old Time Feeling."

Make no mistake, though, *Keepers* isn't Clark's bid for a piece of the "world beat" market. The understated international flavors with which his band spices their performances always serve Clark's talking blues-based narratives, his mastery of which is rarely less than astonishing. On "Texas–1947" and "Homegrown Tomatoes," he delivers his lines with the jazzy insouciance of a beat poet, minus the pretension. On "The Last Gunfighter Ballad," his quicksilver flow evokes a low-key MC—Q-Tip of A Tribe Called Quest, say—however improbable that may at first seem. Nonetheless, the finest examples of Clark's incomparable storytelling come when, towards the close of the record, he updates two of his signature ballads, "Let Him Roll" and "Desperados Waiting For A Train," where even the pauses in his exquisitely paced recitations convey palpable emotion.

Keepers also features two new songs from Clark, one co-written by Verlon Thompson, the other co-written by Darrell Scott. The former, "A Little Of Both," is a bluesy, Zen-like affirmation of the good life; on the latter, the haunting "Out In The Parking Lot," Clark transforms the gravel lot of a roadhouse into a self-contained universe in which nameless characters seek anything—liquor, violence, intimacy—that might lend meaning to their desperate, fragile lives.

Clark plans to tour in support of the record; he may even play several dates with some or all of the band that backed him at Douglas Corner. "I'm just tryin' to get it upscale enough where we at least have a dressing room," he said half-jokingly, before going on to comment on how expensive it is to take a full ensemble out on the road. "But I would love to take that band out anytime that logistics and economics can afford. I mean, I'd do it all the time if I could."

With Clark now back on Sugar Hill Records—the imprint that released *Old Friends* and also reissued some of the singer-songwriter's earlier albums—it isn't likely that he'll have a tour bus when he takes to the road later this spring. Even so, Clark seems content to be back with the North Carolina label, an outfit known for supporting its artists. His previous record label, Asylum, unceremoniously dropped him after he made 1995's peerless *Dublin Blues*.

"That's just business," he said, without bitterness, of what happened with Asylum. "That's a different business, really, than what I do," he added, talking about the bottom-line mentality that drives most major labels. "It would be great to sell a lot of records," he continued, "but if you don't sell records there's no sense for them to sign you. They're not really in the business of supporting the arts. They're in the business of selling records. I know that. I did the best I could, and they did the best they could. We didn't sell enough records to have it make sense. It's just a fact of life. It doesn't change what I do. I'm not sure it even offends me."

Eclipsing everything in Clark's life these days, most of all the exigencies of the music business, was the death of Townes Van Zandt, Clark's closest friend of the past thirty-five years. "He was the best man at our wedding twenty-five years ago," Clark said. "He's my best friend—ever."

After a lengthy pause, Clark went on to discuss his relationship with Van Zandt in greater detail. "I met him with Jerry Jeff Walker one time years and years ago in Houston. He had just started writing songs and I hadn't. And the first time I heard one of his songs I went, 'Yes, that's worth doin'.' He'd only written about two songs or somethin'. But it certainly changed my life."

According to Clark, the two friends tried to write songs together only once or twice. "About 1972 or 3," Clark recalled, "we wrote a song called 'Dr. Rippy' about this old hippie doctor down on Church Street [in Nashville]. I think I might still have it." But when I asked him if either man had ever considered recording it, he laughed and said, "Never finished it, probably never got past the first verse. I think we tried to write something one other time. But Townes, he didn't need any help writing songs. I mean, it would've been fun, but it wouldn't have been the same thing as when Townes wrote."

Clark's assessment of Van Zandt's musical and artistic legacy is both direct and on the money: "It's literature, as far as I'm concerned," he said. "It's not just song-writing because the songs had to work on paper as well. I mean, some of them are easier to understand on paper than they are listening to them. But they work both ways. Nothing was thrown away in his writing just to get a rhyme," he continued. "It was pretty stream-of-consciousness. It was coming from a place that it's really hard to get to. I mean—'His breath was hard as kerosene, his horse was fast as polished steel'—excuse me! But that kind of imagery just rolled off him. I still find it astonishing, some of the stuff he wrote.

"He was the funniest and the smartest guy I've ever met. His IQ was like 170. And he had a neat way of laughin' at himself. One time he was playin' and he was doin' this set of the saddest stuff and some woman in the audience said, 'Townes, could you play a happy song?' And he said, 'Man, these are the happy songs. You don't want to hear the sad ones.'"

"Brave soul," sighed Clark. "Very few people are willing to go that deep and take that hard a look at the darkness."

Hanging on the walls of Clark's kitchen are numerous photographs; most of them depict Van Zandt's gentle, smiling face, surrounded by friends at picnics and barbecues. On "Desperados Waiting For A Train," the song that closes *Keepers*, Clark sings of another kitchen, a far-off place that he and his grandmother's boyfriend—the man who taught him how to whittle, cuss and spit tobacco juice—return to one last time before the old wildcatter slips away. Kitchens often assume the characteristics of sacred space—places where, through shared food and conversation, we nourish our bodies and spirits. It's not by chance that memories of Van Zandt, with whom Clark shared so much, figure prominently in his kitchen.

"Live Album Lends New Vitality To His Time-Worn Classics" first appeared in *No Depression* #8 (March–April 1997).

Selected Discography:

Guy Clark, *Old No. 1* (RCA) 1975, reissued (Sugar Hill) 1991.

Guy Clark, *Texas Cookin'* (RCA) 1976, reissued (Sugar Hill) 1991.

Guy Clark, *Old Friends* (Sugar Hill) 1988.

Guy Clark, *Boats To Build* (Asylum/Elektra) 1992.

Guy Clark, *Craftsman* (Philo/Rounder) 1995.

Guy Clark, *Dublin Blues* (Asylum) 1995.

Guy Clark, *Keepers* (Sugar Hill) 1997.

Steve Earle

by Peter Blackstock

I can still hear them blaring in the back of my mind, those gleaming brass trumpets and trombones, thrusting right and left toward one end zone and then the other, as the University of Texas marching band zipped through "The Wabash Cannonball." Aside from "The Eyes of Texas" and the UT fight song, "The Wabash Cannonball" was the band's most oft-played number during Longhorns games at Memorial Stadium in Austin, so much so that I grew up thinking it was one of the school's official songs.

It wasn't until a couple years ago, when Townes Van Zandt recorded it on his *Roadsongs* album, that I discovered "The Wabash Cannonball" was written by A.P. Carter, the same fellow who wrote the song for which this magazine is named. Heck, before that I never even knew "The Wabash Cannonball" had words.

Neither did Steve Earle—or if he did, he sure didn't know what those words were when he was seventeen years old and had his first encounter with Mr. Van Zandt. And that got him in a heap of trouble with his hero.

"I met Townes at The Old Quarter in Houston, Texas; I was playing there," Earle says, remembering that fateful night in 1972. "There were about eight people there, they were all real drunk, and one of 'em was Townes. He was hecklin' me. I'm tryin' to play my set, and Townes keeps yellin', 'Play the Wabash Cannonball!' He was sittin' right in front of the stage. And I'd just ignore him.

"He wouldn't yell while I was singin'; he'd only yell between the songs, he was nice enough to do that. So I'd play another song, and he'd yell, 'Play the Wabash Cannonball!' And I'd play another song, and he'd go, 'Play the Wabash Cannonball!'

"I finally had to admit that I didn't know the fuckin' Wabash Cannonball. And he goes, 'You call yourself a folk singer and you don't know the Wabash Cannonball?' So I played this song of his called 'Mr. Mudd & Mr. Gold' that has about 19 million words in it. And he shut up."

Stories like that come a dime a dozen with Steve Earle. Saying that Earle's life and career have been colorful is like saying Elvis had a bit of an appetite. If Earle were to die tomorrow, the film studios would probably be lining up to tell his tale in celluloid.

Thing is, a couple years ago it seemed quite possible that Earle might die tomorrow. The movie-script life he has led hasn't altogether been a matter of being too good to be true; indeed, at times it's been too bad to believe. From critically respected, chart-topping country star, to criminally incarcerated, drug-addled washout, Earle has seen both the highest highs and the lowest lows over the past two decades.

That kind of emotional roller coaster can be hell on the human condition, but it sure does have a way of unleashing the muse. Earle's 1995 acoustic album *Train A Comin'* was a refreshing return that, true to its title, got him back on track. Then came the full-on locomotive. *I Feel Alright* is a career effort, declaring the comeback of one of the most vital and vibrant artists in contemporary country music. Or is that in contemporary rock music?

That's the age-old question about Earle's music no one has ever quite figured out with any certainty, and that's because it's a non-issue at heart, as Earle well knows. "I think Hank Williams records have a lot more to do with the Sex Pistols than they have to do with Brooks & Dunn," he suggests, using those artists as an example of why genre tags can sometimes have no meaning at all.

"It's really just about any kind of music that's *real*," he continues. "That was what my argument with Nashville was all along. It's not about country or rock. It's about *real*.

"This record that I've got now is probably closer to a pop record than anything I'll ever do, in a lot of ways. But it's truer to what I think is the *spirit* of country music than most of the records that come out of Nashville. You know, 'Long Black Veil' wouldn't get recorded nowadays. They want uptempo and positive. They want something a little zippy, and that's something I've butted heads with people on these two streets right here all along."

Earle is speaking by phone from Room & Board, a Nashville studio where he's holed up in late January producing a record for The V-Roys, a young Knoxville band. The V-Roys are signed to E-Squared, a new label Earle has formed with his longtime friend Jack Emerson, a veteran of the Nashville music business and longtime champion of blurring the boundaries between country and rock. The fact that Earle is also working as both a producer and a partner in a record label is evidence of how much ground he has regained in the past couple years.

But the most telling testament to that is the perfectly named *I Feel Alright*. The title track, the first cut on the record, lays it all on the line straight and simple from the start, with telling lyrics such as, "Be careful what you wish for, friends/I've been to hell and now I'm back again." It sears with a redemptive fire, a triumphant reclamation of what was once lost now regained. That spirit is reflected in the mostly upbeat nature of the music; there's a hint of darkness in there somewhere, but this is an album about breaking back out into the light, much as John Hiatt's *Bring The Family* was nearly a decade ago.

"These songs, and the recordings, just sort of poured out of me in a six-month period," Earle says. "I recorded most of them as I wrote them. I finally made a record the way I thought records were made when I was a kid listening to records; it finally felt like I've always thought it should."

The opener sets the tone for the rest of the disc, which, true to Earle's statement, is indeed as close to an outright pop record as he has ever made. About a half-dozen tracks on here that could be hits with the rock crowd, the country crowd, or both. "Hard-Core Troubadour" is a rambunctious, instantly catchy tune about living the legends you create for yourself in song. Autobiographical? Perhaps, though he makes a nod to another great wild storytelling songwriter by sneaking in the line, "Hey Rosalita, won't you come out tonight."

"More Than I Can Do" is equally memorable, a declaration of love by a desperate man—or, as Earle puts it, "a happy little stalker love ballad." "Now She's Gone" is a slightly gentler pop ditty that probably will top the charts for some enterprising Nashville star before long, while the string-enhanced ballad "Valentine's Day" could do the same for a mainstream pop performer. "The Unrepentant" is the kind of put-up-or-shut-up anthem that has earned Earle his vaunted reputation, for better and for worse, as one who does it his way or no way at all. And then there's the closing track, "You're Still Standin' There," a duet with Lucinda Williams that's as perfect as a pop song as anyone could hope for.

All those songs aside, it's the handful of tracks that supplement them which lift *I Feel Alright* to classic status. Anchoring the bursting-at-the-seams spirit of the pop tunes are a couple of darker numbers that reveal why Earle wasn't feeling so all right a couple years ago. The clincher is listed on the jacket simply as "CCKMP," which, as the listener discovers upon hearing it, stands for "Cocaine Cannot Kill My Pain." It's a deathly song both in sound and subject, the summation of a drug addict at rock bottom realizing how low he's fallen and how far he has to go to crawl out. And then there's "South Nashville Blues," which musically is deceptively happy, strolling along to a plucky banjo as Earle sings matter-of-factly about taking his pistol and $100 to a drug deal and having "everything I need to get me killed."

That was Earle's life for most of the early '90s, a period he sardonically referred to in the liner notes of *Train A Comin'* as "my vacation in the ghetto." "I was sort of out of touch for a few years," he readily admits. "The last few years that I was using, I didn't even have a guitar. And I listened to a lot of hip-hop because I didn't hang out with any white people; that's just where the dope was in this town, so that's where I was. And also, black people don't listen to my music at all, so it was one place I could be pretty anonymous."

Not anonymous enough, eventually. Arrested on drug charges in 1994, Earle did time both in jail and in a rehabilitation center, where he finally began to kick the habits that had been dogging him for most of his career. He has admitted to reporters that he was a heroin addict as far back as the release of his breakthrough solo album, *Guitar Town*, in 1986.

Guitar Town, which presented the most definitive synthesis of country and rock 'n' roll during the 1980s, is generally considered Earle's debut, but in fact he had released a rockabilly EP titled *Pink & Black* in the early '80s. Furthermore, he had been a fixture on the Nashville scene for more than a decade before *Guitar Town* came out, ever since he had moved there from his boyhood home of San Antonio to play bass for Guy Clark.

"I met Guy the first night I was in Nashville," Earle recalls. "I came up here on sort of a reconnaissance mission before I actually moved up, and I was shootin' pool in Bishop's Pub, and he walked up to me. He liked my hat.

"Guy just sort of took me under his wing. There were a lot of pickin' parties in those days. They went on at John Lomax's house, and also at Jim McGuire's photo studio. And people would just sit up all night and the guitar would go around the room. And there'd be everybody from me and David Olney, who were at absolutely street level, to Neil Young, when he was passing through town in those days. So it was like a university for songwriters. And Guy knew me from those things, and he helped me get my publishing deal. And when it came time for him to make a record and go out on the road, he said, 'You used to play bass, didn't you?' I said, 'Yeah, a little bit.' And he said, 'Well, you're the bass player.' And that was it."

Earle toured with Clark for a couple years before deciding to pursue his own career, but by then it was the late '70s, and his timing couldn't have been worse. "Nashville was slipping into the throes of the whole 'Urban Cowboy' thing," Earle recalls, "and people here were trying real hard not to be hillbillies. That was their major concern. And I didn't fit into that."

Though he wasn't being taken seriously as a performer, Earle was beginning to get recognized as a talented songwriter. "People [publishers] would keep signing me because they knew I could write, but nobody got a lot of cuts on me, so they'd usually drop me eventually, and then somebody else would sign me," he remembers. "I had the odd cut here and there....The first record I ever had that made any money was a Johnny Lee single in about 1980 that I co-wrote."

Actually, he came darn near to doing much better than that a few years earlier, when he was barely twenty years old. A song Earle wrote that eventually appeared on a Carl Perkins album was originally scheduled for an Elvis Presley recording session. "Tony Brown, who produced my first records, was Elvis' piano player in those days, and he was on that session," Earle explained. "They had my song up on the sessions, and it was gonna be the first one they were gonna record. But Elvis never left the hotel and came to the recording studio, and he never recorded again. So, when he died, I was pissed off at him for years."

Nowadays, Earle doesn't have to worry about such make-or-break opportunities as a songwriter. "I've had seventeen or eighteen cuts just in the last year," he says, with a gratified tone that reveals equal amounts of bemused surprise and humble pride. His favorite versions of his songs, out of the thirty or forty that have been recorded to date? "The two Emmylou cuts, without a doubt," he responds without hesitation. (Harris recorded Earle's "Goodbye" on 1995's stunning *Wrecking Ball*, and cut "Guitar Town" on her live *At The Ryman* disc in 1992.)

Financially, Earle points out that "I had a Travis Tritt record that was a single last year and made a lot of money," though he acknowledges that sometimes those benefits are more rewarding to the bank account than to the soul. For the record, he doesn't seem to hold what he apparently considered a less-than-stellar version of his "Sometimes She Forgets" against Tritt. "I wasn't crazy about that record, but I was disappointed because Travis is a really, really good country singer....But the producers went for this bullshit calypso feel, which is what Nashville producers do when they get scared."

That's the kind of no-holds-barred commentary that has often made Earle unwelcome company in the play-polite circles of the country music community, where the unwritten rule is that you don't criticize your fellow musicians. This from a man who admits he has a picture of Reba McEntire taped to the toilet seat in the restroom of his office, and who once called current country-schlock sensation Shania Twain "the highest-paid lap dancer in Nashville."

"Uh, yeah, I did say that," he admits, with a rather sheepish giggle. "I hadn't realized that had gotten into print."

It's an entertaining sound bite, but Earle is more than happy to explain why he has a problem with records such as Twain's recent blockbuster. At the root of it, he suggests, is the production—in this case, the work of Mutt Lange, who's perhaps best-known for his work with Def Leppard.

"You listen to a Shania Twain track, one of the singles, and put it up against, like, a Leppard single off of *Hysteria*, and you'll see a lot of the same elements there," Earle says. "You may think I'm crazy saying that, but the same tricks are all there, the same kind of things with percussion and vocals. He [Lange] knows what he's doing. And I admire what he does, from the part of me that makes records and tries to go in and get a performance on a record to push those buttons in people. But he does it real mechanically, and sometimes I think it's cheatin' a little bit."

It's a mid-January evening at The Backstage in Seattle, and Steve Earle is performing the finale of six West Coast shows that made up the last of three acoustic mini-tours with the accompaniment of Peter Rowan, Norman Blake and Roy Huskey Jr., the band with which he recorded *Train A Comin'*. The place is packed; word has obviously been passed from friends who have seen the tour make its way up the West Coast that Earle is not to be missed on this run.

A handful of rowdy-to-the-point-of-obnoxious fans are hootin' and hollerin' at the drop of a hat throughout the show, obviously drunk beyond the point of reason—not exactly the kind of support a recovering drug addict deserves. For his part, Earle just plows right ahead with his songs and pretty well ignores the fuss. (When asked about it a couple weeks later, he says, simply, "I just don't let it bother me that much. I mean, the point is, I don't tell anybody else what to do. Nobody can tell me what to do.")

As the show wears on, Earle mixes songs from *Train A Comin'* with old classics such as "Someday" and "I Ain't Ever Satisfied," previews a couple tunes from *I Feel Alright*, and eventually takes a break to allow Rowan and Blake their time in the spotlight. Rather than head backstage to grab a drink or a smoke, Earle stands just to the edge of the lights taking it all in, grinning as wide as Texas, glad still to be a part of it all. And still enjoying the pickin' parties.

It's been a long road back.

"Back To His Life's Work After A 'Vacation In The Ghetto'" first appeared in *No Depression* #3 (Spring 1996).

Selected Discography:

Steve Earle, *Guitar Town* (MCA) 1986.

Steve Earle, *Exit O* (MCA) 1987.

Steve Earle, *Copperhead Road* (MCA) 1988.

Steve Earle and the Dukes, *Shut Up & Die Like An Aviator* (MCA) 1991.

Steve Earle, *Train A Comin'* (Winter Harvest) 1995, reissued (Warner Bros.) 1997.

Steve Earle, *I Feel Alright* (Warner Bros./E-Squared) 1996.

Steve Earle & The V-Roys, *Johnny Too Bad* EP (E-Squared) 1997.

Steve Earle & The Supersuckers, *Steve Earle & The Supersuckers* EP (Sub Pop) 1997.

Steve Earle, *El Corazon* (E-Squared) 1997.

Steve Earle, *Early Tracks* (Koch International) 1998.

Ray Wylie Hubbard

by Roy Kasten

Two years ago, "The Messenger" appeared at the end of a tape a friend made for me, sounding with a shock of recognition, knocking me out of some cross-state driving daydream and into a world that was fierce, visionary, and crystalline.

I'm wearing old boots, black Cuban heels
Our soles they are worn and we stand here by grace
My trousers are torn and my jacket is borrowed
And I'm wearing my time behind the eyes in my face

I am not looking for loose diamonds
Or pretty girls with crosses round their necks
I don't want for roses or water
I'm not looking for God
I'm not looking for sex

The story of some traveler, some songwriter, barely fixed in time and place as he makes his journey, becomes intensely visible through pure chord changes over two guitars. The song suggests someone like Harry Dean Stanton's character in *Paris, Texas*: a man who has forgotten what he looks for, or won't or can't say, yet still carries a secret wisdom of hard-won hope. Ray Wylie Hubbard's work often calls upon other voices he carries with him. "It's called 'sampling,' I think," he cracks. There's Leon Payne in "Loco Gringo's Lament," Tim Hardin in "The Real Trick," Gram Parsons and Dylan in "Ballad of the Crimson Kings"—but Hubbard has that rare ability to renew and recast those sources. The message of "The Messenger" flares up in a line from Rainer Maria Rilke's most famous letter—"Our fears are like dragons guarding our most precious treasures"—but the notion was within the song from the beginning, in the figure still standing and still looking after all the trials of time. "After you get through with a song like that," Hubbard says, "you just say 'Thanks.' You don't know where the words and phrases came from."

Hubbard's story begins in Dallas, where he first heard the musicians who were forming one of country music's most important subcultures. "I went to high school in Dallas with Michael Murphey and B.W. Stevenson, and a guy named Larry Gross [now host of "Mountain Stage"]. There was a big folk scene and the influences of that time were Woody Guthrie, Jimmie Rodgers, Bob Dylan and all that. At that time growing up in Dallas, one night you'd go to a little club and see Freddie King and the next night you'd see Willie Nelson. Then we'd go up to Oklahoma City and see Mance Lipscomb." The latter is an oft-overlooked Texas country bluesman who, while not a great innovator, disseminated the elegant melodic fingerstyle work inseparable from the Texas troubadour school. Indeed, Lipscomb is another version of The Messenger.

Hubbard quickly absorbed those influences but was "sidetracked," as he often puts it, for an early recording career of false starts. "Those [first records] don't count," he says. "They were just half-baked projects, under-funded, and with lots of extenuating circumstances. They weren't real....My history of recording was just never complete. My first record on Warner/Reprise, *Ray Wylie Hubbard and the Cowboy Twinkies*, was like that. Though I had been playing a lot of acoustic stuff, I had these friends and we discovered beer and electricity. So, by God, we got us a band. We'd recorded a record in Austin that got us offers from places like Atlantic, and Frank Zappa's label, Discreet, really liked it. But we never could get the record company to release the record we had. They always wanted to go re-record it.

"So we went to Nashville with the band. After we left, they put girl singers on it and tried to make it commercial country. But they had no idea what we were doing, no idea what we were about. We gave them the working art for the cover and they put rope letters on it, and so when the record came out, we listened to it and were just, well, depressed. We worked hard on it and when it came out, it just devastated us. We couldn't go out and tour with it. We waited out that contract and didn't record again. It really hurt."

Yet the record contains material of a depth that outstrips all but a few of his more famous Texas contemporaries. Especially exquisite is "Portales," with its chorus, "It's a hand-woven love song of sadness." Then in 1978, at the request of Willie Nelson and his fledgling Lone Star Records, Hubbard cobbled together demos he had scattered across Texas and released *Off The Wall*. Hubbard made the record on the condition that the follow-up would have a real budget and producer, though when Nelson signed to CBS, all bets were off. *Off The Wall* had no "Portales," but it did contain Hubbard's version of his own "Up Against The Wall Redneck Mother," the most notorious cut on Jerry Jeff Walker's *Viva Terlingua* and a song Hubbard still can't shake. At gigs he'll succumb to the requests and introduce it with a cautionary tale: "Never write a song you won't want to sing for the rest of your life."

No song could be less indicative of Hubbard's art than "Redneck Mother." But perhaps owing to the weird cult status it conferred on him, and certainly because of the strong bands he assembled—including members of Walker's Lost Gonzo Band as well as Bugs Henderson and his now constant companion Terry Ware—Hubbard has been able to continue performing, despite never really having a record to back. Ultimately, touring within progressive country circles came to feed both the restlessness of some of his songs and the comedic wisdom of others. And at least he has stories to tell.

"I was in Nashville and a promoter hired a blimp to fly over the city with a big deal that was supposed to say 'Ray Wylie Hubbard Salutes Nashville' and somehow the blimp came over and said 'Ray Wylie Hubbard Palutes Nashville.' I don't know, somebody said, 'It doesn't get weird enough for me.' We opened for Willie Nelson at the Troubadour in Los Angeles, and this was back in the glitter rock era, and the night before we went into this little club and there was this band dressed up as space guys, right, with green big heads and one guy was silver. So of course we invited them to our show and they came in costume. So we had these four space aliens sitting around talking to us and Willie Nelson."

Hearing Hubbard speak of years in honky-tonks and bars where "the other band didn't like us and threw beer on us" *is* unexpected. His recent works all require an intimacy of hearing—not because the songs are subdued, but because of their power to transfix, to bore straight through and leave you in wonder.

Just as unexpected is Hubbard's spiritual conviction. At heart, he is the most independent of religious songwriters, his voice sometimes declaiming with a steely, Puritan keen, visions only a voice as unaffected and grave as his can capture. "It's more spiritual than religious," Hubbard explains. "I don't follow any one religion. I'm kind of a spiritual mongrel." "This beautiful ancient wisdom has been prostituted for personal gain," he sings in "The Real Trick."

It's hard not to see a slow, spiritual quest throughout Hubbard's career, or better still, redemption through the folk songwriting craft he started out exploring in Texas coffeehouses. "Kinda like John Prine and Jesus, I had my missing years, you know," he quips. "I just didn't do any recording. I just played in Texas and California. Now I think of myself as a songwriter. Before I don't know what I thought; I just couldn't quite get it together. Nine years ago I came out of this honky-tonk fog....I just didn't feel good trying to be a honky-tonker. I made this conscious decision to get back to what I really like doing. I started out doing acoustic stuff. I wanted to be just a songwriter." He calls his 1994 Dejadisc release "my first real record"; Dejadisc also reissued his 1992 album *Lost Train Of Thought*.

On the final cut of Hubbard's new album, *Dangerous Spirits*, "Ballad of the Crimson Kings," he celebrates the songwriter. "It's the story of a band. Kind of a cross between Son Volt and the Dead Reckoners. These bands that go out there and write for the sake of writing. I was talking to Kevin Welch and Jimmy LaFave, and we decided that the writers we liked didn't start writing because they had record deals or had a publishing deal or trying to get other people to record their songs. Later on they did that. They started writing 'cause they had no choice. They were going to write these songs for the sake of writing these songs. All the way from the Louvin Brothers through the Burrito Brothers. You know, old dreadnoughts and drop down Ds."

"Ballad of the Crimson Kings" draws together voices and words which "sparkle and fade away." The song takes in the whole human drama that makes *Dangerous Spirits* such an affecting and expansive document. The album captures and sets side by side the homeless and the relieved, the tempted and the forgiven, those "that rise above blind faith" and those "above the law and outside the bounds of grace."

"Somewhere inside of me there are two people," Hubbard says. "I'm kinda trying to decide between—not trying to decide, but I'm aware of it—trying to put them together. But I don't really have an answer. In that first song, 'Dangerous Spirits,' you've got the hold-up man, a thief, a rascal. All of a sudden he puts down his gun. It's not fear, it's compassion. All of a sudden he starts to see.

"When I came out of this fog, I hopefully developed a conscience. Not so much what I could get out of the world, but what I could contribute. That song is about redemption, but not going through church. The guy just drops his gun and puts on the coat of a pilgrim. The same character is in 'The Messenger.' The guy who walks away from the powder and the flame. Some days I do that, and some days I don't. The days that I do, I have better days."

"Put Down The Gun" first appeared in *No Depression* #11 (September–October 1997).

Selected Discography:

Ray Wylie Hubbard, *Lost Train Of Thought* (Misery Loves Company) 1992, reissued (Dejadisc) 1995.

Ray Wylie Hubbard, *Loco Gringo's Lament* (Dejadisc) 1994.

Ray Wylie Hubbard, *Dangerous Spirits* (Philo) 1997.

Toni Price

by Brad Buchholz

The Continental Club isn't into fashion statements; it's hard to get too carried away with image when you're sharing the block with a business establishment called "Just Guns." The interior is spare, cheesy, the walls decorated with gay, oversized paintings of European capitals. Chairs and tables are obstacles, not enhancements. As you face the stage, the Continental is a little wider than a two-car garage—and almost as comfortable.

Every Tuesday, Toni Price plays the place for tips, at Happy Hour. It's the hottest show in town.

Austin jams the Continental, standing shoulder-to-shoulder, to hear her sing. To see Toni Price, however, you must push your way to the stage—past the guys in power clothes drinking imported beer, past the blonde princess in the black evening gown and plastic tiara, past dancing white-haired hippies with ponytails, past Mr. Nose Ring and the biker and cute little caterpillar head.

Then you see her, seated at center stage. She's a fair, wispy woman in a baggy, sleeveless "peace sign" sweatshirt, persistently tugging at a long wave of sandy brown hair that insists on falling over her left eye. There's a snake tattoo on her left forearm, and a glass of scotch on the floor. Flanked by three acoustic guitarists—seated front-porch style—Toni sings with her eyes closed, immersed in a bluesy trance, wrapping her heart around a song about good times that can't be reclaimed, oblivious to the intimate din that surrounds her. She's totally connected to the soul of the song.

Toni sings plaintive the way Hank Williams sang lonesome. Emotive fuels her shows; the experience is more about feeling than listening.

"I think people are starved for emotion right now," Toni says. "The world we live in is so stripped of emotion, so harsh, it's like we're made to *be* numb. I think people want something acoustic, something real. They want wood. They're sick of plastic and metal and fake and violent. Real people need a release from all the harshness— and that's where emotion comes in."

Like the folks at the Continental Club, Toni doesn't care much about the hottest trends in Nashville or conforming to musical genres. Is her music country? Is it blues? Is it pop? Is it rock? "Who cares?" she suggests, Tuesday after Tuesday. The only thing that matters is that the music works—and that it touches the audience.

Toni's affinity for the Continental, and the exchange that goes on there between artist and audience, reveals a great deal about her priorities. Her label, Discovery, would love to put Toni on the road to support her two critically acclaimed albums (*Swim Away*, released in 1993, and *Hey*, in 1995). They've challenged her to become "video friendly," to let go of her strong Austin focus, and to work with L.A. music producers.

But Toni won't budge.

"I cannot be managed, produced, or directed," she says defiantly. "I have to have freedom, no matter what the cost. My single-mindedness is my saving grace, and it's also my curse. I know what I'm supposed to do if people will just let me do it. But everyone thinks they know better. They want to paint a mustache on the Mona Lisa— and that really bugs me, you know?"

At age thirty-four, Toni Price values her freedom because it took her so long to realize it. A child of Tennessee, she was orphaned as an infant and raised in Nashville by adoptive parents. In school, Toni was the classic "good girl"—a bookworm, artistic, good with paints, eager to please. Her first connection to music was The Beatles, not the Grand Ole Opry; as a girl, she'd fight to be Paul when her friends would sing Fab Four hits. In time, she would discover the power of Aretha Franklin and grow to love Ray Charles' soulful renditions of classic country songs.

After dropping out of college to pursue music, Toni sang in Nashville cover bands and played frat parties, fronting groups such as Mel and the Party Hats. In terms of live performance, she perceived that the rules of the game in Nashville were pretty rigid—little that was daring or different was celebrated. Deep down, she longed to break rules. But the environment wouldn't allow it.

Toni visited Austin for the first time in 1989 to play Antone's blues club during South by Southwest. At the time, she knew nothing about Austin or its music. But the experience changed her life. "It wasn't until I came to Austin that I realized that I wasn't alone in the universe," she says. "I came to understand that I had compadres here—musicians, and audiences—people who wanted and needed real music. I'd been through all the styles, all the gymnastics, without realizing that I was really supposed to just go out and *sing*—sing songs that had meaning to me."

Toni's first shows in Austin were spicy, rowdy, dance-all-night affairs at Antone's— a powerful confluence of her longtime love for melody and her newfound affinity for blues expression. Her stage persona sometimes suggested Bonnie Raitt, but her soulful, husky phrasing was from the Ray Charles school, with wonderfully clipped consonants and long, lovely, marinated vowels. All the while, she paid close attention to the advice of house guitarist Derek O'Brien and the performance of blues divas Angela Strehli, Lou Ann Barton and Sarah Brown.

"I learned a lot from them about style and honesty, and how they carried them-selves—like queens!" says Toni. "When I came in the first time, I was butting in on their scene—which is like royalty—shaking my booty, with no idea where I was. And they accepted me! They were really nice and supportive.

"Nashville is different. It's catty and competitive. It hurts people. It grinds them up and spits them out. But it's not like that here. Austin is very welcoming—as long as you come to give and not to take. I sensed the magic when we drove into the city the very first time."

A single mother, Toni took a waitress job to support her family while honing her craft and putting together material for *Swim Away*. But as her popularity grew and her musical breakthrough became a matter of inevitability, the day job was increasingly awkward.

"Say! Aren't you Toni Price?"

"Yes," she'd answer. "Would you like some more tea?"

When *Swim Away* hit the racks to rave reviews—it was named the top independent pop album of 1993 by the National Association of Independent Record Distributors— Price gave up the day job. At the same time, she also shelved her stand-up performances in favor of a more informal, front-porch approach she'd been experimenting with the past year at the Continental Club. Crowds liked the intimacy of the acoustic shows, and the chair didn't seem to diminish the power of her voice.

"If you've ever studied yoga, or karate, or dance, you learn that the whole power of your body comes from where your legs join your body—not your throat, or chest, or diaphragm," says Toni, suggesting that sitting down actually enhances her vocals. "When you sit, you can totally 'crunch.' Look at Joe Ely when he sings. He does it standing up, but he crunches. Elvis did it, too. That's where the power comes from."

There's power in the voice, and power in the wood, too. Through time, Price's Continental shows have become notable as guitar showcases, spotlighting star Austin players such as Rich Brotherton (Robert Earl Keen's band), Champ Hood (Lyle Lovett's Large Band), "Scrappy" Jud Newcomb (Loose Diamonds) and Casper Rawls (Leroi Brothers). As one who celebrates space in music, Toni eagerly allows the guitarists to take over her songs, stretch, and give them new textures.

In a city that celebrates the singer-songwriter, Toni is the rare acoustic artist who does not write her own material. It's obvious that she loves words—she'll hold her own in any conversation about Mark Twain, Flannery O'Connor or John Steinbeck—but she's never felt comfortable as the writer. In large part, that's the job of Gwil Owen, an old friend from Nashville who's written half of Toni's recorded material. The match between plaintive songwriter and plaintive stylist is so pure that you sense Gwil Owen is Toni Price.

"Gwil writes the things I wish I could write—the things I need to say," says Toni. "When I lived in Nashville, his songs gave me my first clue about connecting song to heart. He is a real person, you know, a great artist in his own right. But the amazing thing is the new songs and the old songs are equally wonderful." Toni points out that "Hey" and "Edge of the Night," two Owen songs on the new album, are ten years old, while "Something" and "Tumbleweed," also on the new disc, are brand new.

"The weird thing is, Gwil and I aren't alike at all. He's kind of a grumpy, quiet guy. And I'm the extrovert, the dreamer. But when he writes a song, we're the same person. Not similar; we are the same *person*."

There's one more thing: Gwil Owen drives to his shows in a Chevrolet. Toni Price walks—or takes the bus. In fact, she hasn't owned a car in almost ten years. Cars are bad, she says. Concrete is bad. Exhaust is bad. Gasoline is bad. Wars over gasoline are bad. Besides, the bus is fun. People fight, and preach, and philosophize. The street is fun, too.

"It helps me feel a part of life, because I do tend to shelter myself," she says. "I don't watch TV. I don't listen to the radio. I make my own world. So it's good to get out there and find I'm still a part of things. I do a lot of creating and planning when I'm out there. I like to observe people. It's very therapeutic."

Toni could easily catch a ride from friends. And she could certainly afford to buy a car of her own. But that's not the point. Put Toni Price in a Volvo, and she's no longer Toni Price. It's a similar message that she's passed on to the record people. Put Toni Price on the road, and she's no longer Toni Price.

"These people who want me to tour—who are they? They're certainly not the people who come to see me at the Continental," she says. "You play in a town, you build up a following—and then you're supposed to leave them? That has never made sense to me. The Continental gig is the most fun on the earth for me. It's such a giving thing. For an artist who needs love, there's nothing better."

Discovery has apparently received the message. Toni says she isn't sure if she's still under contract with the label, or whether Discovery is willing to work with her on a third album. The future, she says, is a mystery. And she can deal with that.

"I don't know what's going to happen next," she says. "But I feel totally successful. I don't aspire to play on the Letterman show, because I don't want to play in a band with what's-his-name. But I have success. I have two records I'm totally proud of. I have a happy home. I have time to spend with my family. I'm not starving. I don't need a day job. And once in a while, I walk down the street and hear somebody say, 'Oh, Toni!'"

In the shadow of Paris and Vienna, under the gaze of Elvis, Toni Price hears that call, again, in the Continental Club. As the tip jar wobbles overhead and the fans shout requests, Champ Hood picks up a fiddle, the singer closes her eyes, and the magic lives on. As she sings, Toni Price gently raises her left arm and lets it glide high in the air, her palm wide open, feeling the beauty of the night, a spirit shared that can never be owned.

"What Price Glory" first appeared in *No Depression* #2 (Winter 1996).

Selected Discography:

Toni Price, *Swim Away* (Discovery) 1993.

Toni Price, *Hey* (Discovery/Antone's) 1995.

Toni Price, *Sol Power* (Discovery/Antone's) 1997.

Bad Livers

by Grant Alden

If the chat around the cooler is to be believed, we are in the throes of another aesthetic shift. That is, we have already moved past post-modernism, which near as I understand mostly amounted to cleverly chewing the past into new bits; reconstituted culture. (It's all about packaging.) The fancy new kid's called deconstruction, which seems to be a highly decorative and utterly dysfunctional movement bent on chewing the past, the present, and the future into utterly unrecognizable and impersonal bytes. Computer-assisted dada, if you will.

Which is probably a long-winded way of saying we're lost.

Adrift and afraid, gasping for substance like fish on the dock.

Or, as the Sex Pistols had it twenty years back, No Future, except this time it's for a failure of imagination, not hope.

This, in part, explains the fond glances we've been taking toward our cultural past: the glorious '50s kitsch (sorry: art modern) which graces so many hip homes and secondhand stores, old metal cars (a British friend thinks his 1974 Plymouth Duster is some kind of classic), BR5-49's wardrobe. I Love Lucy, The Brady Bunch.

Now, believe me, I know that's a lot of trash to throw at three early-middle-aged guys who live in Austin and play banjo, fiddle, bass, tuba, accordion, guitar, whatever, and squirm audibly even at the suggestion they might be a bluegrass band: the Bad Livers, who don't drink. A trio given equally to heartfelt gospel and Surfer-esque chaos. Songwriter Danny Barnes (banjo, primarily) will identify himself as a Christian, though his Jewish comrade Mark Rubin (bass and tuba), who punctuates the conversation with "amen" and no irony, is quick to point out that Danny also practices tai-chi and meditates.

Straight lines rarely happen in nature, and it's the colliding arcs that are responsible for most of what's worth looking at or listening to.

Anyway, that's what good music does: It sweeps you off somewhere and drops you, unexpected, splat in the middle of an idea you didn't know you had. And that's what the Bad Livers—Danny and Mark and Ralph White (fiddle and accordion)—have been up to these last seven years, which amounts to 1,500-plus shows and four full-length releases.

Not without a price, that. There's a new CD, *Hogs on the Highway,* a new label (Sugar Hill), and a new member. "Last fall, when the Bad Livers were out doing some shows," Barnes wrote in an e-mail update, "Ralph woke up one morning and indicated to Mark and I that he was wore out on touring....It was a moment of realization for all of us. Mark and I realized that we were enjoying what we were doing more than ever. And we felt positive about our business and where we were going. Ralph, on the other hand, felt that the rigors of touring and 'the business' had taken a serious toll on his attitude."

The upshot is that, while Ralph and Danny may continue to write together, Bob Grant, an old friend who picks mandolin and guitar and presently lives in New York City, has joined the band.

Beginnings. Pick any spot to start, but mostly it's called living. Rubin began off a tuba player, back in Oklahoma. "It's been a long, strange journey for me," he says over the phone, while Danny chimes in from the receiver on the fax machine. "I was setting myself up for a career as a classical musician when I was in high school, by being a tuba player. Right about my senior year of high school my father passed away, and that just knocked the stilts out of a lot of the plans that I had made.

"At the same time I was getting really involved with punk rock music, and I'd stopped playing tuba and got an electric bass, and hung around the punk rock scene up in Oklahoma City; bands like the Flaming Lips came out of that little bag. I guess I moved down to Dallas in '84, and just kicked around.

"That was about the time I felt that all the promises that were made by the Minute-men and Black Flag and bands like that had pretty much gone to hell. Dallas was a good place to be, because there was a lot of great music going on, and I used to go see this band Killbilly play. I bought a string bass and joined them. Simple as that."

Simple, but Mark still had to relearn to play the bass. "It's a new instrument entirely," he says. "I had been playing electric bass, and I pretty much well-versed myself in a lot of different styles—country-western and blues, and I did two years in a reggae band up in Oklahoma City. With the upright bass you have to totally relearn the instrument from the ground up, and I'll let you know, honestly, the way I play bass is a lot different than, I'd say, ninety-nine percent of the bluegrass players out there. I play a lot more percussively because we have a trio, and everybody's got to work extra hard live."

Barnes, raised in Texas, also comes from slightly off the bluegrass track. "My mom and dad's folks are from Alabama and Tennessee," he says. "Even though we grew up in Texas, I was always inundated from a very early age with Grand Ole Opry acts. Bill Monroe and Lester Flatt, all those kind of guys."

Danny and Mark ended up in Killbilly together, Mark in what Danny describes as the band's first serious incarnation, and Danny for a few tours. Later, they both landed in Austin, where Ralph White was a neighbor. "I met Ralph at a little restaurant by my house," Barnes recalls. "They had a little jam session down there on Sundays, and he played fiddle and accordion. We got to playing—we'd meet on Sundays and play at this little jam—and I just hit it off with him. We got to talking, he liked fishin' and huntin' and stuff like that, and we became good friends and it just snowballed into this little deal we've got now."

That would be the Bad Livers, who began dangerously near to a novelty punk-bluegrass fusion. Which is what happens when you live in Austin and all your friends are in punk rock bands. Indeed, the first single was a cover of Iggy Pop's "Lust for Life," but they grew out of that quickly enough into whatever it is they've become. That part is a bit touchy.

"I used to tell interviewers a long time ago that I have way too much respect for bluegrass music to say that we have anything to do with it," Barnes offers.

"Yeah," says Rubin. "There's certain little hoops that you have to jump through in order to be a bluegrass band. We've probably violated quite a few of them."

Such as?

"Well, the accordion is a certain no-no," Barnes starts.

"No tubas, no short pants on stage, things like that," the well-tattooed Rubin adds.

"We don't have a style created whereby things are held up against this and then tossed away and evaluated through this style," Barnes says. "We're pretty adventurous in what we're doing. That's not really accepted in the traditional form. Because we played to kids, and to people that didn't really have an education in bluegrass music, we were free to do whatever we wanted to. That made it real advantageous for us, because we have a lot of different influences. I look at acoustic music as being this big thing, and bluegrass is like a slice of the pie, but there's so many other things in it."

"I'd like to be able to say that we came up with this great idea, but we didn't," Rubin concludes. "We just did what we did, and we just followed our muse. It dawned on us that people outside of Austin really liked what we were doing, and we put on a good show, and we played real well. They didn't at first get attracted to us because we played bluegrass per se, or because we played folk music."

This constant need to label things is one of several ways we now sort ourselves into tribal clans. Sheila is a punk rocker, little Ramona's gone hillbilly nuts. Otherwise, we all shop at the same dozen stores at the mall. No surprise there; have to belong to something, and odds are these days it's not going to be a family, a church, a neighborhood, a job.

But it makes music—which, fundamentally, is just invisible waves of sound dancing against your eardrums—a curious quilt. We are challenged with the introduction of a new instrument, the computer, which allows, on the one hand, for the synthesis of organic sounds (and the creation of non-organic sounds), and on the other for sufficient market research to identify the segment of society most receptive to those sounds.

Add onto that—and imagine yourself trying to write a song or twelve against this backdrop—the cultural imperative to recycle the past (and the present) at an ever-escalating speed, and utter uncertainty as to what the present or the future might hold, and maybe that's why people view deconstruction as some kind of logical and pleasant exercise. Just tear the whole machine apart so it can't work, and let the parts rust.

Is it just me, or is alienation the central theme of post-WWII Western culture?

The Bad Livers, to their infinite credit, have found a way to expand the hidebound traditions of bluegrass. To look simultaneously forward and backward. And to do so with tremendous joy.

This, incidentally, does not place them in league with New Grass Revival and its extended alumni association. "You know," Barnes says, choosing his words slowly, "I think those guys are great players, especially Sam Bush. I'm a big Sam Bush fan. But that music, to me, is a kind of pitch that I never swung at. It reminds me a bit of Al DiMeola, or something like that. You can't deny that it's great music, or good picking, but it doesn't really speak to me personally."

"What negative thing can you say about a guy who makes a living playing banjo?" Rubin asks.

Still, the Livers are quite obviously headed down a different road. Danny's apt to drop names like Captain Beefheart along the way, but he's hard-pressed to see much connection between the boundaries his songs push and New Grass's experiments. "The light that they were growing to was a different light than what we were growing to," he offers. "We're more interested in organic grooves and relationships between the instruments, rather than creating scenarios whereby you can take good solos."

"I think the key word that Danny used there is organic," Rubin says. "Unfortunately, sometimes when I see bands play I get the idea that they kind of came up with an idea and now they're trying to force that idea into being. Whereas I'm much more interested in music that just kind of happened."

"I think what we're trying to do is, we're exploring the relationships of the instruments to each other, rather than the solo being the main thing," Barnes picks up. "Compositionally, how I'm driven is, I look at what the composition's come from as sort of like theme songs to little movies that I make up in my brain. I'm trying to evoke moods and things like that."

Jars of Clay aside (they're a Christian faux-alternative rock band that mysteriously appeared on the *Billboard* charts last year), it's bloody hard to inject anything resembling rock music with anything resembling spirituality. That is, if you want it to come off.

It's a seamless matter with the Bad Livers, always has been a part of their music, shows up mid-set and amid their recordings. A while back they recorded the cassette-only *Dust on the Bible,* a collection of ageless gospel songs. It's cassette-only because it was recorded straight to cassette in Danny's spare room, and the fidelity's not up to their standards. But the songs flat swing.

"Mainly what I want to do, I'd like to have the opportunity to do that rascal again, you know," Barnes says, while Rubin laughs in the background. "I'd like to try to do that one again, and do it right. That was like the first recording I made in my home studio, and it's pretty rough. I think I spent about twenty-four bucks on the whole thing, and that was just buying cassette tape.

"Also, the more that I do this, the more that I'm interested in composition. I really would like to have the opportunity to make a gospel record that was all original pieces, 'cause I feel like, that's really my voice, and what I feel like I have to add to the world of music is a vision that's sort of an idea, rather than dragging up a bunch of songs and just playing them."

That makes it no less curious to hear Rubin's seconding amens dotting the conversation. "It's kind of an interesting question," he says. "Why do you have to be Christian to sing, or be involved in, gospel music?"

"One of the things I really enjoy about gospel music is it's just this incredible groove and vibe that's just…so much of our music today doesn't really help you out very much in terms of spirituality or philosophy, you know?" adds Barnes, and Rubin's question never does get answered. "Gospel music has always interested me because it has a connection both lyrically and musically. If you ever read interviews with Bill Monroe and Ralph Stanley, even guys that weren't necessarily particularly religious people, they certainly were well aware and quite respected the power of gospel music, in that it has levels of communication in it that are beyond mere music and lyric."

"It also appeals to why I got interested in music in the first place," Rubin says. "It's because it seems to do things you can't touch."

One of my theories about live music is that when it works really well, it has the ability to disintegrate the existential solitude that most of us dwell within.

"Amen," Rubin says. "Absolutely. I was a symphony musician for a long time, and I know that to be true. When you're a member of a big 150-piece orchestra and you're playing in front of 2,000 people, you can break down the walls to where it's all just one."

Another kind of beginning. We're watching another generation of rock musicians re-examine hillbilly music. It's a natural for aging punks who respond to the shared aesthetic demand for absolute honesty even if the standards of virtuosity are different. But the roots of the tree have spread far and wide by now, and the matter of authenticity (witness Gillian Welch, say) becomes murkier and murkier.

For the Bad Livers, who have to some extent done the post-modern thing and swept together a handful of seemingly unrelated musical notions, it hasn't been much of a reach. Even Rubin's tuba, which seems so natural a part of their music that it's hard to remember what a novel approach it is in traditional bluegrass circles.

"When I was ten years old, the first cat I saw that I really liked was Stringbean, who's got a bad rap," Barnes says. "He's a really great banjo player. And I really liked his rhythm; he's just got a super funked-out rhythm. He's sort of like George Clinton in his rhythm. Obviously Earl Scruggs, Ralph Stanley and Don Reno, those are the big three. I really got into John Hartford's playing, especially his music in the '70s. All the clawhammer players I can get my hands on. So yeah, normally one would assume that I would be from Appalachia or something, based on the banjo playing, but I come by it honest in terms of my family."

"I think there's a danger of over-regionalization, too," Rubin adds. "What with the great '60s folk scare, and the fact that we have records, and we all have TV now, all that stuff gets pushed around."

"I think it's important to note," Barnes says, "that there was a part of American music development where you could almost tell what part of the country someone was from, based on the style of music that they played. Mass communication has smeared that all around, where it's hard to tell anymore where your influences are from. Also, you're exposed to all the records at one time. Someone that was playing music in the '30s, he was exposed to innovations in order. Right now if someone's interested in bluegrass music they can go down and buy all the records at one time, which is a different thing."

Likely because their peers were mostly in punk bands, the Bad Livers ended up on Quarterstick, the more experimental imprint of Chicago's louder Touch & Go label

(The Jesus Lizard, stuff like that). That's where 1992's *Delusions of Banjer* and 1994's *Horses in the Minds* were released (*Dust on the Bible* is also available through Quarter-stick, or was).

Still, it was a weird fit. "We're all friends, you know, and they are the biggest fans. When we first started working with them, there was this discussion, I guess it was in '91, where they kind of looked at us and said, 'You know, we don't do this kind of thing. It's not what we do,'" Rubin recalls.

"He reminded us of that, after the second record kind of ran its life. And we all pretty much agreed, well, it's been a great run, and we love each other, and we're all good friends, but we need to attack a little differently, shift course just a little bit in our business."

The process of finding a new label wore on, and *Hogs* went through various incarnations as they wrote songs and sharpened ideas. "It's hard to really call it a bidding war for banjo records," Barnes laughs. "We certainly have talked to a lot of different labels, probably ten or fifteen, but it's just hard to come together on it.

"We sort of got the sense that a lot of the people approaching us were coming to this only because they were trying to cover their ass, which seems to be the big affliction of the music industry. Not to really try to do quality work, but just to cover your ass. So, in other words, somebody was going to get in trouble if we signed to a different label and did well."

Long story short, they ended up at Sugar Hill, which places them at the far edge of a pretty traditional bluegrass label, instead of the far edge of a pretty traditional punk rock label. And while their punk rock leanings may be a little less obvious this time out, that's apt to be as much the ravages of maturity as anything.

"I knew we were in trouble when I went over to Dan's house and he was going, 'I just don't have enough songs,'" Rubin laughs. "I realized when he wrote 'em all out that he had actually twenty-six, all together. And then I looked over at what he had been listening to recently, and he had [Captain Beefheart's legendary] *Trout Mask Replica,* and there are twenty-nine tunes on it. He was just assuming that that's what it took. That was a big slap in the face. We'd been down in the ditch for so long that we'd forgotten what the sunlight looked like up at the top, you know."

And the songs that didn't make the cut onto *Hogs?*

"Um, use 'em for the next record," Danny laughs.

"It's called recycling," Mark finishes.

"Deconstruction Blues" first appeared in *No Depression* #8 (March–April 1997).

Selected Discography:

Bad Livers, *Delusions of Banjer* (Quarterstick) 1992.

Bad Livers, *Horses In the Mines* (Quarterstick) 1994.

Bad Livers, *Hogs On the Highway* (Sugar Hill) 1997.

Buddy Miller

by Peter Blackstock

It arrived innocently and quietly enough in the mail last summer, amidst the relative trickle of new releases that tend to surface between the labels' much busier spring and fall seasons. *Your Love And Other Lies*, by Buddy Miller, some guy I'd never heard of; I set it on the rack of things to listen to that never does quite manage to shrink to zero. Fortunately, someone on the America Online "No Depression" board tipped me off that this one oughta get moved up in the stack. By the time two or three other people had chimed in with similarly hearty recommendations, the disc had made it into the rotation on my CD player, and it didn't leave there for a good month or so. I still hadn't a clue as to where Buddy Miller had suddenly come from, but I knew one thing: *Your Love And Other Lies* was the best true country record I'd heard all year.

In due time I discovered that Miller had been there all along, lurking just beneath the radar, low enough that it was possible to have missed him even if you'd been paying attention. He spent the better part of the last decade playing guitar with Jim Lauderdale, a comrade in that fringe-country community which never quite seems to fit into Nashville's big plans. But one listen to *Your Love And Other Lies* begs the obvious question: With sure-fire songwriting chops and a soulful vocal twang that easily equals his considerable talent as a guitarist, why was this guy merely serving as a sideman for all those years? Why didn't Buddy Miller have his own record deal?

"Nobody asked me," he answers, quite matter-of-factly. "And I didn't know if I had the stamina to go around banging on everybody's door saying, 'Please let me do a record.'…When HighTone called me, it kind of surprised me, but of course I said sure."

Sometimes all there is to A&R is recognizing the obvious and acting on it. In that sense, HighTone's role in Miller's career is quite similar to what the influential independent label did for Jimmie Dale Gilmore. Miller is in his early forties, as was Gilmore when HighTone issued his equally long-overdue solo debut, *Fair And Square*, in 1988. Such on-the-surface evidence might lead one to the conclusion that Gilmore and Miller are simply late bloomers, but in reality, they've been plenty active for most all of their adult lives, playing music in various places and configurations for the better part of three decades.

In fact, when Gilmore first started kicking up dust in Lubbock with his buddies Butch Hancock and Joe Ely as the Flatlanders in the early '70s, a fresh-faced, barely-out-of-his-teens Miller had just arrived on the Austin scene. He spent about eight years kicking around in bands—generally going nowhere but having fun, which has always been the unofficial pastime in Austin, especially back in those days. It seems fitting, then, that our interview took place on a mid-February afternoon in the lobby of an Austin motel. Miller was in town for a two-night stand at the Continental Club, kicking off HighTone's Roadhouse Revival tour (which featured Miller, Dave Alvin, Dale Watson, Big Sandy and Rev. Billy C. Wirtz).

It was also in Austin that Miller met his wife, Julie, with whom he frequently collaborates and who recently inked her own solo deal with HighTone (Buddy's producing her record). His running buddies in 1970s Austin included Shawn Colvin and Gurf Morlix; Morlix later played guitar and bass on *Your Love And Other Lies*. "Gurf and I were playin' in bands, drivin' around in old school buses in 1976 together here," Miller recalls. "And Shawn was playing in a band called Dixie Diesels then; it was like a Western swing band. And I had a different country band. We were just friends; it was a fun time, a good time."

Though they recently settled in Nashville, Buddy and Julie spent most of their post-Austin years living in either New York or Los Angeles. It was during this stretch that Buddy hooked up with Lauderdale. "We're like brothers," he says of his longtime musical ally. "We met in 1980 when we were both playing country music in New

York, which was kinda screwy, and we've been friends since then. I've played with Jim for like the last eight or nine years."

Miller made a point to acknowledge his old pals on *Your Love And Other Lies*, on which he covers songs by both Lauderdale and Morlix. He also unearthed a couple of long-lost chestnuts from the country annals—"You're Running Wild," an old Louvin Brothers hit, and Tom T. Hall's classic "That's How I Got To Memphis."

But it's his originals that really stand out, particularly the ones he co-wrote with Julie. The album kicks off with one of those, a rousing cut called "You Wrecked Up My Heart" that sets the tone as Buddy and Lucinda Williams drawl out the opening line in sublimely spunky a cappella harmony. Equally gutsy and full of glorious grit are "I'm Pretending," which features Lauderdale on backing vocals, and "I Don't Mean Maybe," with Julie providing the harmonies herself. "I Can't Slow Down" is more of a gradual groove, coolly casting a smoldering spell as the great Dan Penn takes his turn as the contrapuntal crooner in the chorus.

Best of all, though, is "My Love Will Follow You," which has that intangible appeal of a timeless classic. The melody is simple and memorable, yet still intriguing; the lyric is well-structured, yet full of passion. "Even on the road that takes you down/ Where the cords of human kindness come unwound/My love will follow you," Miller sings, perhaps the song's most moving and deeply cutting couplet.

In fact, someone recently commented that "My Love Will Follow You" struck them as "a country 'Every Breath You Take'"—and that someone just happened to be Kix Brooks, half of mainstream country's current chart-topping sensation, Brooks & Dunn. Overrated and overexposed as they may be, that twosome deserves credit for plucking this diamond from the rough and covering it on their new Arista disc.

Not that they're the only ones who have suddenly discovered the gems lurking on *Your Love And Other Lies*: George Ducas recorded "I'm Pretending"; and Jon Randall recorded "Don't Listen To The Wind," a song written by Julie.

Despite the extraordinary quality of the songwriting, Buddy says he and Julie didn't expect the attention the album has attracted from Nashville acts. "We were surprised," he admits. "I wasn't playing any gigs under my name, and nobody knew who the heck we were....And we haven't shopped it around. I find it so funny, because the whole Nashville machine, they write their lyrics to be like, 'Please record my song!'—you know, they have the hokiest stuff in there. And we just made a record to make a record. We cut it in the living room."

Ah, yes, we were wondering about this Dogtown Studios place credited in the liner notes; somehow, it didn't quite sound like a name befitting one of Music Row's high-end recording facilities. "We've got this old, old house that was built in 1903, and at some point it was divided into a duplex, so the two halves are pretty soundproof from each other," Buddy explained. "So we just live in half the house and record in the other half. We set the drums up either in the living room or the back room, and we all just play until the neighbors throw rocks.

"It works out fine. The board's marginal, but"—he pauses, before slightly redirecting his train of thought—"I mean, I didn't know anybody was gonna hear this record. I thought maybe it would end up on five or ten people's cassette players in their car running at the wrong speed, and they'd never know where it was recorded. But I think it sounds OK, actually. It's got good old mikes and that kind of stuff that I've collected over some years."

In fact, wheeling and dealing in home studio equipment was how he ended up meeting Dan Penn, once an idol of Miller's youth and now a friend and guest singer on *Your Love And Other Lies*. "He came over to buy a piece of equipment of mine, and I didn't even know it was him," Miller recalls. "He was wearing what I now know is, like, his 'uniform'—which is overalls, cap, toothpick—and, he was looking at this two-inch, 24-track machine I had. He was saying things like, 'Sounds good, don't it'—no technical questions. And on the way out of the house, he said, 'OK, I'll probably give you a call. My name's Dan, Dan Penn.'

"And at that point, I said, 'Step inside, close the door and sit down!' He's been a hero of mine forever. I'd had his old record that came out on Bell in the '60s, and I would just buy records when I was growing up looking at the back to see if there were any Dan Penn songs on it. So we became friends after that."

It's no wonder, then, that he was able to surround himself with such a remarkable supporting cast on *Your Love And Other Lies*. "Lucinda and I lived in L.A. at the same time, and through Gurf I've kinda known her for a long time," he says, referring again to his old Austin pal Morlix, who has played guitar with Williams for years. Also a fixture in Lucinda's band is Donald Lindley, who handled most of the drumming duties on Miller's record. Tammy Rogers and Don Heffington, from the

Dead Reckoning camp, show up on a few cuts. Nashville great Al Perkins contributes steel guitar on several tracks.

And then there's the queen herself, Emmylou Harris, adding her trademark Midas-touch harmony to "Hold On My Love." Which brings us to Miller's most recent digression—since March 1997, he's been playing guitar on Emmylou's world tour to support her *Wrecking Ball* album. Miller plays hard-country counterpoint to the Acadian-soul/funk rhythm section of Daryl Johnson and Brady Blade, who frequently work with *Wrecking Ball* producer Daniel Lanois.

The unlikely combination has proven to be a brilliantly effective vehicle for Emmylou's music, despite Miller's overly humble concerns during our February interview that he might not be good enough for the part. "If I stink after a week, they could say, 'Gosh, we're really sorry, but, what's Steuart Smith's number, do you know it?'" he cracked, before eventually acknowledging that "I think I'll probably be able to keep that gig. I listened to *Wrecking Ball* and heard what he [Lanois] was doing on guitar....I wasn't gonna imitate it, because he's nuts," he says, with a smile that makes clear his admiration for Lanois' abilities.

"He's out on the edge of the limb at all times, and doesn't care if he comes back. And I've got a lot of respect for that kind of player. Richard Thompson does the same kind of thing with his playing. It's a much different style, but they just take chances. But I can hear what he's doing tonally and know the sound he's getting, and I can kind of get that. And I can play the country stuff. Her records are like *the* classic records that brought in such a high level of integrity to country music, and I know all that stuff."

The Emmylou tour will keep Miller busy through the summer, after which he plans to finish working on Julie's record and then get started on his second disc for HighTone. "I've got a bunch of songs and I'm ready to cut the next record right away," he says. "It was probably almost ready when this one came out. And as soon as this next one's out, I'll probably have another batch of songs ready to go."

Given the excellent appetite-whetting mini-set Miller cranked out on the Roadhouse Revival tour, it seems reasonable to expect some live dates to support the second album. That never really materialized after *Your Love And Other Lies* came out, mainly because, like me, most people just didn't know who he was at the time—a problem that hopefully has been largely eradicated by his significant accomplishments of the past year.

"I did everything I could [to tour behind the first record]," Miller says with a laugh of resignation. "I *begged* people to book me. I don't know how these bands get booked. And a lot of 'em don't, or a lot of 'em go out and lose a lot of money.

"I did go out with Lauderdale; we went around the country, and I opened for him. They wouldn't let me have a band play; I just got up with a cue stick and sang for a while. And that was fine. Any way I can, it's nice to play."

"It's Miller's Time" first appeared in *No Depression* #9 (May–June 1997).

Selected Discography:

Julie Miller, *Invisible Girl* (Street Level/R.E.X. Music) 1994.

Buddy Miller, *Your Love And Other Lies* (HighTone) 1996.

Julie Miller, *Blue Pony* (HighTone) 1997.

Buddy Miller, *Poison Love* (HighTone) 1997.

Jason & the Scorchers

by Bill Friskics-Warren

The year is 1982, on the Sunday before Labor Day; the place is Cat's Records, on West End Avenue in Nashville. A thousand people have packed the store's parking lot to see Jason & the Scorchers, who in the past year have taken the city by storm with their shotgun marriage of country music and punk rock.

"We had flatbed trucks pulled up in the parking lot," remembered Steve West, who promoted the Cat's show and now runs Nashville's 328 Performance Hall and Go West Presents. "We didn't have backdrops or anything—just a P.A." The lack of pageantry only heightened the immediacy between audience and performer, emphasizing the anything-could-happen mood that marked Scorchers shows at the time. On this particular night, the crowd's excitement was at fever pitch; the band had just pulled back into town after a series of road dates promoting the release of their debut EP, *Reckless Country Soul*.

"During the first song," West recalled, "Jason slammed the microphone into his mouth and broke his tooth off."

Adrenaline must have masked singer Jason Ringenberg's pain, because he performed like a man possessed, even by his own maniacal standards. During one of guitarist Warner Hodges' lead breaks on "White Lies," Ringenberg, an American flag in tow, shot up the store's signpole like an explorer who had just discovered some uncharted frontier.

Jason & the Scorchers' historical moment had come and gone long before "Americana" became a radio format and *No Depression* became a magazine, but the Nashville-based rockers have as much claim to being founders of today's alternative country movement as any group to emerge in punk's wake. No other band boasts the Scorchers' country pedigree, none rocks as savagely, and none has a recorded legacy that can touch the mid-'80s triptych of *Restless Country Soul, Fervor* and *Lost and Found.*

The Scorchers' influence on Uncle Tupelo, the Bottle Rockets and countless others is undeniable. It may be commonplace now for roots-rockers to perform cover versions of classic honky-tonk songs, but back when the Scorchers were running Hank Williams, Jimmie Rodgers and Eddy Arnold through their punk blender, it just wasn't done—it might even get you hurt or run out of town.

"Literally, you could go into certain places and do what we were doin' with country music—forging it, melding it, slamming it together with punk rock and rock 'n' roll—and get beat up. And we almost did several times," said Ringenberg, recalling the band's early '80s heyday during an interview in the back room of Tootsie's Orchid Lounge in Nashville, two weeks before the early October release of the Scorchers' inspired new album, *Clear Impetuous Morning* (Mammoth/Atlantic).

Whereas *A Blazing Grace*, the Scorchers' 1995 reunion album, proved that the band could still rock and still had something to say, their new record finds them kicking their way back to the top of the cowpunk—or, in today's parlance, alternative-country—heap. Raging with affirmation and insight, and playing with relentless mid-'80s intensity, *Clear Impetuous Morning* is the Scorchers taking command of the musical subgenre they all but invented.

While the new album finally may earn them the recognition they're due, Ringenberg isn't exaggerating about the hostile reception the Scorchers often encountered back when they were taking early-'80s Nashville by storm. At the time, many believed the Scorchers were poking fun at country music. Little did they know that the foursome were devoted to the sounds they grew up listening to on the Grand Ole Opry. Nor were they aware that guitarist Hodges' parents played with Johnny Cash, or that drummer Perry Baggs' father sang old-timey gospel.

Others, like the Vanderbilt coeds who almost booed the Scorchers offstage when they opened for the Talking Heads in 1982, simply missed the point. But nothing, not even the prospect of getting their asses kicked, could stop Ringenberg, Baggs, Hodges and bassist Jeff Johnson from unleashing the glorious noise they heard banging around inside their heads.

"Mixing country and punk seemed a natural thing to do," Ringenberg said. "Warner, Jeff and Perry—they knew country music and played it a lot. But they were also fierce, ferocious rock 'n' rollers. Then here comes this kid off an Illinois hog farm that's never even been south of the Mason-Dixon Line who still's got hog poop on his shoes. You put all that together and it was just an outrageous chemistry."

Early live dates at such Nashville punk clubs as Cantrell's, Phrank 'n' Stein's and the Cannery were more like explosive chemical reactions. "Those shows were totally spontaneous," Ringenberg said. "The rock community in Nashville was just discovering itself and the Scorchers were discovering what we were. Some of those shows were really bad and some of them were transcendent, brilliant." The Cat's Records show in '82 certainly fell into the transcendent category, as did a second performance there in 1985, which drew 5,000 fans and brought traffic to a halt on the city's major East-West corridor.

Ringenberg's electrifying Jerry Lee Lewis-meets-Iggy Pop stage attack was what attracted Johnson and Hodges—and, later, Baggs—to the singer in the first place. Johnson was the first member of what eventually became the Scorchers' classic lineup to see the edition of the band Ringenberg assembled upon arriving in Music City during the summer of 1981. The fledgling Scorchers were sharing a bill at Cantrell's with then-regionally acclaimed indie-rockers R.E.M. Immediately after the show, Johnson called Hodges and invited him to Ringenberg's next gig. This time, it was a slot opening for rockabilly legend Carl Perkins.

"I went to the Carl Perkins show and thought, 'God Almighty, this guy is nuts,'" remembered Hodges, referring to Ringenberg's incendiary performance. "He spent the entire night in the crowd with this long guitar cord. Everybody else up onstage was scared to death. But Jason, man, he was the show."

It wasn't long before Hodges and Johnson had replaced the Scorchers' original guitar and bass players. Several weeks later, Baggs took command of the drum kit, and the classic—and still current—edition of Jason & the Nashville Scorchers was born.

"We went real fast in those days," admitted Ringenberg. "In a couple of months we were gettin' songs together and fillin' rooms, and we said, 'We need to get a record out.'" added Hodges: "It was like you had to have a record to play."

Former bassist turned manager Jack Emerson was very insistent, explained Ringenberg. "Jack said, 'We gotta get a record out to prove that you guys are the founding fathers of modern country. And we gotta get it out now. We gotta get it out before the first of the year so that we have a 1981 date on the record.'"

The EP, *Reckless Country Soul*, didn't hit stores until the second week of 1982, but it immediately sent shock waves through the Nashville rock underground. Originally released on the Praxis label, it featured gonzo covers of Hank Williams and Jimmie Rodgers classics and an early version of "Broken Whiskey Glass," a song the Scorchers later re-cut for *Lost and Found*, their first and finest full-length album. The band also tore apart the Willie Nelson-penned Faron Young hit "Hello Walls," though the recording didn't see the light of day until Mammoth reissued the complete sessions, along with outtakes from *Fervor*.

"We cut *Reckless Country Soul* in four hours in somebody's living room live to four-track," Ringenberg recalls. "We had to hurry because Perry had to go to work at the bowling alley that night. It was five songs, four hours, just raisin' hell." If the record didn't quite live up to Emerson's claim that the Scorchers had founded modern country music, definitive proof came with the release of *Fervor* and *Lost and Found*, two of the finest weddings of id-driven punk and hard-core country music ever recorded.

"They called themselves Scorchers for good reason: They kicked butt," commented country music historian Robert K. Oermann, senior music writer for *The Tennessean*, Nashville's morning newspaper, at the time the Scorchers burst onto the local scene. Oermann also penned a *USA Today* story that helped break the band to the rest of the nation.

"Their shows were so physical," said Oermann. "Jason acted like a guy who had been attacked with a cattle prod. And I still maintain that Warner Hodges was one of the most charismatic lead guitarists of his generation. The two were like twin poles of electrical energy. You could almost see the bolt of lightning that connected them. The Scorchers never sold more than a million records, but nobody who saw them will ever forget it."

"If Hank Williams were alive today," observed Scorchers co-manager Andy

McLenon back in 1984, "he would be playing with the same intensity as Jason & the Scorchers, because for the pre-rock era, Hank Williams' music was equally as intense and on-the-edge."

Ringenberg, Johnson, Hodges and Baggs were as electrifying as they were outrageous. Looking back now—and having experienced the visceral thrill of those early '80s shows—there's no denying that the Scorchers, the first modern rock band out of Nashville to sign with a major label, galvanized a formative moment in the city's storied musical history.

But if in 1985 the Scorchers were poised to conquer the world, by decade's end the bottom had dropped out. Excess, personal problems, the fickle winds of the music business—all contributed to a fall that was as dramatic as the band's rise was meteoric. It started with Capitol's ineffective marketing of 1986's *Still Standing* just as the record's first single, "Golden Ball and Chain," was getting some airplay. Soon Johnson left the group; by the time the band's lukewarm *Thunder and Fire* surfaced in '89, the Scorchers were all but finished.

"We worked on *Thunder and Fire* for two years," said Hodges. "Jason wrote like seventy songs and we demoed and demoed and demoed—just busted our butts putting the band back together [after Johnson's departure]. I didn't think it was that bad a record. Maybe not quite the direction we should have gone, but we gave the record company the record that they quote/unquote wanted. We put a lot of time and effort into it and then it just fell flat on its face. And then Perry got sick with diabetes and we said, 'The hell with it.'

"The Scorchers didn't break up, we fell apart," continued Hodges, who, after the split, moved to New York and then California, working in the video business. "I ran," he admitted. "I guess I hid and ran. I didn't know how we could try any harder and be any less successful. I seriously didn't know how we could put any more effort into it for so little return. We just couldn't play the game anymore."

"If you talked to each of us independently," said Ringenberg, "I think all four members of the band would tell you it wasn't a good time in anybody's life. I did a solo record for Capitol/Nashville, a watered-down Scorchers kind of record, and went through a bad divorce. It just wasn't a good time at all."

In 1992, EMI reissued *Fervor* and *Lost and Found*, along with a couple of B-sides and live recordings from the mid-'80s, under the title *Essential Jason & the Scorchers, Volume 1: Are You Ready for the Country.* Johnson was so far out of the Scorchers' loop that the label didn't bother to send him a copy; he had to go out and buy the record at Tower. Amazed at how vital the band's early music still sounded, he pushed for a Scorchers reunion. His former bandmates weren't interested at first, but Johnson didn't take no for an answer, and it wasn't long before they were practicing, putting a tour together and talking about making a record.

The Scorchers' 1995 comeback album, *A Blazing Grace* (Mammoth), symbolized their spiritual rebirth. It didn't break new ground musically or lyrically, but it rocked harder than either *Thunder and Fire or One Foot in the Honky Tonk,* Ringenberg's 1992 solo effort for Capitol. "What *A Blazing Grace* did for us, way beyond what it may have sold, was make people aware of the band again," Ringenberg said. "It also got us back together as a band." Indeed, enthusiasm for the record—and for the Scorchers' reunion in general—got the group's members looking again toward the future.

Today Ringenberg and Hodges, both nearing forty, exude an emotional and spiritual maturity that's almost disarming, coming from two of post-punk's wildest showmen. But both agree it is this growth that makes *Clear Impetuous Morning*—recorded this past spring at Bakos Amp Works in Atlanta—such an uplifting record.

"*Clear Impetuous Morning* was just a great labor of love," Ringenberg said. "We never talked about sales. We never talked about what we were gonna do with it until it was done. After it was done, we said, 'OK, let's get this thing out there.' But while we were making it, we did it just for the pure joy of making it.

"That's not to say every song doesn't have its share of pain, heartache and suffering in it," he continued. "But there's an element of joy and exuberance behind every song and every lick on there. *A Blazing Grace* was an answer to the past. *Clear Impetuous Morning* is definitely charging into the future with very few inhibitions. It's remarkable for what we've been through, personally and as a band."

Indeed, the delight with which Ringenberg kicks off the album, singing "Oh what a rush," is enough to get anybody's heart racing. Co-producers Johnson and Hodges sustain that immediacy and sense of abandon throughout. The rhythm section is devastatingly tight, and Hodges' guitar work, which avoids what he calls "pyrotechnic, whammy-bar crap," is as muscular and imaginative as ever.

"I made a conscious effort to stay out of ground I've already covered," he said. "When Jeff and I were working on the guitar tracks, I said, 'If you hear something that you've heard 400 times before, just stop me.'" Songs such as "Uncertain Girl" and "Tomorrow Has Come Today" reveal that Hodges' playing has taken a melodic turn, at times reminiscent of Bob Mould's phrasing from the mid-'80s glory days of Hüsker Dü. Elsewhere, Hodges' fretwork suggests the punked-up Chuck Berry aesthetic of kindred spirits Keith Richards and Johnny Thunders.

Ringenberg's singing and command of narrative are likewise undiminished. "Going Nowhere" and "Cappuccino Rosie," both co-written with Nashvillian Tommy Womack, exhibit as much humanity, humor and pathos as such early Scorchers classics as "Still Tied" and "Broken Whiskey Glass." But these new songs don't merely evoke timeless verities about longing and loss, they flesh out their themes with characters and stories listeners can connect with. Today, Ringenberg sings less of sin than salvation: The resiliency and hope that can be heard on "Self-Sabotage" and "Everything Has A Cost"—the latter a gorgeous duet with Emmylou Harris that seems a lock for Americana programmers' playlists—are no doubt born of the band's struggle and rebirth.

But the moral and musical high point of *Clear Impetuous Morning* is a demolition of "Drugstore Truck Drivin' Man," the Gram Parsons/Roger McGuinn sendup of Ralph Emery, the Nashville deejay-cum-veejay who in the late '60s dismissed the Byrds' visionary synthesis of country music and rock 'n' roll.

"We started playing 'Drugstore Truck Drivin' Man' during the *A Blazing Grace* tour," said Ringenberg. "We try to work up at least one or two covers for every tour. The song worked really well live. We had a lot of fun with it. Conceptually, it's a crime that the Scorchers never did a Gram Parsons song. But this one seemed like the perfect choice. We're from Nashville and we've been slammed by Ralph, you know, the whole nine yards.

"We sing it with a lot of pride," Ringenberg continued, "because we feel like you have to have a lot of confidence in yourself to sing 'Drugstore Truck Drivin' Man' and to remake it. We're proud of the fact that people are saying that we've done the song justice."

The Parsons connection also rings true from a legacy standpoint: From the rock side of the equation, only Parsons can match the Scorchers' influence on today's alt-country movement. The Scorchers may have enjoyed plenty of acclaim during the mid-'80s, but if the Americana chart had been around back then, they likely would have reached a wider audience.

"I have no bitterness or darts to throw," said Ringenberg, referring to the lack of convergence between the Scorchers' heyday and the current alternative-country boom. "I'm kinda proud that people point to us as one of the pioneers. It's validation, and that makes us feel good."

Ringenberg has obviously kept up with the current crop of country rockers, some of whom probably formed bands in part because of the Scorchers' influence. "There are some awfully good people out there," he said, singling out Wayne Hancock, the Backsliders and Uncle Tupelo offshoots Son Volt, Wilco and Courtesy Move, among others. "Any time you have a form of music or movement, there are good bands and bad bands, people copying and people leading the charge creatively. But I've gotta hand it to folks who are trying to make something viable out of this, because it's hard for artists who are doing this kind of thing because you can't get on country radio and it's hard to get on rock radio. So I think it's a good thing.

"One thing I do resent," he added, "is how a lot of people in the alternative country world still slam Nashville. That really bothers me because there's a lot of great music here. I mean, Hank, Sr. came out of Nashville. Sure, there's been a lot of bad stuff. But there's also been a lot of brilliant, brilliant music that's come out of this town. Even lately, there have been some great things. Steve Earle came out of Nashville, you know. It always bothers me when people take this anti-Nashville stance and say that everything out of Nashville is corporate schlock. That's not the case at all. This is a great, great town for making music. The Scorchers are proud to be from here.

"We're from the other side of the tracks, no doubt—but those are beautiful tracks."

"The Scorch Will Rise Again" first appeared in *No Depression* #6 (November–December 1996).

Selected Discography:
Jason & The Nashville Scorchers, *Reckless Country Soul* EP (Praxis) 1982, reissued (Praxis/Mammoth) 1996.

Jason & The Scorchers, *Fervor* EP (Praxis) 1983, reissued (EMI America) 1984, reissued (Mammoth) 1996.

Jason & The Scorchers, *Lost And Found* (EMI America) 1985, reissued (Mammoth) 1996.

Jason & The Scorchers, *Still Standing* (EMI America) 1986, reissued (Mammoth) 1996.

Jason, *One Foot in the Honky Tonk* (Liberty) 1992.

Jason & The Scorchers, *A Blazing Grace* (Mammoth) 1995.

Jason & The Scorchers, *Both Sides Of The Line,* (Mammoth) 1996.

Jason & The Scorchers, *Clear Impetuous Morning* (Mammoth/Atlantic) 1996.

BR5-49

by Phil Fuson

In the shadow of the new metroplex behemoth (what one distinguished local has dubbed "Y'all Hall"), emerging from a block-wide hole, lies a serious strip of American music history. Known as Lower Broad, this is where giants once walked among us, stomping on the terra from the back door of the Opry to Tootsie's World Famous Orchid Lounge.

Many moons have since passed. The lower end of Broadway has fallen into fits of decay and kitschy renewal. Three doors down from Tootsie's is a place called—what else—Three Doors Down, a.k.a. Robert's Western World.

In the past year or so, the Lower Broad scene has received an infusion of young blood. One of the most promising acts, a charter member of this roots revival of live music in downtown Nashville, is named after the phone number on the sign country comedy savant Jr. Samples held up while selling used cars on Hee Haw: BR5-49.

These folks are mining the classics with real love and a feel for the stuff, but not to the point that the compositions feel like museum pieces. Ray Price shuffles and Webb Pierce whiners can be found alongside the songs of young upstarts like that Parsons boy from Florida. Sprinkled in amongst these gems are their original tunes. It's sometimes difficult to distinguish between what's a classic and what's homemade. Their compositions are straight outta honkdom. Often, the only way to identify their originals is by hearing someone on the stand declare, "THAT'S a true story!"

Head yodeler Chuck Mead once told a confused and horrified Crook & Chase, "There's not that much difference between Hank, Sr. and the Ramones." Another oblique comparison could be made between the evolution of this band and the Beatles during their Hamburg days. "We've just kept on pickin'. Up until August we were playin' six nights a week," Mead says. Then and now, all compensation for live performance derives from a jar labeled TIPS. So, uh…they aren't playing this music for the money. (At least not yet.)

"It all started a little over a year ago," Mead said. "I got there [Nashville] in April of '93, and Gary landed in May," he says, referring to Gary Bennett, the other primary songwriter in the band. "I first saw him at a writers' night audition at the Bluebird. We both passed the audition but wound up on Lower Broad. We both knew about twenty of the same Johnny Horton songs."

Mead later ran into Bennett at Robert's Western Wear. "Robert [the owner] had him in a band. He [Robert] got 'em all together," Mead recalls. "One night the guitar player got sick so I got invited. We sang together and liked the same songs."

Smilin' Jay McDowell became the next permanent fixture. "He was playing in a band called Hellbilly at the time, but one night we played with Nick Lowe at 328 [Performance Hall], and afterward I saw Jay and said, 'Why don't you get a dawghouse bass and come play with us?'," Mead said.

Rounding out the orchestra are Shaw Wilson ("stirrin' up the beats") on drums and "The Professor" Don Herron on fiddle, mandolin and vintage Fender steel. "I talked Shaw into moving down around June of '94, and Gary knew Don from playing around Washington and Oregon," Chuck said.

In performance, they are a joy to behold. They appear to be a traditional country-western string band—"We started out just wearin' ties on the weekends but…if you're gonna play hillbilly music, you gotta wear a suit!" Mead says—but after a few tunes, like an old big block gettin' warmed up, you start to notice things.

The rhythm section of Shaw and McDowell is like a steel cradle (with tuck-and-roll-interior by Nudie, of course) that carries the rest of the band. Bennett's solid rhythm on his old arch top Gibson makes you realize what Freddie Green of Basie's band might've sounded like in a tonk situation. Mead focuses the blast of his Gretsch through an old blond '62 Fender Bandmaster with a Duane Eddy-cum-Billy Zoom vibe at times. And last, but certainly not least, is The Professor. Whether it's Bob

Wills-esque fiddlin' or Speedy West-channeling-Hendrix steel playing, there's never a dull moment when Don Herron is settin' the house a far!

All this sonic firepower backs up some of the finest high 'n' lonesome vocal stylings heard in Nashville in a long time. Mead and Bennett blend nicely, swapping parts flawlessly. "Gary's one of the best singers I've ever heard," says Mead, who can holler with the best of 'em himself. Mead's words would be high praise from anyone who's spent more than a week in Nashville, let alone somebody who has closed tonks on Lower Broad six nights a week for over two years.

And now for the silver lining: BR5-49 recently signed with Arista.

"All of a sudden these music biz types started showin' up," Mead says. "We didn't think they'd be interested…just look at the stuff they're turnin out. I mean, I'm not knockin' Garth or anybody. Obviously he's workin' hard to be that successful. We just wanted to play more homespun music."

A live EP is scheduled for release this spring, with a full-length disc due in stores by summer. Many are hopeful this could signal the demise of "test your motor skills here" boot-scootiesque recordings being churned out in Nashville. Then again, as you read this, some guy is having his head measured for that Resistol, thus endearing him to Ralph Emery and all those drugstore truck drivin' guys and gals. If this gives you the blues, just dial BR5-49. Your faith will be restored.

"Honky-tonk Heroes Of The Western World" first appeared in *No Depression* #3 (Spring 1996).

Selected Discography:

BR5-49, *Live From Robert's* (Arista) 1996.
BR5-49, *BR5-49* (Arista) 1996.

Gillian Welch

by Bill Friskics-Warren

Music critic Ann Marlowe once noted that the Louisville string band Freakwater had cornered the market on child-death songs. Gillian Welch's debut album, *Revival*, boasts only one dead baby song; nonetheless, her breathtakingly austere evocations of rural culture, though not as attentive to politics of gender and class, bear more than a passing resemblance to those of principal Freakwater songwriter Catherine Irwin. And while Welch's record has a more commercial feel than the rough-hewn, lo-fi music of her Kentucky counterparts, it drinks just as deeply from the mountain wellspring of country music's pre-commercial era.

Somewhat surprisingly, Welch's portraits of the darker side of rural life aren't based on firsthand experience. The twenty-eight-year-old performer grew up in relative comfort in West L.A., where her parents scored music for "The Carol Burnett Show" and sang Irving Berlin and Rodgers & Hart standards around the family piano. But, despite the fact that Welch wasn't raised dirt poor in some East Tennessee hollow, her grasp of the emotional and spiritual reach of old-time country music is undeniable.

"I must just have a natural inclination toward the stuff," she observed during a Nashville interview. "I've listened to a lot of pretty rural stuff, so I guess I had the groundwork—the sponge—to absorb it. From the very first time that I heard the Stanley Brothers, it rang a bell with me. I didn't know it until I discovered bluegrass and Appalachian stuff that everything I liked was in that music, all rolled into one."

The hauntingly soulful voices of Ralph and Carter Stanley—as well as the close harmony singing of the original Carter Family and brother duos like the Delmore Brothers and the Blue Sky Boys—are an obvious inspiration for Welch's older-than-her-years vocals, especially when paired with those of her musical partner, David Rawlings. But Welch's songs draw as much on the Celtic origins of Appalachian music as on its hillbilly roots. "David and I always go in for the more pitiful ballads," confessed Welch, "the darker tunes that go back a long way and probably have their roots overseas."

Indeed, songs such as "Orphan Girl"—which Emmylou Harris included on her *Wrecking Ball* album last year—as well as "Annabelle" and "Acony Bell," could easily pass for popular English and Scottish ballads compiled by nineteenth-century collector Francis Child. Some of the more contemporary sounding material on *Revival* also brings to mind Richard and Linda Thompson's 1974 album, *I Want to See the Bright Lights Tonight*, perhaps the most exquisite synthesis of the traditional folk music of the British Isles and rock ever recorded. On "Only One and Only," "One More Dollar" and "Tear My Stillhouse Down," Welch wrings untold emotion out of her lyrics in much the same way that Linda Thompson's stately vocals do on "The Little Beggar Girl" and "Has He Got a Friend For Me" from *Bright Lights*. And on the songs where the deft flatpicking of Rawlings and Welch is fired by the fretwork of guitar legend James Burton—who was almost certainly an influence on Richard Thompson—the effect is strikingly similar to Thompson's modal excursions of the mid-'70s.

Welch and Rawlings met in the early '90s while living in Boston, where Welch was enrolled at the Berklee School of Music. "We'd known each other a year," she recalls, "but we'd never worked as a team until we moved down here in July of '92 and started arranging traditional [country and bluegrass] tunes. We were pleased to discover that our voices sounded pretty good together. Dave was really never a singer before that, but he was kind enough to agree to working up my four songs and to slogging it out in the writers' nights around town."

The duo's days of playing three to four open mike showcases a week—not to mention Welch's job at a bed and breakfast in nearby Franklin—ended abruptly one night at the Station Inn in Nashville where, opening for Peter Rowan, they caught the ear of ubiquitous producer T Bone Burnett. "T Bone came back after our twenty-minute set and said, 'Gee, I'd love to make a record with you guys,'" remembers Welch. The relationship felt right from the beginning. "We talked to some other producers," Welch admitted, "but just felt so at ease with him. He came and saw us live a couple more times, we had some dinner and just really hit it off."

Welch's account of working with Burnett at times takes on an almost dreamlike quality. For one thing, he recruited heady company—the aforementioned Burton on guitar, Roy Huskey Jr. on upright bass, Jim Keltner and Buddy Harmon on drums—to back Rawlings and Welch on the songs they didn't record simply as a duo. But, as Welch is quick to point out, perhaps more important than the presence of such luminaries was the way Burnett "always worked from the angle that he loved what he heard the first night—just Dave and myself. That was always the core."

Preserving what he first heard at the Station Inn was obviously important to Burnett—so much so that, to ensure they re-created that sound, he suggested Welch and Rawlings record some of the album's songs in mono. "The first day we got in the studio, they were wrestling with some of the older gear," Welch recalled. "T Bone had wanted to get an old Wollensak like the kind that Hank [Williams, Sr.] recorded on, but he tracked one down and the heads were funky so we ended up working with a slightly more modern machine." The team's inability to locate vintage equipment notwithstanding, they still went ahead and recorded four songs on *Revival* in mono. "It was an extraordinary experience," Welch said. "That first week was really intense. It was just T Bone, Rik [Pekkonen], the engineer, and Dave and myself. We got so inside our little world. There was very little distance between our singing and playing. The sound was very immediate. It was so light and small."

It was very important to Welch to work with a producer who was in tune with her and Rawlings musically. "I was always really afraid," she said, "that if someone took Dave and I into the studio, just the two of us, just four elements—two voices, two guitars—that they would make that really big lush acoustic guitar sound where it fills up the spectrum so as to compensate for the fact that there's very little going on. Dave and I always felt strongly that it should be tiny—that, if anything, it should go the other way and be contracted."

Things have opened up considerably since Welch and Rawlings started playing writers' nights around Nashville a couple years ago. The week before *Revival* was released, the duo played the Ryman Auditorium, the original home of the Grand Ole Opry. They'll also be opening for Son Volt on a number of dates during the band's spring and summer tour. As if that wasn't enough, Welch was up until 5:30 A.M. the morning before our interview, picking and singing with Guy Clark, Townes Van Zandt and others after their gig at Green's Grocery, an old-time country store in Leipers Fork, just outside of Nashville. Welch insists Clark is responsible for her lack of sleep, but who could blame him? She has the makings of a songwriters' songwriter; couplets such as "The night came undone like a party dress/And fell at her feet in a beautiful mess," from "Barroom Girls," sound as if they were inspired by Clark's muse herself.

Welch approaches her lyrics like someone who writes short fiction for a living: always striving to say more with less, finely honing miniatures that are fairly pregnant with meaning. She's particularly fond of story songs, especially those with religious themes, or what she calls "gospel fodder." "What else can happen in the third verse of a song?" she asked rhetorically. "Your main character can die or your main character can kill somebody or, if things are going really bad, you can always appeal to God. I'm not saying that it's purely a storytelling thing, but, when you're reaching for where a story can go, a spiritual side is always a good option. By the same token," she added, "there's no way that I could sing the songs if I thought, well, that's a load of crap."

That's good, because Nashville has more churches, per capita, than any city in the United States. Despite the town's pervasive, sometimes suffocating religiosity, Welch seems perfectly at home living in Music City. "I love it here," she admitted. "I was much more at home here in a couple of weeks than I was in Boston. Boston was a big shock. I was living in a very urban area and it was very tough. Nashville was easy, except that I couldn't understand some of the local dialects."

If the timeless stories and melodies on *Revival* are any indication, Welch's ear for the rhythms and cadences of rural speech and culture is adapting just fine. In fact, except for the past couple of Freakwater and Iris DeMent albums, Welch's debut is about as distinctive and satisfying as Americana gets.

"Orphan Girl Of The Hollywood Hills" first appeared in *No Depression* #4 (Summer 1996).

Selected Discography:
Gillian Welch, *Revival* (Almo) 1996.

Freakwater

by Allison Stewart

Before leaving on Freakwater's last, ill-fated tour, singer Janet Beveridge Bean went to a new age healer, who promised Bean she would cleanse her aura. "She told me she would open my third eye," Bean remembers. "I'll tell you, from that day on, everything has just been a disaster." The ensuing mini-tour became a nightmare of fraying tempers and canceled shows. "Maybe it was someone's way of telling me to get out of this business," Bean says. "I think I either have to go back and get that eye closed, or face life with it open."

The past year has been particularly trying for Freakwater, with the band delaying their just-released fifth record, *Springtime*, as well as waging a very public war with Steve Earle and his record label, E-Squared. But Bean has been threatening to quit the record business, by her own recollection, since the day she started fifteen years ago. "I'm always closer to it than I was," says Bean. "It's like the rabbit and the carrot; you never quite seem to reach it. I'm sort of delusional, anyway. At thirty-three I still think I could join NASA and be an astronaut. I could do anything, if I could just figure out what it is."

Given the trauma surrounding its birth, it's a small wonder that *Springtime* is Freakwater's lightest record yet. Though full of the mournful folk ballads and Gothic bluegrass numbers that have become the band's stock in trade, Freakwater also makes fine work of several bustling, almost peppy folk-pop numbers on *Springtime*.

"It's like we're getting perky all of a sudden," says Bean, with some trepidation. "I don't know where *that* comes from."

While *Springtime* is the band's most accessible record, if only by default, no one expects the relative upsweep in record sales for alternative country artists to reach as far as Freakwater, whose raw, starkly pretty Appalachian folk bears little in common with, say, Son Volt. Stubbornly anachronistic and seldom seen, Bean and fellow front-woman Catherine Irwin tour rarely, briefly, and under great protest. They release an album every couple years or so and have spent the latter part of their creative lives at Thrill Jockey, a small Chicago indie that houses similarly iconoclastic acts such as Tortoise and The Sea And Cake.

It was to everyone's surprise, then, that major-label interest, in the form of Earle's E-Squared label (affiliated with Warner Brothers), came calling last winter. To hear Bean tell it, Freakwater, enticed by the prospect of a label run by a respected artist, came close to signing with E-Squared until concerns over the amount of artistic control the band would retain scuttled the deal.

"It put our lives on hold for the longest time, although I'm sure it didn't stop Steve Earle for a minute. It's one of those things where you go in, and you think you have a certain idea about a situation, and then they'll say, 'How about firing your band and taking it to the next level?'" Bean said. "That made us kind of nervous, but we were willing to go down there and work with session musicians. [Bassist Dave Gay] was even willing to let them play on the record. That was the first stumbling block. We were gonna sign, and then we got a lawyer and things fell apart, and they insinuated that that was why. I think they needed a band that felt comfortable being controlled a little more."

The resulting public dust-up, which led to, among other things, a Bean-penned article in a local paper detailing the experience, and a protracted online skirmish, prompted Earle to tell a Chicago audience during a show last winter that the Freakwater women (who did not attend) "can kiss my ass."

"Steve Earle's had a rough time of it," says Bean. "I don't bear him any ill will, even today. It was just something that happened, you know? I still think we could have worked together."

For their part, representatives from E-Squared have claimed that the deal fell apart not over matters of artistic control, but over far more prosaic things, like

Freakwater's demands for larger advances and tour buses. Though that seems unlikely for the women of Freakwater, who have survived this long on shoestring recording budgets and second jobs (Bean waits tables; Irwin paints houses). The lack of money has been a bone of contention since the band's early days in Louisville, Kentucky.

"It's like this ambiguous ground we ride where it takes up a lot of our lives, but we don't do enough with it to take it to the next level," says Bean. "It's like, we can't get jobs because we're not around enough, but we aren't gone enough to make money. And it's always been that way."

Best friends now, Bean and Irwin weren't immediately drawn to each other when they first met growing up in Louisville. Irwin vaguely remembers being nasty to Bean; Bean remembers Catherine as a "nice little punker girl." It would take a mutual antipathy towards the bagpipes, of which both Irwin and Bean's fathers were overly fond, to eventually unite them. "Those things were incredibly loud. I mean like a truck," Irwin remembers. "But I still say the bagpipes can be used for good, not evil."

While Irwin had cut her teeth on country music, "I was an album-rock chick," Bean says. "Pink Floyd, all that sort of stuff. I didn't have a certain mindset about country, or anything. I didn't actively dislike it, except for the Statler Brothers. It represented something I didn't really want to be interested in when I was a kid. It was all around me growing up in Alabama and Kentucky, and I wanted to separate myself from it."

Irwin soon talked Bean into performing at an open mike night at the now-extinct Beat Club in Louisville. "It was in an area downtown where there were a lot of strip bars, and we went and did 'Pistol Packing Mama' and 'Divorce'," says Bean. "We were pretty well-received, although whether it was because of the music or our low-cut dresses I still don't know."

The Beat Club gig would mark a turning point, if only because it may have been the last time Irwin and Bean, given the current deathly seriousness with which they approach their music, displayed anything remotely resembling irony. "Well, the whole thing started out with a love of those songs, with enjoying them," says Bean. "But being eighteen years old, everything is ironic. Everything was sort of meant to piss people off, I guess."

Although Freakwater's songs—which are, almost without exception, lonely, lovely ballads about divorce, hardship, and dead babies—could do with some leavening,

Bean and Irwin seem to have, unwittingly or not, cast themselves in the role of musical preservationists. Their desire to protect early twentieth-century country and bluegrass traditions—things, like mountain folk hollers, that even predate oft-cited Freakwater archetypes such as Bill Monroe—is almost palpable. Whatever else Freakwater are, they aren't kidding.

Most any question about their songs is met with a recitation of historical precedent. When asked, for example, where the band picked up its overweening death fixation, Bean will say: "I think the history of Appalachian balladeering is almost nonchalant about it. You would sing a song about death, but it's almost a part of life. It was such a predominant issue in a lot of the old mountain songs."

In Louisville, Bean and Irwin spent hours plowing through Louvin Brothers and Carter Family records and harmonizing around a basement four-track, until Bean left for Chicago with soon-to-be-husband Rick Rizzo. Bean and Rizzo eventually formed Eleventh Dream Day, an occasionally sublime indie-rock outfit that resembles classic X during its finer moments, a country version of Tortoise during its worst. Living in separate cities ("It's good in some ways. Otherwise we would have killed each other by now," says Irwin), Bean and Irwin would sing on the phone to each other, mostly, until officially forming as Freakwater in 1989. The trio, with Gay on board as bassist, released two records on local indie label Amoeba before moving to Thrill Jockey a few years later. It took the release of 1995's *Old Paint*, which remains perhaps the definitive Freakwater record, before the band was seen as anything more than the bastard stepchild of Eleventh Dream Day.

Though Eleventh Dream Day was ostensibly the more successful outfit (although their major-label flirtations would prove in vain as well), its frequent forays into traditional country felt trailer-trashy, meant to tweak. Freakwater explored the flipside: The aggressively traditionalist, deathly earnest *Old Paint* was steeped in dobros and pedal steels and national guitars, full of bleak, mournful ballads about drinking, murder and dread. Lyrically, like its predecessors, it made only cursory references to the latter part of the twentieth century. Occasional allusions to waitressing, cars, or atheism (most notably in *Old Paint*'s now infamous "There's nothing so pure/As the kindness of an atheist" couplet) seem the band's only tie to the present.

Bean and Irwin perfectly echo the gentle, world-weary fatalism of Appalachian folk hollers, replacing coal-mining disasters with car wrecks, and injecting occasional bits of feminism along the way. "Catherine is never the victim," says Bean with admiration. "Some of her songs are full of a lot of venom and can be really ugly and caustic, but it's never this 'Pity me' sort of thing. I think a lot of women writers in the past have come from vulnerable positions like that. But she doesn't."

Bean and Irwin split the songwriting and singing duties; in Eleventh Dream Day, Bean and Rizzo do the same. "My husband's really good at writing allegories, but it's hard," Bean says. "You don't want to reveal too much and hurt people, but [if you're afraid of that] then you're paralyzed. My songs, if they're not narrative stories, they're things I write to punish myself, to reinforce the way I'm supposed to behave. I need to impose discipline upon myself because I don't have enough from the outside world. Sometimes I think between Catherine and me we could keep a lot of soap operas going. It's hard to capture how poignant day-to-day life can be in a song."

Springtime is only vaguely cheerier than *Old Paint*, thanks in part to new multi-instrumentalist Max Johnston (late of Wilco), who even contributes a lead vocal track on the song "Harlan." "Catherine and I were probably out of our minds to let him do it," says Bean. "Because now everyone will probably be like, 'Let that guy sing,' you know?"

Bean also points to *Springtime*'s lack of dead baby songs—a onetime Freakwater staple—as further proof the band is lightening up some. "She said there were no dead baby songs?" asks Irwin in delight. "She just doesn't know what she's singing about. The record is perkier sounding, but lyrically, I don't think it's any perkier. I don't think this record is any less, um, evil."

The women of Freakwater, rarely cheery, one suspects, under the best of circumstances, seem to approach the mere act of being in Freakwater as if it were a bit of a chore, an intrusion into Actual Life. Recording is unpleasant; touring, as Bean once said, is like giving birth. Bean swears she will never again tour as she once did, playing in Eleventh Dream Day and Freakwater at the same time, opening for herself and wreaking havoc on both her vocal chords and her psyche. Her five-year-old child with Rizzo provides an added complication. And Catherine "has a life she likes, and doesn't want to leave," Bean says.

Irwin stays in Louisville, writing songs, and painting to pay the rent ("My goal in life is to do less, actually, not more," she says). Louisville has been kind to Freakwater, one of the few cities that seems instinctively to know what to make of them. "It's because

Louisville is full of perversity, and they love of that sort of thing," explains Bean.

Audiences in other cities have not been as understanding. Freakwater is regarded as far too twangy for all but the most progressive college/hipster crowds, and for Top 40 country audiences, Freakwater is, of course, out of the question.

Louisville once gave a start to acts such as Slint and Palace; Will Oldham, in fact, can be seen as Freakwater's only living sonic equivalent. (He also has the distinction, along with Richard Buckner, of being one of the few artists Catherine likes who is still alive.) But the city hasn't offered up much since. When asked if there is a music scene in Louisville, Irwin says, "I don't know, there may be. I, um, don't go outside much. There probably isn't one. I mean, someone would have told me."

On "Louisville Lip," the song that serves as the centerpiece of *Springtime*, Muhammad Ali throws his gold medal into the river when a restaurant wouldn't serve him. It is one in an endless string of true events—car wrecks, house fires that kill children—that find their way into Freakwater's catalog of universal woe. "So far I haven't had to make up anything in my songs," Irwin says. "I keep hoping someday awful things will stop happening to me and I'll have to make things up. But not yet."

In years past, Freakwater's schedule—long periods of hibernation followed by short bursts of activity—lent the band's records a tentative feel. One reason *Springtime* sounds more assured, Irwin and Bean will tell you, is because the extended legal wrangling with E-Squared postponed its release and gave them more time to learn the songs. In years past, Bean and Irwin were able to rehearse together only when time and travel money permitted. Recording sessions were similarly brutish and short. Surprisingly, given its budgetary limitations, *Springtime* is a clean, decidedly un-lo-fi recording, much more polished than even the Brad Wood-produced *Old Paint*.

Bean and Irwin debuted several tunes from *Springtime* at a show in Chicago last winter, where the band has a sturdy fan base. "We never [play] to be more popular," says Bean. "It's usually to make money, like, 'If we do this show, we can pay our insurance next month,' or whatever." Freakwater will, with great reluctance, play their first-ever Los Angeles headlining show in their extended history sometime this spring, as well as a few weeks' worth of roadshows. No one seems to know what happens next. Bean speaks wistfully of getting her teaching certificate and moving her family to Greece for the summer.

"There's a certain amount of instability when you're involved in music. It's not like you get a 401(k) plan or something," she says. "You get screwed sometimes, and things turn out great sometimes, and if you love what you're doing, it doesn't really matter. I love singing, and I love playing my guitar, but I love doing it in my house just as much. Sometimes I think I need to figure out whether I need to do it beyond that level. Apparently I do. Sometimes I'm just not sure why."

"Spring Forward, Fall Back" first appeared in *No Depression* #13 (January–February 1998).

Selected Discography:

Freakwater, *Freakwater* (Amoeba) 1989.

Freakwater, *Dancing Underwater* (Amoeba) 1991, reissued (Thrilljockey) 1997.

Various Artists, *Keep On The Sunny Side: A Tribute to the Carter Family* (Amoeba) 1993.

Freakwater, *Feels Like the Third Time* (Thrill Jockey) 1993.

Freakwater, *Old Paint* (Thrill Jockey) 1995.

Freakwater, *Springtime* (Thrill Jockey) 1998.

Blue Mountain

by Jon Maples

These days are truly the dog's days for Blue Mountain.

The Oxford, Mississippi band is currently touring in support of their second album, *Dog Days*, and husband and wife Cary Hudson and Laurie Stirratt are also raising their six-month-old part-chow, part-lab Willie. "We found him on our road, right down from our house," Stirratt says. "We didn't want to give him away, so we took him on the road with us."

The band is finding acceptance with audiences as they open for the Jayhawks, Wilco and Son Volt. Raising the puppy, however, has been more trying. "We lost him for a while in San Francisco," Stirratt explains. "We let him off the leash on a walk and he got ahead of us."

After searching in vain for hours, Hudson and Stirratt gave up in order to open for the Jayhawks at the Fillmore. After the concert, on a whim, Stirratt called her Oxford answering machine, as Willie had the number on an ID around his neck. "Someone called and had him. He had run about a mile away. It was terrible; I thought we were going to have to leave without him."

Calling on a lost dog is the kind of neighborly, down-home touch that Hudson and Stirratt can relate to. Blue Mountain's formation came about from the couple's experiences in Los Angeles. They moved out west after the breakup of their band the Hilltops, a more punk-leaning rock band that included Stirratt's twin brother,

John, now bassist for Wilco. The L.A. experience left the couple longing for home—and their musical roots.

"When you get taken out of the environment that you grew up in," Hudson says, "you start to realize who you are. And you start thinking about things that aren't there. You start thinking about rain, green trees." After ten months of working dead-end jobs merely to pay rent, and living in a crime-riddled neighborhood, Hudson and Stirratt returned to Oxford and started concentrating on Blue Mountain. "We actually came up with the name and played a few gigs out there [in L.A.]," Stirratt says.

The soulless environment of Los Angeles pushed Hudson back to what he calls his own soul music: country. "Yeah, I started hearing country or Southern-type music in my head," Hudson says about living in Los Angeles. "And it made me realize that being able to play that kind of music with soul is important."

Named for a small town near Oxford, Blue Mountain blends country, blues and rock into an original sound. The band has been together for about two and a half years and features lead vocalist-guitarist Hudson, bassist-vocalist Stirratt and drummer Frank Coutch.

Dog Days includes several songs that were first recorded on a self-titled, self-released album. "We recorded it for $1,000, and it sounds like a $1,000 record, too," Stirratt says. "But that was probably the best thing we could have done to attract a record label."

Indeed, the album got the attention of Jeff Pachman, director of A&R for Roadrunner. Pachman, who signed Uncle Tupelo for Rockville, says Blue Mountain's live show convinced him to sign the band. He first saw them perform at one of Uncle Tupelo's last shows in Columbia, Missouri.

"They have the capacity to play all kinds of music, and play with a lot of soul, which is pretty good for some white folks," Pachman says. "They can play softer, more melodic songs and have no problem with just kicking out the jams." He was surprised there wasn't a small bidding war for the band's services. "To me it was a no-brainer," he says about signing the band.

Yet a major bidding war was never the aim of Hudson and Stirratt. "You want to work your way up so that you have some clout when you start dealing with a major label," Stirratt says. "I believe in starting off on a small level. If you have some records under your belt and a fan base, then you have some clout. If you don't, you're at [the major label's] mercy. If you look at all the bands that have [built up clout], they've had good careers. Uncle Tupelo did it really well, Hüsker Dü did it well, and the Replacements did it well, up until the last couple albums."

"We didn't want to come out and have a huge first, second or third record," Hudson says. "We want to grow organically, by word-of-mouth and touring. Many times you can have a video and the video song will be huge, but people might be responding to more what the video director's doing than what the music is about."

Hudson believes there will be a time for the band to do a video, but this isn't it. He cites R.E.M. as setting a good example to follow in that regard. "I haven't always been a fan of all the music they've done, but I've always admired how R.E.M. handled their career. They didn't even start doing videos until their fifth or sixth record."

The deal calls for five records, which might have been more than Stirratt wanted, but she says the band is interested in having a long career, not making a big splash. "I hope when I'm sixty I'm still playing, so I really don't mind putting out as many records as possible. I would have preferred a three-record deal, but you've got to give and take. And the five records, that's fine."

Hudson hopes the slow-growth plan will also help with the time-consuming and sometimes painful process of songwriting. "[Writing songs] is a lot of work. In fact, it's so much work that I put it off a lot." He'd like the band to stay out of the trap that many bands fall into when they become successful. "I think a lot of bands get so busy that they don't have time to work on the songs," he says. "They get more popular, and ironically enough, their songs get worse. Hopefully, that won't happen to us."

Produced by the over-worked Eric "Roscoe" Ambel (Bottle Rockets, Go To Blazes, etc.), *Dog Days* was recorded quickly—two weeks—and mostly live. Stirratt is happy with Ambel's job and with the album, especially having the luxury of getting the sound right compared to the more slapdash way the first album was recorded. "He managed to get us relaxed and let us do pretty much what we wanted. There were only a few things he was adamant about."

Dog Days travels the entire spectrum of Blue Mountain's influences. With Ambel adding mandolin, acoustic guitar or a second lead, some of the softer tracks on the album, like "Soul Sister" and "Blue Canoe," exude a full and summery sound. "ZZQ," "A Band Called Bud" and "Slow Suicide" rely on a stronger, more Hilltops-like influence. "Jimmy Carter," which Hudson wrote as much as an homage to the bicentennial summer of 1976 as to the Georgian president, is a pure country hoedown. "Let's Go Running," with its soft, sad guitar, emphasizes Hudson's plaintive lyrics: "Have you ever met a stranger/On the corner of your bed?" Even Skip James' blues jam, "Special Rider," gets a twirl on the disc.

Because Blue Mountain is a trio, many of the softer touches on the album disappear live. It's an issue Hudson and Stirratt understand. "I wonder sometimes about people who come out to the shows and have only heard the record," Hudson says. "I can see someone saying, 'That's not what I was expecting at all.'"

Yet the harder-edged live show reveals another side of the band. It showcases the strong working relationship between Hudson and Stirratt. The couple has been playing together for eight years, and it clearly shows live. Hudson's electric guitar playing melds cleanly with Stirratt's bass lines. Her sweet backing vocals stand out as one of the few soft touches that remain from the album. After employing a series of drummers, they've settled on Coutch behind the kit.

"We really enjoy being a three-piece band," Stirratt says. "You don't see many bands playing the music we do [as a trio]. We've always been a three-piece and we'll stay that way for awhile." The band does plan to work an acoustic set into the show and include some more rock tunes into the next album to give a more even representation of the band.

Blue Mountain recently received a showering of good reviews and some Triple-A radio play after the late July release of *Dog Days*. Magazines from *Billboard* to *CMJ* expressed admiration for the solid roots sound of the album. Hudson admits that the mini-boom of roots-rock bands, *Gavin*'s Americana chart and Triple-A radio could put the band at the forefront of a developing format.

"But there's another side of me that doesn't really give a shit if it happens or not," he says. "If we always kept playing at a small level, I wouldn't really care. Just as long as I don't have to work a day job. What more could you ask, really."

Both Stirratt and Hudson approach this band as part of a long career. "That's the good thing about music, too. If you don't become a heroin addict, you can age really slowly," Hudson says. "I was hanging out with Gary Louris [of the Jayhawks] recently...and in the course of the conversation he mentioned that he was forty. Now that blew my mind. Gary doesn't come across as what you'd think of as a forty-year-old. He looks great and he's got a very youthful outlook.

A music career is good that way. It kinda keeps you in that state of perpetual adolescence."

An extended adolescence may soon take the form of an old-fashioned European trip for the band. *Dog Days* recently sold seventy-five copies in one week at a Paris record mega-store, an extraordinary number, according to Pachman. There's also been interest and airplay in Germany. A short tour may be in the works for the spring.

As for Willie—he'll probably miss the overseas trip and return to Mississippi to rediscover his roots, much like Blue Mountain did. "Cary's sister is coming up to Oxford to go to school, and we may leave Willie at home with her," Stirratt says. "We do take good care of him, but the road is hard for him."

"Oxford Blue" first appeared in *No Depression* #2 (Winter 1996).

Selected Discography:

Blue Mountain, *Dog Days* (Roadrunner) 1995.
Blue Mountain, *Home Grown* (Roadrunner) 1997.

Son Volt

by Peter Blackstock

Catchin' an all-night station
Somewhere in Louisiana
It sounds like 1963
But for now
It sounds like heaven.
  —"Windfall," Son Volt

It's a warm, incandescent, comforting burnt-orange blur. The slim needle of the AM radio dial in that old Chevy station wagon, dimly lighting the dashboard as we coasted along the winding river road, heading home from another serene Sunday afternoon at the lake. The flickering embers of a once-blazing fire at summer camp years ago. The soft glow of the cathode-ray tube glimmering through cracks in the back of the old black-and-white, fading ever so slowly even after we had switched off the set and drifted into dreams.

"Trace"—definition eight, *Webster's New World:* a) the visible line or spot that moves across the face of a cathode-ray tube; b) the path followed by this line or spot. Definition number one: A way followed or a path taken.

It's a fitting title for the debut album by Son Volt, the path taken by Jay Farrar after he left Uncle Tupelo in the spring of 1994. The band appeared to be poised at the brink of a commercial breakthrough when Farrar simply up and split, to the surprise of seemingly everyone except himself.

Perhaps all's well that ends well. Jeff Tweedy and the other Uncle Tupelo members have found a new groove as Wilco, mining Tweedy's more pop-oriented songwriting instincts to a fuller extent, while still mixing in the traditional instrumentation and influences that made Uncle Tupelo the beacon of a dynamic and substantial country-rock revival. It took some gumption for Tweedy to take the wheel and steer Wilco back onto the highway, but he's done it.

Farrar, meanwhile, has headed for the back roads with Son Volt. Sometimes it's wide-open stretches of rural two-lane with the pedal to the floor: "Live Free," "Route," "Drown," "Loose String" and "Catching On" burn rubber with the intensity of a desperate man fleeing the scene of disaster. But there comes a time for quiet reflection. "Windfall," "Tear Stained Eye," "Ten Second News," "Out of the Picture" and "Too Early" take a turn down rambling dirt roads, where the dust of dobros and fiddles and accordions and steel guitars is carried off by a wind that takes your troubles away, way down into the streets of the smallest towns in America.

Flat River. Times Beach. Ste. Genevieve. Festus. Farrar.

Yes, Farrar—population 90, Perry County, Missouri. It's one of several tiny burgs south of St. Louis that comes up in an interview with Jay Farrar a few weeks before the release of *Trace*, the band's debut album for Warner Brothers.

"My dad has a hat from that town, from some general store or something like that," Farrar says, though he's unsure if there's any tie between Farrar, Missouri, and his family history. "I don't really know; I think my dad's family is from around that part of the state, though."

Notoriously tight-lipped in interviews—not because he's rude or insensitive, but just because he apparently prefers to let his music do the talking—Farrar does manage to open up ever so slightly when our conversation turns to small-town stories and myths. Like the place where *Trace* was made. "We recorded at a studio in Northfield, Minnesota. I guess Northfield is the place where the James Gang got turned back by the locals. The studio's across the street from a bank where they still have bullet holes circled in the wall outside, supposedly bullets from the James Gang."

Another anecdote relates more directly to the music. Asked about one of the most memorable lyrics on the new album—"There's a beach there known for cancer waiting to happen," from the hauntingly hushed "Ten Second News"—Farrar readily offers up the inspiration for the line. "There's a place off of Interstate 44 [in Missouri] on the Meramec River, a town called Times Beach. I guess years ago it had dirt streets, and someone had sprayed oil on the streets to keep the dust down, and the oil had dioxin in it. And then when the river flooded once, the whole town had to be evacuated. So it's a ghost town now. And I think they're building some kind of incinerator there now to burn off all the topsoil and debris that's dioxin-tainted."

Not that the entire song is necessarily about that. The biggest difference between Farrar and Tweedy as songwriters is that Tweedy generally takes an up-front and straightforward approach, whereas Farrar's lyrics are couched in poetry, imagery and metaphor. Exactly how the Times Beach tragedy relates to a chorus that simply states "Only you'll ever know/As day by day disappears/Only you'll ever know" is a mystery—but it's the feel, the emotion, that counts, and Farrar delivers that in spades.

Even more oblique is "Tear Stained Eye," which mentions Ste. Genevieve, a small town (pop. 4,411) on the banks of the Mississippi River. "It's a historic town, and in the song, it's just referring to the fact that every time the river floods, the town is in danger of being flooded," Farrar says. Which doesn't quite explain the line in the chorus: "Ste. Genevieve can hold back the water, but saints don't bother with a tear stained eye." And it doesn't need to, what with equally elusive but beautiful lines in the verses such as "I will meet you anywhere the western sun meets the air."

As for Flat River and Festus: The former is the town where Farrar was heading the day after our interview to meet up with his bandmates—brothers Jim and Dave Boquist of Minneapolis, and former Tupelo drummer Mike Heidorn of Belleville, Illinois, who has rejoined his old friend after a couple years of domestic anonymity. Flat River (pop. 4,823) is the site of a rehearsal space normally occupied by the Bottle Rockets, who hail from nearby Festus (pop. 8,105).

Between the two of them, the Bottle Rockets and Uncle Tupelo were the much-ballyhooed St. Louis country-rock scene of the late '80s and early '90s, even though neither of them actually lived in St. Louis (Heidorn, Farrar and Tweedy all had addresses across the state line in Belleville). "At the time we were getting into it, St. Louis had the worst music scene in the world," says Brian Henneman, guitarist and primary songwriter for the Bottle Rockets. "We always played on the same bills with Uncle Tupelo because we were the only two bands that they could figure out to put together. Because there was nothing else going on like that in St. Louis."

What the scene lacked in quantity, it more than made up for in quality. It was clear from Uncle Tupelo's first album, 1990's *No Depression*, recorded when Tweedy and Farrar were barely old enough to drink (though age regulations probably didn't stop them in those notoriously hazy days), that we were witnessing the development of a great American rock band. From the anthemic opening lurch of "Graveyard Shift" to the perfect porch-song closer "Screen Door," and spotlighting a brilliant exhumation of an old Carter Family chestnut (the title track), *No Depression* was the launching pad for what has now become a bona fide movement.

The 1991 follow-up *Still Feel Gone* kept the ball rolling in the same direction, with Tweedy's passionate "Gun" and Farrar's aching "Still Be Around" highlighting another solid collection of hard and heartfelt tunes. But Farrar and Tweedy were wise enough to avoid falling into a rut and subsequently made their third album, *March 16-20, 1992,* an all-acoustic affair produced by R.E.M.'s Peter Buck. The next step was a move to the majors: Sire/Reprise signed Uncle Tupelo and released *Anodyne*, which found the trio expanding to a quintet and striking an ideal balance between its acoustic and electric personas.

In the meantime, Henneman—who had toured with Uncle Tupelo as a guitar tech and contributed mandolin, banjo, bouzouki and slide guitar parts to the acoustic album—began gearing up for his own career by assembling the Bottle Rockets from former members of his old band, Chicken Truck. When their debut album came out on East Side Digital in 1993, the St. Louis—er, suburban-St. Louis—scene seemed primed to recharge the new alternative mainstream with a two-pronged assault of country-tinged rock 'n' roll.

And then Farrar quit Uncle Tupelo.

To this day, the reasoning behind his decision remains hidden to about everyone but Farrar. "It's as big a mystery to me as anybody, and I was pretty much hanging out with them during that whole time," Henneman told me in a recent interview. "I don't know what the heck ever came between 'em to make 'em split up. It was like, out of the blue, they were gone. And I thought they were set to really do something huge."

Even Tweedy appears to have been in the dark, judging from the honest bewilderment he has expressed in interviews when the subject of his old band is raised. "I think it was a personal decision for Jay, but he wasn't very communicative about anything to us, which was fairly normal for Jay," Tweedy told Alan Sculley of the *St. Louis Post-Dispatch* in April 1995. "I mean, a lot of things that were used as explanations were fairly contradictory, so I really wouldn't be able to comment on it."

For his part, Farrar pretty much sticks with the straight "artistic differences" party line. "It just seemed like it reached a point where Jeff and I really weren't compatible," he says. "It had ceased to be a symbiotic songwriting relationship, probably after the first record."

Looking to the music for clues is always a dicey proposition—it's easy to misinterpret lyrics or read too much into them—but it seems reasonable to suspect that the Son Volt song "Drown" might deal with Farrar's departure from Uncle Tupelo: "When in doubt, move on/No need to sort it out." Maybe it was just that simple.

For Farrar, moving on included relocating from Belleville to New Orleans. "It's been about a year, last August," he said. "My girlfriend got a job down here. And I was ready to do it."

Musically, Farrar says he didn't have any sort of master plan in mind when he left Uncle Tupelo. "I just knew that I had the songs, and I felt fortunate that I had an outlet for the songs," he says. "I feel fortunate that I met Jim and Dave, and of course Mike."

The Boquist brothers entered the picture as a result of an Uncle Tupelo tour with Joe Henry, for whom Jim had been playing bass. "When the tour was ending, we all exchanged numbers and everything," recalls Jim, a veteran of mid-'80s Minneapolis band the Mofos who more recently had gigged with current Jayhawks drummer Tim O'Reagan. "And then I went down and saw an Uncle Tupelo show in Des Moines; this was after Joe Henry had finished touring with them. I basically went to visit, and I had a drink with Jay later on that night. This was not long after certain decisions had been made [about Farrar's departure from Uncle Tupelo]. He had some recording he was going to be doing, and he asked me about doing it. And I said that if I could, I would."

When Farrar began looking for another guitarist who could also play instruments such as fiddle and banjo, the natural choice was Jim's brother Dave, who had met Farrar once at a show in Minneapolis. "I'm not really sure how we all got connected, but it just sort of all made sense," says Dave, who spent the early '90s playing with Minneapolis band John Eller & the DTs. "Jay and I were talking, and I think Jay was talking to my brother, and my brother was talking to me. It's kind of a small world up there in Minneapolis."

Playing with Farrar seems almost a stroke of destiny for Dave, who grew quite attached to Uncle Tupelo's *Anodyne* while on vacation in France in the winter of '93. "It was an album that kind of carried me through a lonely time in Paris," he remembers. "I thought it was just a beautiful record."

Drummer Mike Heidorn, of course, had much deeper attachments to Uncle Tupelo's music. Heidorn left the band a couple months after the recording of the *March 16-20, 1992* album, a decision he says was prompted by conflicts between a family and a career. "I had just gotten married, and we have a couple of kids, and I didn't really want to hold the band back in getting their music out and all that stuff," he says. "We had some offers from some bigger labels, and Jeff and Jay were writing some really good songs, and I figured maybe they could use somebody at that juncture who could just go, go, go."

Ironically, it was Heidorn's wife who encouraged him to get back in the music business when the opportunity to work with Farrar again arose last year. "I had pretty much clocked out and never thought about it at all until Jay had this album to do. And my wife was actually talking to me and said something like, 'Give him a call, see what he's doing.' So I just called to see if he needed any help to record…and he said, 'Sure.'"

Playing drums in Son Volt has been like slipping back into a comfortable old sneaker for Heidorn. "I've only played with him or Jeff in my life, so I just fell into automatic mode. I guess it was just like I thought it would be."

It's mid-June of '95, and Son Volt is onstage at 7th Street Entry, kicking off a two-night stand at the storied Minneapolis club. They had played an impromptu acoustic gig at the Uptown a couple nights earlier, but for all practical intents and purposes, these are their debut live performances, their first chances to showcase songs recorded a few months earlier in the studio across the street from the bank with the bullet holes of the James Gang in the wall.

The band is tight—maybe a little too tight, perhaps a shade nervous about their first gig, concentrating on playing everything right. But it hardly matters. When you've got a guy who may well be the best songwriter of his generation at the helm, it's hard to go wrong.

They run through a set of about twenty tunes, including nearly everything from *Trace* and a well-chosen smattering of Tupelo standards—"Grindstone," "Slate," "True To Life," "Fifteen Keys," "Chickamauga" among them. A few overzealous fans call out way too many times for "Whiskey Bottle"; Farrar skips it the first night and plays it the next, probably because nobody screams for it.

But it's the new songs I'm digging most. At that point, I had listened to *Trace* only a couple times, yet it was clear that every song on it was a keeper. The urgently crashing "Drown" hooks you in so instantly that these guys may well have a hit single on their hands. The heart stopping ballad "Too Early" addresses the tragedy of burning out too brightly as eloquently as any song ever written (and I'll bet my bottom dollar it's about Townes Van Zandt, by the way). "Live Free" shows the other way to go, and how that move to Louisiana has given Farrar room to grow: "Someday we'll be together, farther south than the train line/The Delta mud will be there....The rhythm of the river will remain."

And then there's "Windfall," the first song on the record and an instant classic if ever I've heard one. It shines with an irrepressible warmth and a truer sound, like the TV's glowing cathode-ray tube, the AM radio in the dashboard, the ashes from the dying campfire drifting into the distance on a southbound summer breeze. May the wind take your troubles away.

"Dim Lights, Small Cities" first appeared in *No Depression* #1, Fall 1995.

Selected Discography:

Uncle Tupelo, *No Depression* (Rockville) 1990.

Uncle Tupelo, *Still Feel Gone* (Rockville) 1991.

Uncle Tupelo, *March 16–20, 1992* (Rockville) 1992.

Uncle Tupelo, *Anodyne* (Sire/Reprise) 1993.

Son Volt, *Trace* (Warner Bros.) 1995.

Son Volt, *Straightaways* (Warner Bros.) 1997.

Wilco

by Peter Blackstock

I'm just a soul whose intentions are good
Oh Lord, please don't let me be misunderstood.
    —"Don't Let Me Be Misunderstood," Eric Burdon & the Animals, 1965

Misunderstood.

We all feel that way sometimes. In the beginning, it's inevitable, with only varying tones and volumes of bawling to distinguish the point you're trying to get across to mom or dad. As a teenager, it's practically a rite of passage; nobody seems to understand what you're going through (which is what leads so many of us to rock 'n' roll). It doesn't get any easier as an adult; the potential disasters of misunderstanding loom in wider and deeper chasms, capable of swallowing up once-blooming relationships between souls whose intentions were good.

Jeff Tweedy knows the feeling. The first track on Wilco's new record is called "Misunderstood," and it's unlike anything the band has ever recorded. The introduction is a cacophonous assault. After about ten seconds it fades into a simple piano ballad of vignette verses, before transforming once again several minutes later into a cathartic, screaming, final chorus of Tweedy crying that he's "so misunderstood." The song ends with Tweedy declaring, "I'd like to thank you all for nothin' at all."

Welcome to the new Wilco.

The buzz about *Being There* began building early. For starters, it's a double album—an ambitious undertaking for a band at any stage of their career, much less their second release. The material, meanwhile, is all over the map, dropping numerous veiled and obvious references to classic '60s rock and pop acts such the Rolling Stones and the Beach Boys. Furthermore, guitarist Jay Bennett spent a significant amount of time in the studio playing piano. (Another shift in instrumentation probably will be evident on tour, as mandolin/fiddle/dobro/banjo player Max Johnston was dismissed from the band in early August.)

That said, *Being There* isn't so much a departure from Wilco's past as an extension of it. About a half dozen songs on the record are country/folkish acoustic numbers that would have seemed at home on the band's 1995 debut *A.M.* or a latter-day Uncle Tupelo album. It's clear that such songs and sounds are still important to the band. It would have been easy to eliminate those tracks and pare down the new release to a single disc if they had wanted to make a complete musical break from their past.

Emotionally, however, breaking from the past does seem to be much of what *Being There* is about for Jeff Tweedy, who turned twenty-nine in August, 1995. Last winter, he and his wife Sue Miller, co-owner of the storied Chicago nightclub Lounge Ax, had a son, and fatherhood seems to have had a profound effect on Wilco's frontman. "I really wanted the record to close that chapter of my life where music was the only thing in my life, forever. I wanted it to be like, 'See ya later!'" he says. "But at the same time, I ended up feeling more excited about it again, with just a different perspective on it, but in a really healthy way."

"Hold on a second, I've gotta turn this baby monitor off," Tweedy says on the other end of the phone line from his home in Chicago as we begin our interview. A baby monitor? "It's like a walkie-talkie for your sleeping baby; it's this receiver you can carry around with you, but it's not good for cordless phones." Which explains the static that suddenly besieged the line.

Granted, having a kid throws a few logistical curve balls at those ever-present music-biz duties such as interviews—or, for that matter, touring, which Tweedy touches upon when discussing a recent tour with his side-project band, Golden Smog, that was extended a bit longer than expected.

"It seemed like there was no real legitimate excuse to turn the shows down, other than I wanted to stay home with my son—which I felt was pretty legitimate," he says.

Fortunately for Tweedy and his newfound domesticity, most of the recording of *Being There* was done in Chicago. "That really felt great, because I'd come home every night, and instead of popping in a rough mix of what I did that day and sitting around and stewing about it, I didn't have any time to think about it. I was changing diapers and playing with my baby and totally excited about that being way more important all of a sudden. It felt like it really contributed to being a little bit freer about the whole process."

The initial recording was done in November of last year at a Chicago studio called War Zone, known primarily for industrial-rock projects. "It was in this huge live room, but I can't understand why they have this live room because they never track anything live. They do mostly industrial stuff; it's all synths and MIDI and drum machines," Tweedy said. "I think they were kind of freaked out having a band play live in there. They didn't have any monitors; we just did it all in the same room, without any headphones, just trying really hard to hear each other."

Though Tweedy was already starting to fit some of the songs together in his head, a double album wasn't part of the plan going into the sessions. "I kind of had these songs all worked out as a sequence, and we recorded them like that; it was like eight songs or so. And at that point I felt like, well, it's going to be really easy to finish this record, because I felt pretty good about most of the stuff we got out of that session.

"And just to be safe, we decided to just have some fun and track for a couple more weeks—dig up all kinds of stuff and track it, and not feel a whole lot of pressure, because we felt like we only needed maybe four more songs to finish out a record....And then when we got done, we looked at how much stuff we had to mix, and we had almost thirty songs. So we had to prioritize, because we really didn't have enough time to mix all of them. We got it down to about twenty-one songs, and we ended up mixing nineteen.

"The idea was, for a while, to try and whittle it down to fourteen or fifteen songs. And then I just started feeling like I really had an idea of how I wanted the record to be, and I realized at the end that it made more sense to include everything and not really edit it—just let it be this kind of bulky conglomerate. There are so many different styles attempted, and some of them come off better than others, but for the most part, it just felt like when you started taking elements away, the overall feel of it wasn't as free. It just felt like it was trying to force it into one category or another, and it seemed more honest to just try and let it be what it is."

Which is all well and good from an artistic standpoint—but this is about the time you'd expect the powers-that-be (Warner/Reprise, in this case) to start hemming and hawing at such an unorthodox proposition. Was it a struggle to sell the double-album idea to the label? "Surprisingly not," Tweedy answers. "For the most part, once the few people that were involved in it got to hear it, they were amazingly supportive. We really didn't get too much of a battle out of them. In fact, we kind of left it up in the air with a couple of them—like, if it was gonna be an enormous problem, we'd consider making it a single CD. And we actually got a couple calls back saying that they thought it was a really cool idea trying to get it to work as a double CD."

With a little number-crunching and decisions on packaging—the discs will be released in a cardboard case that's "kind of like a mini-record, it folds out and has pouches for each CD"—the label and the band worked out a way to keep costs down enough for the double album to be reasonably priced. "I think it's going to be like the high end of a single-disc list price," he said. "The only way I think it would go up to a regular double-disc price is if it sold like 500,000 copies. And that probably won't happen," he added with a modest chuckle.

Probably not—but then again, there is a song on here that could potentially launch Wilco into the commercial stratosphere. It's called "Outtasite (Outta Mind)," or "Outta Mind (Outta Sight)," depending on which version you're referring to. It appears on the record twice, first in a straight-ahead, immediately catchy, rocked-up version that just might be Wilco's ticket to massive rock-radio acceptance. The second version is a delightfully laid-back, easygoing take that sounds straight off of a classic Beach Boys record.

Latent and/or blatant Brian Wilson influences are apparent elsewhere as well, while the backing-vocal chants on "I Got You" and a couple other tracks are clearly patterned after vintage Rolling Stones cuts. The swirling moods and changes of "Misunderstood" recall some of the Beatles' later pop experiments; on "Sunken Treasure," meanwhile, Tweedy's plaintive voice seems a dead ringer for Paul Westerberg.

"I wanted it to be really obvious that our influences are there and acknowledged," Tweedy readily admits, "because I don't hear people quoting each other very much anymore, or being really up-front about stuff like that. And it all comes from somewhere, you know. I wanted it to kind of sound like we were playing our record collections—like this garage band is just plowing through their record collection and pillaging it, and having a good time doing it."

The lyrical content of their new songs is equally direct, though it draws explicitly from their own lives. Several songs speak from the experiences of a lifelong musician—which, though it sometimes results in rather insular subject matter, is an honest portrayal from a guy who has been playing in bands since his high school days.

Tweedy says their lyrical perspective was intentional as well. "Without being overly arty about the whole thing, I really did have a lot of ideas about how I wanted people to hear this collection of music," he says. "And along with wanting it to sound like, as a band, that we were playing through our record collection, I also really wanted there to be songs where I totally came out of character, completely straightforward, and said, 'Look, this is all I know.' Like in a movie—a comparison would be when somebody looks at the screen and comes out of character and says, 'Don't listen to me. I've really no idea what I'm talking about. Except that I really care a whole lot about what I'm doing.' And right now it's a struggle for me to come to terms with people paying attention to me, on any level."

Which brings us back to "Misunderstood." If it's a struggle nowadays for Tweedy to deal with what people might think of him and his new work, it's nevertheless an improvement over the transition days from Uncle Tupelo to Wilco, and the emergence of his solo voice. And though Tweedy still seems not quite to have resolved those past conflicts completely—with Jay Farrar, and with Uncle Tupelo's audience—hindsight has allowed him to see some things more clearly.

"In the back of my mind, I was still wanting Uncle Tupelo fans to like me," he says of the days that followed the band's June, 1994 split. "That wasn't a thought that I allowed myself to say out loud; I just kind of recognized it later. And that's not really me. I never dug that whole somber approach to making music. I think it's bullshit. I think it should be fun. Music is entertainment. It can be serious, it can be sad, but for the most part, I want to feel better, and I want to feel good when I'm doing it.

"As Uncle Tupelo evolved, it became more and more repressed to kind of fit into Jay's world. Which is a hard world to fit into, for anybody. I felt like I was just trying to be more and more like him for years, and in the end, that's the thing I blame myself for the most. You know, I think, 'Why didn't I just stand up and be myself all along?' The personality of the band was definitely in debate, whether I knew it or not....The whole approach became way more serious. And at the same time, I understand that it works for Son Volt in a lot of ways, and I know some people really believe it and appreciate the lack of showmanship or whatever, or just the plainspoken nature of the band. But I personally don't buy it."

Tweedy also doesn't buy the notion that Uncle Tupelo was a particularly influential band. "I appreciate the fact that people are remembering the band and are enjoying the music—and more importantly, that they got something out of the songs, that we succeeded in connecting with people," he says. "But I think as far as it being described as a band that was pioneering a type of music, or claiming that the first two records are great, I think that's just totally off the mark....I mean, we maybe felt a little bit alienated from the rest of what was going on in the independent music world, but we also felt like there were dozens of bands before us and along with us doing very similar things, or that had similar feelings. The other word I think that's really funny when it's attached to Uncle Tupelo is 'visionary.' Like, I wish I was that smart! I really do. And I'm sure Jay wishes he was that smart, too.

"But the first couple records, especially, are overrated to me. I think you can really hear a young band trying to decide whether or not it wants to be Dinosaur Jr, or Hüsker Dü, or whatever band you want to think of from the time—deciding whether we wanted to be that, or play this country stuff that we really just discovered on our own and came through us kind of naturally. I don't know why that happened, but for some reason, folk music and country music really connected with us in a big way, and it felt right to do it."

In his effort to downplay the importance of his former band's earlier work, Tweedy ironically hits on the reason that has given them the reputation he feels they don't deserve. Indeed, on *No Depression* and *Still Feel Gone*, there is a great conflict going on between a band torn by its loves for two seemingly disparate kinds of music. It is precisely this conflict—and the willingness ultimately to toss the rules out the window by pursuing both avenues simultaneously—that made their fans stop thinking about "alternative" and "country" as a matter of Us vs. Them.

"That's probably something I can't hear; I can't hear it as a beautiful thing," Tweedy replies, acknowledging that one of the defining principles of art is that it's open to interpretation beyond the artists' original intentions. And even if he disagrees with those interpretations, he seems quite willing to accept them.

He's certainly heard them voiced plenty of times. "I hear everything you guys say about me," he says, somewhat slyly. "From one source or another, I get it. Like, my mom says, 'Well, want to hear what's on the Internet?' I'm like, 'No, not really—but, yeah, OK.' And some people will come up on tour and go, 'Hey what'd you say about blah blah blah.' And I don't ever want to seem unappreciative about it at all. I just think I have a right to say what I feel about it, honestly. But I definitely don't want to take away from anyone's enjoyment of it, or make somebody think that I take it for granted. You know what I mean?"

Yeah, I think so. He's just a soul whose intentions are good.

These days, there's really only one fan Jeff Tweedy has to answer to. "Could you hold on a minute? Spencer woke up, so I have to take him to his mom and his grandma," he says, his voice shuffling off momentarily as he juggles receiver in one hand and baby in the other. "I'm sitting in here and he just popped up while I was talking on the phone. Sorry Spencer, I woke you up."

Later, Pops Tweedy reflects further on the positive impact his son has had on his ability to rediscover his own love for music. *Being There*, it turns out, was a narrow victor over *Baby* as title for the Wilco album.

"I have a captive audience all the time now," Tweedy beams. "I can sit and play with Spencer for hours, and play guitar for him, and he's just totally excited by it. And I can play anything!"

And he probably won't ask whether or not it's alternative country.

"Yeah, he's not gonna say, 'Dad, is that another No Depression song?'"

"Being There, Doing That" first appeared in *No Depression* #5 (September–October 1996).

<u>Selected Discography:</u>

Uncle Tupelo, *No Depression* (Rockville) 1990.

Uncle Tupelo, *Still Feel Gone* (Rockville) 1991.

Uncle Tupelo, *March 16–20, 1992* (Rockville) 1992.

Uncle Tupelo, *Anodyne* (Sire/Reprise) 1993.

Wilco, *A.M.* (Sire/Reprise) 1995.

Wilco, *Being There* (Reprise) 1996.

Bottle Rockets

by Grant Alden

The sign reads "Haircuts $6," painted across the window so boldly as to obscure the interior and with no especial concern for aesthetics. Inside, the salon is decorated much like the back room of a thrift shop at the edge of a bad neighborhood: A doll-sized chair made from a Budweiser can on the counter, generic cleaners used so often they've left their own trail of gray, ashtrays, clutter. The barber in back is giving a trim to a uniformed cop, in silence. Three beauticians up front trade tequila war stories from the night before, which would have been Monday.

The woman in tight pink with the free chair doubtless turned heads twenty years back, but is far enough removed from those days that the memory no longer concerns her. She has lettered "Brushes Not Garbage" across a small plastic trash can at the foot of her chair, is playing a St. Louis new country station on the solid state stereo in the corner and is smoking a long, unfiltered cigarette between deep, fluid coughs. Her scissors don't draw blood, quite.

"You making fun of my music?" she jokes with a regular. "I like this new country, not that old cry-in-your-beer stuff."

One forgets to ask if she likes the Bottle Rockets.

Brian Henneman, principal singer and songwriter of the group voted St. Louis's best country outfit two years in a row, lives only a few blocks from the salon. (So, for that matter, does Jay Farrar of Son Volt, only on a nicer street.) He shares a comfortable apartment atop a neighborhood bar with someone he identifies only with deep and wry affection as "mah wo-man" until she comes home from work. Sometimes Brian whiles away the nights sitting in the kitchen playing his guitar along with the jukebox below.

See, it's been a long time since the Bottle Rockets had much of anything to do, except wait.

But at last they have a release date for *24 Hours a Day*, their third long-player, which means it will come out almost exactly one year after it was recorded, and fourteen months after the band last formally toured.

During those intervening months, the Bottle Rockets flirted with bankruptcy (the unwritten sequel to *The Brooklyn Side* track "1000 Dollar Car" involves a $250-a-day diesel bus), changed management and booking agents, watched as Atlantic re-absorbed the TAG imprint to which they were signed and spent some months wondering if they would be among the acts dropped in the restructuring Atlantic (and virtually every major label) has gone through.

All of which follows two years of touring behind *The Brooklyn Side*, a process extended when TAG chose to re-release the album in the fall of '95 after signing the Bottle Rockets from East Side Digital (which originally released the album in the fall of '94). Oh, and ESD, for whom the Bottle Rockets recorded their eponymous debut, recently evaporated, which leaves their first album in some kind of limbo. Henneman and Tom Parr (drummer Mark Ortmann lives in Minneapolis; bassist Tom Ray lives in Chicago) just look at each other and laugh.

"That's a good question, what will happen with the first album?" Brian says. "Who knows? Should we make it again? We'll make it as our next album."

"Only 5-10,000 people bought it anyway," Tom shrugs.

"There was some small little contract," Brian says, rubbing his beard, "but...I don't know. We could probably call a lawyer somewhere and find out, but I don't know."

"Well, we've got plenty of lawyers," Tom says, emptying a can of Busch.

For those keeping score at home, that makes three labels with whom the Bottle Rockets have been associated that are no longer active, counting the Rockville release of their first single, "Indianapolis." Happily enough, they've re-recorded "Indianapolis" for their latest. Kind of had to, the way things worked out.

"We figured the song could stand a little better chance," Brian says. "And it kind of fit with the whole vibe. By damn, we were recording in Indiana, and it had the whole John Cougar reference, and we were doing it in Mike Wanchic's studio, who's Coug's guitar player. And he played the rhythm guitar part on the very guitar that was used on 'Jack & Diane.' So that was enough reason to do it right there."

"So when you listen to it, just when you think of the acoustic guitar, think of…" and Tom starts singing the Cougar guitar part.

"That's the one," laughs Brian. "I was playing through a silver-faced Fender Deluxe Reverb that actually had 'Cougar' stenciled on the back of it. The Coug was all over the place, man, it was just like the ghost of…"

So why isn't he singing on it?

Brian drops his voice into a smoker's drawl. "Well, Coug don't do that."

"It's his guitar player's studio, he won't go there," Tom says. "He's never been in that studio."

"You gotta keep thirty feet back from the Coug," Brian says. "That's a fact, too, 'cause we opened for him one time. The band's cool as hell, they're hangin' out in the dressing room. Then it's like, okay, Coug's coming, get the hell out of the dressing room. Including his band. Then we go out in the parking lot, and some guy's saying, OK, thirty feet, you gotta keep thirty feet back."

"He needs his space," Tom says.

"That's right," Brian nods. "Keep thirty feet. That's why he only plays big stages, because the band's got to keep thirty feet away." They laugh for a time, then Brian looks up. "Naw, I'm not trashing the Coug. I've seen more Coug concerts than anything else. I've always gotten free tickets somehow. I thought he was the best thing at Farm Aid, not this year, but the year before."

So much for fashion, but then St. Louis—much less Festus, thirty-five miles or so south, where Brian and Tom and their friends all grew up—isn't much concerned with the tyranny of style.

See, the Bottle Rockets' roots go back to a few crucial nights in Festus when Brian caught Cheap Trick and then, mere weeks later, the Ramones, on "Don Kirshner's Rock Concert" and decided maybe he really could play guitar. A previous fondness for Rush somehow eroded his confidence. "Here I am with this guitar my parents bought me and I'm listening to Rush and Aerosmith and I'm not relating with this G chord I learned from the Mel Bay book. But after Cheap Trick, it was like, man, I gotta pick this thing back up. Originally, I wasn't going to play guitar, it was going to be bass. Bass has got four strings, and you're watching the Ramones and Cheap Trick, and you're going I can *definitely* play that," he chuckles.

"And I woulda got a bass, except I found a Stratocaster for less money. The bass was going to be like $375 at Robert's Music in Festus, Missouri, and then in the *Trading Times* they had a Fender Stratocaster, $275. Damn, for the same money I could get that *and* an amplifier. So it was teenage economics that made me a guitarist."

Tom Parr's brother Robert bought a bass, they found a singer and the usual string of drummers and they dubbed themselves the Blue Moons. The apogee of their success as a cover band came the same day Ricky Nelson died. "Our biggest gig ever was $250 on New Year's Eve," Brian chuckles. "And there was like eight people in the bar. The bar owner called me aside after the third set, and I thought he was going to tell me he couldn't pay us. Instead he says, 'Look, man, I'll give you $210 if you leave right now.' I said, 'Buddy, you got a deal.'"

That was about the end of the Blue Moons. Brian and Robert hung out in Festus for about a year, pretty much doing nothing. "I think the punk excitement was over by like '85," Brian recalls, "and the rock coming out at that time was just not doing anything for me at all. So it was time to find something else." That was when Bob stumbled across John Anderson's hit single, "Swingin'," on the radio.

"We got the album, and there were better songs than 'Swingin'," Brian says, opening another can. "So we got infatuated with John Anderson. It was like, whoa, that's it! We don't look like Aerosmith, let's be country, that's the answer, that's why we failed. Look at John Anderson, that's us. We can do that. Those chords are as easy as these chords, and they don't even go as fast. So that was our big plan, to get down in the trenches and decide to be country. But we didn't want to learn country songs, we wanted to take what we knew and write our own country songs."

So they re-enlisted the last Blue Moons drummer, made Robert's little brother take up the guitar and named the new band after John Anderson's single, "Chicken Truck." ("We made sure it was one of the ones he wrote," Brian said.)

But Anderson was only half the new equation.

"John Anderson was the woodpile," Brian says, struggling to get the history in order, "and Jason & the Scorchers was the gasoline and the match on the woodpile. I've always been lucky with MTV, seeing the one video that they might play once, and I saw them doing 'Absolutely Sweet Marie.' And then, just by fate, I was driving somewhere and I heard on the radio that Jason & the Scorchers were coming to Mississippi Nights, which is the big club here in St. Louis. So it cost $4 and they were great, just totally great." Connect that to an early fondness for ZZ Top, Lynyrd Skynyrd and a binge of Kinks, and you get the picture.

Chicken Truck went on to acquire a small kind of legendary status, though Brian shrugs it off. "It's a local thing, a band that had an entire career in one tavern in St. Louis. Did the whole thing, got crazy, did punk rock, performance art, the whole bit. We'd just get out of hand. And it was all country, though, all country music."

Well, sorta country. "We tried to be a country band, tried playing country songs, but nobody liked us," Brian admits. "We didn't know about the whole country dance thing. There's certain rhythms that you two-step to, the whole bit. We just knew that Buck Owens was cool and John Anderson was cool and…"

"Neil Young was cool," Tom chips in.

"Yeah! Neil Young, that's country." Brian shakes his head and laughs hard. "People just hated us, so we failed as a country band. We tried it for a while, tried to come to St. Louis and get a gig, it didn't work out.…It ended up Uncle Tupelo, who used to be the Primitives, which we played with when we were the Blue Moons—see, this is all shit that's getting forgotten and remembered in bad order. We opened for them, blah blah blah, turned into a punk rock band, blah blah blah, the whole bit. Opened for Meat Loaf."

Later Brian digs up the tape of a Chicken Truck show, offering the explanation that the band got four pitchers of beer and, at the time, he was the only one who drank. The second set opens with Springsteen's "The Ties That Bind," segues into the Stones' "Waiting For a Friend," then drifts through Gene Davis into Chuck Berry, through a Ted Nugent medley into Hank Thompson, then Webb Pierce, then their own "Wave That Flag," a Paula Abdul cover and a closing Neil Young shambles. (That's right, Paula Abdul.)

And, yes, "Wave That Flag" is the same song, more or less, that shows up on the first Bottle Rockets record. Indeed, the Bottle Rockets are still pulling tracks from a ninety-minute tape of original Chicken Truck compositions. Including "Perfect Far Away" ("I wonder if she's real/I really couldn't so/Well I don't wanna know/'Cause she's so perfect far away") on their latest, one of the cuts being considered for release as a single, though Brian had to find his advance copy of the CD to remember which tracks were on it.

"There's a whole 'nother album that didn't get put out on this one," he explains, looking down at the pre-release disc. "We recorded twenty-something songs out there."

That's almost Wilco-length.

Brian laughs again. Over dinner later, he recalls having first heard the Wilco two-disc set over CB radio, one Bottle Rocket tour van transmitting it to the other, and whoever else happened to be listening as they drove to Minneapolis.

"Well, if we really wanted to, I guess we could go back and do a triple," says Tom. "We've got enough songs sitting around."

"This record's been so long, I'm totally ready to go make another one now," Brian says. "It's interesting now because we have played this stuff live maybe five or ten times in the last year." He pauses, blinks. "Oh boy, we played five times last year. But the songs are already goosing up. Just from the five times we've played it, it's already like leaning forward and poking you in the chest. If we were on the road for a week straight, it would definitely be poking you in the chest and stealing your lunch money."

On disc, anyway, the newest Bottle Rockets songs are less rambunctious than their predecessors. In part this is because it is their second outing with producer Eric Ambel, and in part it's because they had more time in the studio. Mostly, though, the songs are more personal this time out. Brian and Tom look at each other, nonplused by this assessment, their memory of the disc fogged by time and the number of unreleased tracks it produced. "Maybe the stuff that didn't get on there is the crazy-ass stuff," Brian decides at last.

"There was no desperation, other than our own personal desperation," he adds, struggling to remember exactly. "The thing was, we had twice as much time to make this one."

"And *The Brooklyn Side* had twice the amount of time as the first one," Tom picks up. "Really, we did that one in three days. All the tracks were down by Tuesday morning, and we came in there Monday evening."

"Yeah, the first one was done and finished in three days," Brian says. "The second one was finished in eight days, and this is like one of those sprawled out major-label affairs. It was finished in three weeks, and then it was finished again six months later, after three days of mixing."

He pauses, reflects for a moment. "I kind of like the panic of the fast, I don't like that slow stuff. Too many choices."

Some of that abundance came from the six songwriters who play with and/or contribute to the Bottle Rockets (and the still-open-for-plundering legacy of Chicken Truck). Bob Parr is now a fireman, but chips in the odd song, as does Scott Taylor, a record-collecting schoolteacher back home in Festus who sometimes co-writes with Brian.

And, despite the joyous bluster of their live shows (there's a reason Brian wears a Mötorhead T-shirt), it's the songs that make one take notice of the Bottle Rockets. Those of us with more education than sense tend to romanticize the virtues of the working class; either that, or totally discount their wisdom and survival skills. At the same time, there is nothing more desperate than a scrawny dog roped to the porch of a sagging double-wide.

It is the Bottle Rockets' virtue that they are able to render their world hard and smart, in plain English. It's tough to get confused when, as Tom must eventually, you've got to run off to your job as a janitor at the insurance office. ("It's the cockroach of jobs," Brian says, and he knows.) *24 Hours a Day* comes straight outta South St. Louis, complete with an homage to "Slo Toms," one of those bars you can get tossed out of for not drinking enough or fast enough. Or "One of You," a curiously touching love song about the drive home.

Mostly, there's a kind of world-worn resignation to the thing, wrapped up nicely in "Rich Man" and "Turn For The Worse." The protagonist of "Rich Man," to paraphrase, dies of a heart attack without ever having made time to use that organ. "Turn For The Worse" is the other side of the coin, a commentary on the fragility of what Henneman calls "the Taco Bell lifestyle."

There is still the sense, in other words, that the Bottle Rockets are getting away with something by not quite having normal careers.

No, that's just where ideas come from. "Smokin' 100's Alone," for example, is probably the best song of the set. It's the story of a woman who's tossed out her worthless boyfriend, again, waiting and wondering if he'll come back, again. A touching song, nearly conventional country in its structure, it's written with wonderful detail and from her perspective. It is almost a sequel to Tom Parr's "What More Can I Do?" from *The Brooklyn Side,* an almost tongue-in-cheek explanation of domestic violence from the batterer's perspective.

"Smokin' 100's Alone" marks a quiet breakthrough for Brian. "That was the first time I've written from a fictional perspective, other than the silly songs," he says. "We were sitting at Bob Evans restaurant eating breakfast one morning, and there was a lady sitting behind us, smoking. Well, my friend, this total character, he just says [in a deep voice] 'Oooh, she's smoking 100's alone. You should write a song about that.' Well, it sounded too cool, so I had to totally make it up."

He stops for a second. "Well, you know what? That is not the first fiction. The first fiction was 'Financing His Romance,' which was recorded for this album but didn't make the cut. But the thing about 'Financing His Romance' which was funny was that it was totally fiction, but it turned out to be a true story in my life about six or maybe eight months after it got written."

In the right hands, real life and fiction come to about the same thing. In the Bottle Rockets' hands, the Ramones, John Anderson and Neil Young come to about the same thing. And the beauty of South St. Louis—other than cheap rent, and $6 haircuts—is that it doesn't seem like anybody much cares.

"All Day And All Of The Night" first appeared in *No Depression* #9 (May–June 1997).

Selected Discography:

Bottle Rockets, *Bottle Rockets* (East Side Digital) 1993.

Bottle Rockets, *The Brooklyn Side* (East Side Digital) 1994, reissued (Atlantic) 1995.

Bottle Rockets, *24 Hours a Day* (Atlantic) 1997.

Old 97's

by Tom Skjeklesaether

It struck me right outside of Waco, Texas, that world-famous American center for the furthering of religious understanding and human compassion. On my way down Interstate 35 in the early morning hours, bound for Austin and the annual cacophony of music called South By Southwest, I was wrestling with a musical riddle of the caliber that can drive you crazy: Where did I hear that song? Who does that voice remind me of? The voice of Rhett Miller, the energetic singer and acoustic guitar player in the Dallas quartet Old 97's had bugged me since I heard their debut album, *Hitchhike To Rhome*, while I was living in Austin in '94.

Driving down from meeting the band on their home turf, I was listening to their much-anticipated major-label debut, *Too Far To Care*, when the black truckstop coffee suddenly cleared my mind. Miller could easily have stepped in as Robert Smith, the singer for English pop-gothic band The Cure, had he only been willing to trade his nerd-looking glasses for lipstick. But of course my initial angle on the Old 97's, their utterly cool version of Merle Haggard's "Mama Tried" off their debut album, hadn't exactly pointed me in the right direction.

This annoyance off my mind, I was able to turn up the volume of the most downright entertaining album so far from the already over analyzed current generation of alt-country aficionados and rewind the tape three quarters of a year back to the summer of '96, when the Old 97's visited Norway for the first time. The band did four gigs in a short week and started out by blowing the ears off of a selection of major record company label managers who were instructed by their American home offices to treat the band generously, to aid the ensuing bidding war in the wake of the band's showcase at SXSW '96.

During the weekend, at the festival Down On The Farm, they hooked up with fellow Texan Jimmie Dale Gilmore for the first time and did rousing versions of Gilmore's "Dallas" as one of many high points in sets which made it clear that country did not necessarily have to be music for an older generation. But the real upper-cut came when the 97's performed a late-night set on Monday at the Oslo celebrity nightspot the Smuget, mainly in front of seasoned musicians, journalists and music biz people. The owner of the club was there, and when the Old 97's exploded all over his stage, I realized he'd had a flashback to the night in 1977 when the Sex Pistols tore down his club.

The Old 97's took their name from "The Wreck of the Old 97"—a song by Henry Whitter dating back to 1923—after a suggestion by the band's resident train buff and bass player Murry Hammond. The song describes a mail train railroad line leading from Virginia to North Carolina, where the wrecking of the Old 97 occurred. The song was immediately made into a million-selling hit by one of the earliest country recording artists, Vernon Dalhart (1883–1948). The Johnny Cash version is best-known to current country listeners.

I met up with the quartet at Hammond's house just north of downtown Dallas, a couple of days before they made their way down to SXSW and a big showcase at the outdoor stage of Stubb's Barbecue. Scattered around Murry's living room are drummer Philip Peeples, and lead guitarist Ken Bethea. Their mood is very upbeat; it seems 1997 just has to be the year of the Old 97's. "There is a lot more work behind this album than it was behind our last record, *Wreck Your Life* (Bloodshot, 1995)," Miller says. "Back then we were scrounging for songs. This time we had way too many."

Too Far To Care was recorded at the end of 1996 at a studio on a pecan orchard in Tornillo, Texas, about a half-hour outside of El Paso, with producer Wally Gagel, a musician/producer best known for his work with alternative rock bands. Before the band settled on Gagel, they had been in contact with a couple of big-name producers, Don Was and T Bone Burnett. (Was even did some rehearsals with the band but had to drop out when he was called in on short notice to work with that other insurgent country act, The Good Ole Rolling Stones Boys Band.)

All of the songs on *Too Far To Care* are originals, including re-recordings of one track each from their two earlier albums—"Four Leaf Clover" off *Hitchhike To Rhome,* and "Big Brown Eyes" off *Wreck Your Life.* The first one has been upgraded as a duet with punk icon Exene Cervenka of X. (The well-versed punker will recall that Exene showed an interest in country back in 1985 with the X side project band the Knitters.)

The new album is no big departure from the two first albums. The group's signature sound has simply been expanded, the twang digs deeper, and the distinctions of Miller's acoustic guitar and Hammond's acoustic bass are clearer. On top of that sits their trademark vocal harmonies. Hammond, rumored to have been a card-carrying metal fan some years ago, brings the band furthest into country territory with his song "West Texas Teardrops."

The Dallas/Fort Worth metroplex has, since the 1970s, been overshadowed by much smaller Austin when it comes to music. While Austin became known as ground zero for Willie Nelson, Jerry Jeff Walker and progressive country, Dallas remained most famous for the TV melodrama that bore its name and for the assassination of President Kennedy ("No guns allowed on these premisses [*sic*]" is the message on the door to the Kennedy Assassination Museum in the Book Depository). Yet the city has fostered rock legends such Stevie Ray Vaughan (who nevertheless is most associated with his glory days in Austin), Stephen Stills, Sly Stone and Marvin Lee Aday (also known as Meat Loaf). But a lesser-known Dallas act figured most prominently in the development of the Old 97's.

"The band responsible for bringing our attention toward country is without a doubt Killbilly," says Hammond, referring to the late-'80s/early-'90s group that mixed bluegrass and punk with sometimes explosive results.

"Both me and Murry spent time touring as members of Killbilly," Miller adds. "So did Danny Barnes and Mark Rubin of the Bad Livers." Today Killbilly's drummer, Mike Schwedler, is the manager of the Old 97's.

There's no doubt that the Old 97's (and their formative incarnations as, among other names, the Sleepy Heroes) took serious detours before they found their way back to the real folk music of their area. An early demo tape indicates that Miller and Hammond would have been more at home on London's Carnaby Street than on the open prairie.

"For a while, me and Murry played as a regular coffeehouse duo as well," Miller recalls. On this live circuit that also includes the band's number one home club, the Sons Of Herman Hall, they met up with local legend Homer Henderson, who took his stage name from a local intersection where his wife runs a clothing shop. Two of Henderson's most known songs are "Lee Harvey Was A Friend Of Mine" (the very definition of politically incorrect, Dallas-style), and "Pickin' Up Beer Cans On The Highway." (The latter was recorded by the Old 97's during the sessions for *Too Far To Care* but will only appear as maybe an extra track on a single.)

Bloodshot previously issued two Old 97's vinyl singles with only one track available on a regular album, and in 1995, Idol Records released a split ten-inch EP with the Old 97's and fellow Dallas band Funland, on which each band took a turn at the other's songs. But the crown jewel in Old 97's expanding catalog of one-offs was recorded just recently in Nashville. Two tracks were recorded with John Croslin (formerly of '80s Austin popsters the Reivers) as producer and with country legend Waylon Jennings as the lead singer of the band.

Jennings has been a fan of the band since they crossed tracks at a radio convention sponsored by *Gavin* magazine a couple years ago. The band played a brief showcase at a seminar for which Jennings was a panelist. "Later, he was asked about his thoughts on alternative country and he gave our showcase a thumbs-up," Miller said. "And he talked about us in an interview with an Austin newspaper."

Jennings' camp first suggested recording a single together. One song, "The Other Shoe," was taken from *Wreck Your Life;* the other, "Iron Road," was made to order by Hammond while the band was mixing the new album.

The result is perfect—simply Waylon as the singer, with the Old 97's sound intact. The single was paid for by Elektra but will be released by an as-yet undetermined indie label. "At the end of the session, Waylon told us that he wanted to use us as the band for his next album," Bethea beams, not even trying to hide his pride.

In Austin, the Old 97's showcase takes the form of a graduation party. Although Bethea starts out with guitar trouble, the show goes on out of sheer enthusiasm from a loud crowd of hardcore sing-along fans. The band members take their energetic stage antics to new levels, leaving one to wonder if Miller and Hammond actually glue their nerd-glasses to their heads. When Exene Cervenka is introduced by Miller as the band comes back for a rare SXSW encore, the field in front of the stage erupts in total chaos. Two songs later, they have proven that they truly deserve their position among the front-runners in the alternative country crowd.

Although they actually play rock with country elements thrown into the mix, bands such as the Old 97's can make younger people understand that country was as essential an influence as blues on the original musical blend that came out as rock 'n' roll—a true American art form.

"The Year Of The Old 97's" first appeared in *No Depression* #9 (May–June 1997).

Selected Discography:

Old 97's, *Wreck Your Life* (Bloodshot) 1995.

Old 97's, *Too Far to Care* (Elektra) 1997.

The Waco Brothers

by Linda Ray

"When it started, the whole purpose of this band was to get beer and money," Waco Brothers ringleader Jon Langford says of the band's $50-a-gig beginnings a couple years ago. In the bargain, club owners in the band's home base of Chicago got not only Langford, co-founder of underground British legends the Mekons, but also Jesus Jones bassist Alan Doughty and Poi Dog Pondering drummer Steve Goulding, late of the Graham Parker band and an alumnus of the Gang of Four.

"It was not until Nan said, 'Make an album,' which we thought was such a ridiculous prospect to just do a lot of really horrible cover versions, that we thought we'd better try and write some songs," Langford continued. "Then the band sort of really turned into a band."

"Nan" is Nan Warshaw of Bloodshot Records, whose 1994 compilation *For A Life Of Sin* documented Chicago rock projects heavily influenced by traditional country and bluegrass music. A pre-Waco Brothers project, the disc included a track from Langford credited to "Jon Langford's Hillbilly Lovechild," and also sported his painting "Deck Of Cards" on its front cover.

"It's important to note how magnanimous Jon has been to us," says Eric Babcock, who co-founded Bloodshot with Warshaw. "He invited me over, offered me beer and then let me choose from his paintings what we wanted for the cover [of *For a Life of Sin*]. The Waco Brothers wouldn't exist if the label hadn't suggested an album, but the label wouldn't exist if Jon Langford hadn't lent his credibility."

According to Babcock and Warshaw, this influence even extends to how Bloodshot's business is organized. "Jon's approach with the Mekons helped us realize possibilities in the different ways he looked at a band's structure," Babcock says of the famously collaborative punk icons who have miraculously survived twenty years of hard drinking and progressive idealism.

Those Mekon politics carry over into Langford's country-flavored incarnation as well. Rob Miller, the third Bloodshot partner, just comes right out with it: "The Waco Brothers are fucking Limey socialists." This summation of the band's world view nicely illustrates a distinction between the character of Bloodshot's country-punk stable and that of their counterparts in the alternative-country world.

As if to underscore Miller's point, Langford bellows good-naturedly from the stage of the Lounge Ax: "Yeah, we like your milk and honey! We'll take your milk and honey and spit it right back at you!" Langford has just been holding forth on the subject of capital punishment: "In Europe, we all think you're barbaric!" Capital punishment is the focus of this night's fund-raising concert, one of many the Wacos perform over the course of a year to support a wide range of progressive causes. The band then rips into the gallows classic "25 Minutes to Go" in a manner to raise the dead.

But Langford doesn't need a forum tailored to a point of view to launch one. Earlier in the month at the Beat Kitchen, an exuberant burst of stagecraft put him in mind of another. Concluding a cover of "Baba O'Riley," the Wacos took turns in the air, solo and in twos and threes. "Yes, we leap," Jon Langford ranted in red-faced good cheer. "We're not like you Americans who have to pay for your own health care if you fall down. We're from Leeds and we *leap*."

Those raucous Wacos pass through rooms with the energy of an eighteen-wheeler sporting polished chrome exhaust pipes and a major attitude. They're pissed off about the human condition: the numbing dehumanization of common labor, the corrupting influence of wealth and fame, the hypocrisy of religion, and the perennial power of plain vice. Indeed, the anger in almost any Waco Brothers song could fuel that truck from Natchez to Poughkeepsie.

So how did it get to Chicago? Mostly for love. Three of the four real Brits married Chicago women. The fourth, mandolinist Tracy Dear, insists he came here to escape a woman. It's Dear who sets the girls' hearts palpitating when he removes his shirt mid-set to reveal a well-shaped muscle-T. And it's Dear who sings the infectious, crowd-pleasing "Do As I Say, Don't Do As I Do," the emancipation proclamation of a love interest as seen from the flipside, the aggrieved lout's point of view.

"Do As I Say…" is just one of fourteen catchy ideological bottle-bombs delivered by the Waco Brothers for your dancing and drinking pleasure on their new *Cowboy in Flames*, a just-under-fifty-minute hard-country collection recorded at Chicago's King Size Sound Labs. It's Dear who seems to hold the band's only romantic view of cowboys and the old west.

"I think people like Guy Clark, just by their philosophy and their songwriting…," he trails off. "He's an unbent man, very true to his word. It's not about dressing up in a hat and all that. I think this is where it taps into the whole punk thing. It's about morals, beliefs. We're just trying to tap into the emotion of it."

Such sincerity is met with hearty derision from his bandmates. "Whatever he said, it's wrong," they chide, howling. "Forget about it."

"The cowboy is just sort of this weird figure," Langford says. "It's been used by a lot of people to represent the situation here [in America]. If somebody comes and does your roof and charges you like 3,000 quid and the roof falls in, they're cowboys. That's what a cowboy is in England."

In fact, the new record's title track isn't a metaphor for the defamation of an ideal or even the corruption of country music (that comes in a later track, "The Death of Country Music"), but rather a scathingly suggestive rant on government cover-ups, specifically related to the crash of TWA Flight 800. "It was about what happened when they shot down that plane with an American missile," Langford says, his voice trailing off wistfully until he catches himself. "They think terrorism comes *to* America, like the Oklahoma bombing when they were looking for Arabs. It's like, we're looking for these *white* Arabs in cowboy hats."

Growing up in England, the future Wacos apparently never associated Johnny Cash or Buck Owens or Merle Haggard with either country music or the American West. "It's white man's urban blues," Langford says. "It's just raw music, honky tonk. Merle Haggard never was on a horse."

Tracy Dear recalls that Cash was a favorite of his father, a member of the rough-neck Irish folk Dubliners from whose groundwork grew the Pogues. "The Dubliners were the tough boys of Irish pub drinking music, and Johnny Cash was one of the tough boys of American music. It was about blue-collar honesty," he says.

"I remember, in the mid-to-late '60s, Buck Owens & the Buckaroos," says Steve Goulding. "When we used to listen to it in England, we weren't really aware of it being country music. It was just American music. Johnny Cash was like Chuck Berry was like Jerry Lee Lewis."

Goulding's considerable range gives the new record a remarkable variety in tempo, from rumba to hand-jive to straight country and honky-tonk to almost arena-scale rock. He deserves much credit for the fact that it never really matters whether you understand what a Waco Brothers song is about. Steel player Mark Durante says, to the nodding agreement of his Brothers, "Steve is the best guy in the band."

Durante, on the other hand, is breaking new ground on steel. His interest in country music derives from youthful devotion to the ersatz weekly WLS Barndance television show in Chicago, where he grew up. Never mind that he toured with hard-rock bands on his way back to it, including KMFDM, on his way back to it. His interest in steel encompasses its history as well as current practice, which he keeps up with through active membership in both the steel players' and Hawaiian guitar players' national associations. His efforts to insinuate real twang into the Wacos' trademark blasting, churning, country-hearted punk deliver mixed, if usually interesting, results.

Durante's playing is just plain poetic on the gorgeous "Dry Land," one of only two songs on Cowboy in Flames that have no apparent political message beyond an interpersonal one (the other being Johnny Cash's "Big River"). On "Dry Land," rather than yield its churning intensity, the band channels it into the rhythmic surge-and-clap of a disturbed sea, with the vocals and the steel guitar gentling over the changes.

Schlabowske, one of two native Chicagoans (along with Durante) counter-balancing the band's four Brits, came to the Waco Brothers from a guitar noise outfit called Wreck. "We were sitting around our bass player's loft and I was playing *Curse of the Mekons.* I liked the production on it and I was telling him we ought to find Jon Langford to produce our record. A guy who was hanging around there developing pictures just kind of shouted over, 'Well, he's spinning disks at Crash Palace [a punk hipster hangout] tonight.'"

In addition to "Dry Land," Schlabowske cops to two other standouts on *Cowboy in Flames*: "Out There a Ways," about what he calls "the bizarre effects" of celebrity, with Michael Jackson as a metaphor; and "Fast Train Down," the most traditional country-sounding song on the record. The latter gives voice to the despair and alienation of a man stuck in a dehumanizing job, knowing that even his dream of escaping it is an illusion fostered by those who would profit from it. "'The boxes go in and the boxes go out,'" Langford muses, quoting a line from the song. "It's what I like about country music—the politics of that. It's like a Merle Haggard song."

"I can't claim to have ever listened to much country on the radio growing up in the Midwest," says Schlabowske, the one Waco whose voice occasionally, and convincingly, opens a country crack as wide as the interstate. "For me the initial figure was Hank Williams. For some reason, all the people who were into punk rock were into Hank Williams. It makes a certain amount of sense because they're both real raw, simple. The themes stem from the frustrations of everyday life in the working class."

The *Cowboy in Flames* track "Take Me to the Fires" concludes with an outright subversion of Hank's classic line "I Saw the Light," going completely over the top with hand-clapping, soul-stirring, old-time gospel call-and-response. Tracy Dear makes the fires of hell sound at least inviting as the wake enjoyed by the survivors, with the best booze and the loudest damned band you ever danced to.

In the record's rendering of the Dorsey Dixon classic "Wreck on the Highway," it's impossible to tell if Langford is angrier about drunk driving or religious hypocrisy. Throughout the song, Goulding's drumming sustains the level of intensity at which U2's Larry Mullen Jr. climaxed "Hawkmoon 269," mimicking the heart-pounding shock of coming upon broken bodies dying, faithless, their blood mixed with traces of their booze in glass smashed by the impact. Langford's delivery implies a dare: Who would save them?

In such classics as this, as well as "Big River" and "White Lightnin'," the significant, if unorthodox, contribution of Alan Doughty's bass is clearest. The Wacos' first record, *To The Last Dead Cowboy*, featured the Bottle Rockets' Tom Ray on bass. By his third or fourth gig with the Waco Brothers last year, on the Beat Kitchen's roomy stage, Doughty was still bumping into his bandmates. There was not yet quite space for his lurching, roving, altogether alarming stage presence.

Within a couple of months, though, Doughty showed the stuff of which he was made when Goulding missed the first set of a gig at Schubas Tavern. The famously hard-and-fast Wacos played percussion-free and, apart from the impossibly syncopated

"Honky Tonkin'," held together. Langford allowed that the mellowness suited his mood; Schlabowske quipped, "These kids today, they don't want to hear all that racket."

An Alan Doughty bassline does handsprings and loop-the-loops where a proper one would thump along the bottom with some discipline. "It's all nervous energy," Doughty explains. "I really have no idea where I'm going next with something. I don't know anything about theory. It's all new to me every time I play." Doughty continues to work on the next Jesus Jones album. "It's been four years and two months since the last one, so this almost qualifies as a comeback record," he says.

Long a favorite with hard-drinking country music lovers, "White Lightnin'" takes on new meaning performed by a band that took its name from an inflammatory incident involving "G-men, T-men, Revenuers, too." The theme of government malfeasance runs throughout the Wacos' work, particularly in songs Langford sings. Besides the title track, *Cowboy in Flames* features Langford on two songs with obvious messages related to government and big business: "See Willy Fly By," which touches on the "us vs. them" paranoia of government leaders; and "Dollar Dress," which treats the general bankruptcy of the American Dream.

One Tuesday night in October, a basement stage in Wicker Park morphed into something like a private living room where songwriters and guitar pickers supported, then lifted, polished and outshone each other's music. Just at the edge of the theatrical lighting onstage, Langford sat hunched thoughtfully in black over his white guitar. He picked out delicate, mandolin-like fills for Chris Mills' cover of a Hank Williams tune. Langford had just finished his turn, with former Texas Rubies singer Jane Baxter Miller providing harmony on his own "Half Past Drinks at Half Price 8," a song he claims was vetoed democratically by the Waco Brothers for their new album. The song is all about counting and includes the line, "At last count there's nothing I want at all." The repose of an angry man.

Mills, a much-buzzed-about Chicago songwriter who just turned twenty-one, is one of the many younger musicians, including Schlabowske and the Handsome Family's Brett Sparks, who have benefited from Langford's mentoring. "A lot of musicians around town think of Jon like sort of a nurturing father, like a really cool dad," says Julia Adams, co-owner of Chicago's legendary Lounge Ax nightclub. "Jon and Susan [Miller, her Lounge Ax partner] and I have a camaraderie because we're sort of the old people in the business [age thirty-nine, she says]. But we all can still rock!"

If Langford's age has anything to do with anything other than inspiring young musicians, it at least doesn't seem to slow him down. He continues working with the Mekons, most recently on a collaborative show, Mekons United, involving an art exhibition and combination show catalog/essay collection, with accompanying CD. He also has a side project, Skull Orchard, with Doughty, Goulding and Durante.

While not without ambition—"We have set out to be the most extreme hard country band," he says, with competition barely in view—Langford and the Wacos have discovered the value of enough. "If you set out to make things bigger and bigger," he says, "you never actually get to the point where you can say, 'This is quite a good size to be.'

"Before the last hundred years, music was a lot of people sitting around playing in a lot of bars. Your favorite band was the band that was playin' in your little tavern or whatever on a Friday night. That's kind of what it is for us. I think there's no reason why it has to be any bigger than this if it works successfully. We're at a point where we sell enough records to make the next one. I don't care if we sell more. It doesn't mean anything to me."

"Beer & Whiskey In The Land Of Milk & Honey" first appeared in *No Depression* #7 (January–February 1997).

Selected Discography:

The Waco Brothers, *To The Last Dead Cowboy* (Bloodshot) 1995.

Sally Timms w/ Jon Langford and others, *To The Land Of Milk And Honey* (Feel Good All Over) 1995.

Rico Bell w/ Jon Langford and others, *The Return Of Rico Bell* (Bloodshot) 1995.

Sally Timms with the Waco Brothers, the Handsome Family and others, *Cowboy Sally* (Bloodshot) 1997.

The Waco Brothers, *Cowboy In Flames* (Bloodshot) 1997.

The Waco Brothers, *Do You Think About Me?* (Bloodshot) 1997.

Jon Langford, *Skull Orchard* (Sugar Free) 1998.

Whiskeytown

by Peter Blackstock

You could see it in his eyes.

"Hey, hop in the van, let's have a shot," Ryan Adams beckoned, and who was I to argue with that Peter Pan gleam and Pied Piper smile. It was Saturday night of the 1996 South by Southwest Music Conference in Austin, and a handful of A&R reps were milling around the van with North Carolina plates parked in front of the Split Rail, just after Whiskeytown had delivered an impassioned forty-minute set to a room so packed that even conference badge-holders were turned away at the door.

You could tell things were heading in this direction ever since Whiskeytown released their first album, *Faithless Street,* the previous fall. Issued on Mood Food, a tiny indie label for whom it was a challenge just to get the disc in stores outside the band's home region, *Faithless Street* nevertheless made waves nationally, simply because it was too good not to be heard. Firing twin barrels of the rawest rock 'n' roll and the grittiest country, it was the kind of debut that signals something truly special is on the horizon.

And so, six months later, record label folks who had gathered in Austin were curious to see what all this "alt-country" buzz was about. Industry pressures be damned, Whiskeytown delivered that night—albeit nervously and tenuously at times, but in a way that only underscored the emotional intensity rather than detracted from it. His microphone slipping from its stand at one point, Adams crouched and staggered awkwardly as the mike dangled ever more precariously, nearly crashing to the floor, struggling to still be heard, somehow holding everything together even as it all seemed to be falling apart before his eyes.

I don't really recall what we talked about in the van that night we first met, before I headed off to catch another band down the street. Something about sending me a tape of some new stuff he'd recorded recently, which of course never happened. Probably a little guffawing at the gaggle of weasels lingering on the sidewalk just outside the windshield. Mostly, though, I remember the sense of excitement that exuded from this twenty-one-year-old boy wonder—and that irrepressible shine in his eyes.

Ryan is the perfect frontman, irreverent and passionate both, a great singer and a charismatic little twerp too. I can't take my eyes off of him.
    —Shawn Barton of Hazeldine
        (from her web-page diary of Hazeldine's tour with Whiskeytown)

Several months later, when the dust eventually settled from the major-label jockeying in the wake of that SXSW '96 show and a showcase three months later at L.A.'s Spaceland, Whiskeytown had landed on Outpost, a relatively new subsidiary of Geffen. (Quite a bit happened to the band in the interim, including a change in rhythm sections, but we'll deal with that later.) They entered a Nashville studio in February '97 with producer Jim Scott and emerged a month later with an astounding thirty-six songs recorded; thirteen of those eventually made the final cut for *Strangers Almanac*.

The magic is evident right from the heartbreaking strains of the opening track, "Inn Town," an acoustic tune on which the voices of Adams, guitarist Phil Wandscher and fiddler Caitlin Cary coalesce in richer and fuller harmonies than they'd previously hinted they were capable of. The pedal steel that kicks off the second track, "Excuse Me While I Break My Own Heart Tonight," sews the band's country influences firmly on its sleeve, with Texas songwriter/rocker Alejandro Escovedo chiming in as a duet partner on the last verse to charge the song with an unexpected spark. The fire continues on the rocked-out third track, "Yesterday's News," Adams avowing at the top of his lungs, "I can't stand to be under your wing/I can't fly or sink or swim."

Despite Whiskeytown's clear grounding in no-bullshit rock 'n' roll and country,

Strangers Almanac is perhaps most notable for its pop songs. "16 Days," the fourth track and likely the album's first single, is a mostly midtempo number, opening with Cary's sweet fiddle drifting over acoustic guitars and gradually building to a sure-fire sing-along chorus. "Everything I Do (Miss You)" shimmers with a pop-soul richness that recalls classic Motown and Muscle Shoals recordings. "Turn Around" is spooky, cloaked in sonic layers and recalling nothing so much as mid-late-'70s Fleetwood Mac (an influence Whiskeytown readily acknowledge with their cover of the Mac smash "Dreams" at recent shows). "Losering" is a masterful mood piece, nonlinear lyrics wrapped around an initially unassuming melody that slowly reveals itself like a sunlight-shy flower, a few more petals opening up each time it spins back around.

Then there are the ballads, achingly spare and desolate and sad. "Houses On The Hill" tells the story of a woman who has never quite recovered from losing her lover decades ago, "when Eisenhower sent him to war." On "Avenues," a beautiful loser wanders the streets alone while "All the sweethearts of the world are out dancing in the places/Where me and all my friends go to hide our faces." The most haunting cut of all is "Dancing With The Women At The Bar," a letter-perfect lament of nature's pull toward the deeper and darker side of the night, the town, and the soul.

If you see the moon and hear the sound of the strip
Call out my name, and call my friends' names too
  —"Dancing With The Women At The Bar"

It's a warm spring night along Hillsborough Street in Raleigh—a.k.a. "the strip"—and, sure enough, a full moon is beaming brightly in the sky above as we head west toward the Comet. It's a familiar hangout at the far end of the strip situated next door to The Brewery, a longtime fixture on Raleigh's live-music scene that has played host to no shortage of Whiskeytown gigs in the past couple years.

With North Carolina State University spanning its southern side and a string of bars, coffee shops, restaurants, record stores and the like scattered over several blocks across the street, Hillsborough is like many such avenues across America. "There's a strip in Jacksonville, too," Adams says as we walk along, referring to the small North Carolina town (pop. 30,013) about an hour and a half southeast of Raleigh where he grew up. His comment sheds a little light on another line in "Dancing With The

Women At The Bar": "My daddy saw the moon and heard the sound of the strip/It called out his name, and it called his son's name too."

Most of Adams' life has revolved around this definitively slackerly stretch of Hillsborough since he moved to Raleigh shortly after quitting high school and getting his GED about five years ago. Presently, we pass the Rathskeller, a restaurant where Adams worked as a dishwasher shortly after he moved up from Jacksonville. A block or two down is Mitch's, a warm, friendly tavern where a few scenes from the movie *Bull Durham* were filmed; "Phil's probably up there right now," Adams guesses of his guitarist, pointing toward the bar's upstairs window. Just off the main road a block or two is a large grassy triangle flanked by a couple of neighborhood streets lined with low-rent houses, a couple of which Adams used to live in. "That's *Faithless Street*, right there," he says of the desolate block, revealing the source of his songs on Whiskeytown's first record.

Down on the eastern end of the strip, shortly before Hillsborough segues from an edge-of-campus boulevard into a commuter thoroughfare leading to downtown Raleigh and the North Carolina state capitol building, is a modest little sandwich shop called Sadlack's. Regulars idle up to the wide-U-shaped diner-style counter for cheap eats and a beer, or lounge around on the wooden picnic tables populating a patio area that's more spacious than the limited confines of the indoor room. In the late afternoon and early evening hours on a balmy North Carolina spring day, the patio is an ideal place to sit around and pick a guitar, as a couple of hippie-looking stragglers are doing on this mid-May afternoon. Something's slightly askew, though. Instead of the requisite classic-rock nugget or trail-mix folk song you'd usually hear being played in such a situation, these guys are strummin' and singin' Robert Earl Keen's "You Keep A' Swervin' In My Lane…"

I consider us to be more of a rock 'n' roll band, but we are country. I'm a country boy from West Virginia. And Ryan's a country boy, too. The country comes more from ourselves, because we are country.

—Steve Terry, Whiskeytown drummer

"The whole premise of the band started when I was walking by here one day, and Skillet was leaning over the deck, and he goes, 'Hey Ryan! I hear you wanna start a country band,'" Adams recalls of a chance encounter at Sadlack's in the fall of 1994 with Skillet Gilmore, who was the owner of Sadlack's at the time. "And I said, 'Yeah, that's what I wanna do, man.' And he said, 'I'll play drums.' I said, 'All right then, meet me here tomorrow at 11:30.'"

Adams had spent the previous couple years playing in a punk band called Patty Duke Syndrome with Jere McIlwean, who befriended Adams when they both lived in Jacksonville. "I was growing up a freak, this weird music person, and in that town, there was no one like me. Except Jere. He worked at Record Bar; he was already twenty-something years old. I was going to the record store and buying, like, Half Japanese albums and Sonic Youth records. And one day he just asked me, 'Why in the hell are you buying these records?' I said, 'Because I like 'em.' We hit it off, and next thing I knew he took me out to his place and he had all this musical equipment, and we started that band. Our drummer, Alan, had this big ol' barn where we played music at all hours of the night."

Patty Duke Syndrome had a brief run in Jacksonville before Adams moved to Raleigh, where he played in a couple of bands he describes in hindsight as being along the lines of the Replacements and the Minutemen. McIlwean eventually moved to Raleigh as well, and Patty Duke re-formed, with Brian Walsby on drums.

"Its official Raleigh time was about a year and a half; we broke up four times," Adams recalls of the band's off-and-on tenure.

"But we were the shit in Raleigh for a while. And I was just 18. I couldn't believe it....They got mad at me because I started drinking. If I had one beer, Jere would get mad as hell at me. And then I come to find the whole time he's a closet heroin addict. And he ended up dying.

"The song 'Theme For A Trucker' [issued by Bloodshot Records earlier this year on a double single] is actually about Jere. He was in a band called Trucker after Patty Duke Syndrome broke up. They were like an MC5 and Bad Brains-influenced band. Hearing them would give you chills; you could feel something was gonna happen, like they were gonna change the world.

"And damned if he didn't go and die on everybody. I wanted to write about it for a long time, and then finally I started writing that song. He'd hate that song so bad; he hated country. Well, he didn't hate country music, but he didn't like my version of it, anyway."

There's a motel with a vacancy
But there is no possibility
That you could drive yourself to ever be
The man you once were.
    —"Theme For A Trucker"

So I started this damn country band
'Cause punk rock was too hard to sing.
    —"Faithless Street"

"The band started with me and Skillet and this guy named Rags playing banjo," Adams says. "And then, his roommate, Brian, became the bass player, and we were a coffee-country band. That's what Skillet called it. It was a three-piece electric band; it sounded kinda like the Gun Club, a little bit like Uncle Tupelo. We called it coffee-country because we were really wired. We'd get a twelve-pack and drink about three cups of coffee, and get stoned and get drunk. And by the time all the chemicals got in us, we were playing pretty fast.

"And then Phil joined the band. I always hated Phil, and I still do. He walked up to me one night in a bar and we were both drunk, and he said, 'Hey man, I think I wanna play guitar for your band.' He bought me a beer and we talked about it for a few minutes, and I was like, 'All right.' He hated my guts, and I hated his guts. I thought he was a fuckin' jerk."

This, understand, is the nature of the relationship between Ryan Adams and Phil Wandscher. For the record, Wandscher makes similar comments about Adams; in the band's official bio issued by Outpost/Geffen, Wandscher recalls the first time he met Adams by saying, "He was like sixteen or seventeen, a real brat....He's still a brat."

However much they may engage in their punk-rock revelry of pretending to despise each other, the magic of their musical relationship is the spark at the heart of Whiskeytown. Eventually, they both fess up to that.

"It was perfect," Adams recalls of the first time he and Wandscher got together to jam. "It just worked. His guitar playing and my guitar playing, and his sensibilities and my sensibilities, they were perfect."

"We came from different angles musically, and we still do, but it just kind of meshes," Wandscher concurs. "I respect what he does and I try to understand it, and he tries to understand where I come from. Like, it's kinda funny that he's so gung-ho into the Rolling Stones now, and he never really was before—because that's my favorite band. And ultimately he's grown attached to them as well, partly because of how much they've influenced me."

Unlike Adams, who brought his experiences with Patty Duke and a scattering of side projects to the table, Whiskeytown was Wandscher's first real band (though he does admit to a six-year tenure with the North Carolina Boys Choir in his grade-school days).

"I kinda used to be in a band, but I didn't play guitar, I just sang and played harmonica," he explained. "We had a bass player and a drummer and I was singing, and we just needed a guitar player, and could never ever find one. All these people always came over and tried out, and finally I was like, 'Fuck it, man, *I'm* gonna learn how to play guitar. Because I know what I would wanna hear, and this is probably what would work the best, and these guys can't do it, so I'm gonna do it. So I sat down and started noodling around and started teaching myself how to play."

Wandscher presently invited his friend Steve Grothman, a bass player, to join in the jam sessions he'd been having with Adams and drummer Gilmore. "And the next thing you know, Caitlin Cary walks in with her fiddle, just off the street," Adams says. "Nobody knew her. She just walked in, she didn't know anybody."

Well, it wasn't quite that fateful. "A mutual friend that was in my department in grad school somehow leaked it to them that I played fiddle," recalls Cary, who was attending North Carolina State at the time. "He came up to me and said, 'My friend Ryan wants a fiddle player for his band, are you interested?' And I said, 'Oh, sure,' and gave him my number to give to him, and I never really expected to hear anything. But he called the next day, and said, 'We're practicing tomorrow,' and I went in and started playing."

The intangible musical magic that ties Adams and Wandscher was immediately apparent with Cary as well—particularly in the way their vocals intertwined. "Oh, definitely, right off the bat," she affirms. "I've never found anybody, outside of my family, who was that easy to sing with. I have a pretty good ear for singing harmony, but I've certainly tried to do it with other people since playing with Ryan, and found it to be harder."

Adams' new musical companions, meanwhile, were helping to turn him in a different direction from the punk and indie-rock that had dominated his previous endeavors. "Phil introduced me to country blues, like the Rolling Stones," Adams says, "and Skillet introduced me to a lot of Gram Parsons and George Jones and people like that—I mean, I knew of them, but I really got turned on, I got tapes to listen to. And Caitlin turned me on to bluegrass."

The spontaneous combustion of Whiskeytown's earliest days was captured almost instantly: Less than two months after they started playing together, they recorded a four-song, seven-inch EP that was released in the spring of '95 by Mood Food. This past April, several other outtakes from those first sessions were released by Mood Food under the title *Rural Free Delivery*—against the band's wishes, as their relationship with Mood Food appears to have soured irreparably over the past year.

Nevertheless, the worthiness of those early recordings—regardless of their spotty sound quality—hinted that Whiskeytown was capable of greatness in the not-too-distant future. They delivered when they returned to the studio in July 1995 to record *Faithless Street*, which came out later that year.

I'll ride with you tonight, I'll ride forever
There's no way to predict this kind of weather
　　—"Midway Park"

From the opening line of the opening song, *Faithless Street* radiated with a reckless emotional force, tangled up in a beautiful mess of hard-charging honky-tonk rockers, irresistibly catchy pop songs and gorgeously lilting laments. Nevermind they'd been together less than a year: Whiskeytown had arrived.

"I love it. I think it's a masterpiece," Adams says confidently when asked what he thinks about *Faithless Street* with a couple years of hindsight now in his periphery. Musicians often tend to cringe at recordings they made in the infancy of their bands' careers, but Adams clearly has no regrets.

"I think it's a strong youth album. It's crazy. It loves what it borrows from musically: It tips its hat to Gram Parsons, it tips its hat to the Stones, it's shaking hands with Uncle Tupelo on some levels. I don't think of it as an 'inspired' record or an 'inspiring' record—I think it's both. That's what albums should sound like; that's what a record is, to me. *Faithless Street* is a proud, proud thing for me. ("I cared about it enough to where I asked Geffen to buy it [from Mood Food]," he adds later; Geffen agreed to do so, and now owns the rights to reissue it in the future.)

The haphazard circumstances under which the album was recorded simply serve as evidence that one need not spend a lot of time and money in a fancy studio to get artistic results. *Faithless Street* was recorded at a place called the Funny Farm, which Adams describes as "a big barn out in the country where they make records. We were in there for like a week and a half, and that was it, we were done, we made a record. It was all a big blur. That was *Faithless Street.*

"My version of recording is, when I get in there, you can't stop me. I'll keep people in there till six in the morning, going, 'I got a guitar part, I'm ready, let's do it,' and they're like, 'Whoa, we gotta set up.' And I'm like, 'I don't care, you ain't settin' a mike.' I'll just throw a mike right in front of the amp and go, 'That's your sound, fix it.' And they'll record it. I mean, I'm a bastard in the studio, just because I go like time is everything."

Wandscher confirms that. "Oh yeah, it was always, how much can you do in this little time? It's all basically live recording, and then it's like, 'Overdubs? We don't have time to overdub, man!' And a lot of times, that worked out better, because you don't have time to mill around and think about it and then fuck stuff up."

Though no one is listed as producer in the liner notes, Adams claims that "Phil produced it, pretty much….At that point, Phil's ear for recording was genuinely amazing. He made our first album to be recorded the way *Exile on Main Street* would be recorded….When we went back to find all the original signals, the drums sounded horrible and things like that, but we got all the levels to be good enough to where we actually got to make a good record with it."

To end the night, Ryan tossed his Vox guitar into the middle of the room with the cable jerking tight. I was right at the side of the stage and saw Ryan running my way, but he veered off to the side to skid on the guitar as if it were a skateboard. The Vox didn't seem terribly damaged until their guitarist, Phil, jumped straight from the stage and landed his boot heels flat on Ryan's guitar. It was still plugged in and made this sound which could only be described as Eugene Chadbourne's rake caught in a lawn mower.

Ryan was on the patio and had not seen his axe being stomped to splinters. I picked it up and took it to him and he proceeded to finish the job against the back steps.

    —Jeff Hart, recounting the finale of a Whiskeytown gig in at the Berkeley Cafe in Raleigh in October 1995

However haphazard the recording sessions for *Faithless Street* may have been, Whiskeytown was quickly earning a reputation for their utterly volatile nature as a live band. Some nights were transcendent, some were disasters; some were a little bit of both, scattered amidst the mayhem and destruction.

All of which made for legendary entertainment, but also hinted at deeper problems within the band. Even as Whiskeytown's star was beginning to rise nationally and major labels were expressing interest, the increasing pressures and personal conflicts were starting to widen rifts within the band.

Pedal steel player Nicholas Petti was dismissed in June of '96, but he had been performing live with the band only for a few months; Bob Rickers laid down the pedal steel tracks in the studio on *Faithless Street*. Things began to fall apart more dramatically about three months later, when bass player Steve Grothman quit the band for what Adams says basically boiled down to "artistic differences." A bigger blow came when Gilmore followed Grothman's lead: "Skillet came in and quit that same day, two minutes later," Adams said. "About three weeks later, he asked to rejoin, and I declined him the opportunity, because I believe that, if you quit, you're gone, you don't come back."

Given that the band's origins could be traced back to Gilmore and Adams hanging out together at Sadlack's, the loss of Gilmore was a particularly trying turn of events. "It hurt pretty bad," Adams admits. "It compromised a lot of the integrity of the band, and it compromised my stability in being able to do the band. I was pretty damaged because of that." (The personal wounds have since healed a good deal, enough so that Gilmore served as the band's road manager on a nationwide tour this spring and even sat in with them on a couple of occasions.)

"I remember me and Phil sitting on the front porch going, 'What are we gonna do?'" Adams continued. "I almost signed as a solo artist to A&M, I almost quit the whole thing. And then I said, 'No, I can't give up the ship. I've worked too hard, and Whiskeytown is still a good band.'"

The continued interest and support of Outpost also helped hold the group together. "Outpost just said, 'Hey, we'll still sign you guys, and if you need a bassist and drummer just to be in the studio, we'll work with you,'" Wandscher recalls. "And that was just like the biggest thing. Because, you know, most people don't even get this opportunity, and then, if something like that [the near-breakup] happens, you definitely don't get that opportunity."

Oddly enough, the personal conflicts that epitomized Adams and Wandscher's relationship ultimately helped them keep Whiskeytown together just when everything seemed to be falling apart. "There was a lot of friction between me and Ryan, and there was some dramatic shit that happened at shows," Wandscher recalls. "But ultimately, that stuff made our relationship stronger, because there was a fire there to fuel every now and then. Which is sometimes pretty good—rather than nothing ever happening, and people keeping stuff inside. That was what happened with our band breaking up…. And that was never the case between me and Ryan. We would just blow up upon each other, but it was good to get all that out in the air right then and there."

Cary came close to quitting as well—close enough to where an interim Whiskeytown press photo issued by Outpost/Geffen, which appeared on the cover of *Billboard*, pictured only Adams and Wandscher. "At that particular time, she wasn't even sure what she was gonna do," Wandscher said. "She never really even knew until we went to make the new record in Nashville."

Take a second to stop
Think about it again
See what you would be losing
   —"Losering"

Somehow all the falling apart fell back into place by February of this year, and Whiskeytown—with new drummer Steve Terry and bassist Jeff Rice (who has since been replaced by Chris Laney, formerly of Ithica Gin and the Adams side-project Freight Whaler)—headed to Nashville to record *Strangers Almanac* with producer Jim Scott.

Not that things were any less fly-by-the-seat-of-their-pants than usual. "Steve and Jeff really just came together as a rhythm section about a week before we went to make the record," Adams recalled. "We didn't practice to make the record. We just said, 'We're going to Nashville to make a record, are you guys ready to go?' They said 'All right,' we got in the car, and there we were. The first three days of rehearsal, I thought he [Scott] was gonna cry. Because we sounded like shit. We sounded horrible."

Furthermore, Scott had a fundamentally different approach to recording than the band experienced during *Faithless Street*. Adams explains: "We're good with first takes; we're good with, 'The guitar part was wrong, but it was great.' Jim's not like that. Jim's like, 'You're not gonna wake up in ten years and call me and tell me what a bad record I made, or that I listened to you and I shouldn't have because you were dumb.' He's like, 'Quit jerkin' me.' That was his line the whole time: 'You're fuckin' jerkin' me. Are you gonna play something good, or are you gonna jerk me?' And we jerked him for about a month, and then we finally did some good takes."

True to form, different band members had different perspectives of the *Almanac* sessions. Wandscher described the experience as "fuckin' great; we just ended up loving him [Scott] to death," and says he appreciated the chance to use a variety of amps and effects to come up with sounds that would have been impossible on *Faithless Street*. On the flip side of the coin, Cary observed that the making of *Faithless Street* "was much more spontaneous.…The other guys in the band might say it [making *Almanac*] was really great fun, but a lot of my stuff had to be done in overdubs, so I didn't get a whole lot of that vibe of the first take of the song. Even though almost everything was recorded live as far as basic tracks went, for me it was mostly in the box later that I got my moment."

Whatever the pros and cons, some of the exchanges between Adams and Scott were classic. "He'd listen to a couple takes, and he'd say, 'I believe this guy.' That's how he would talk about it. He wouldn't ever put it on me; he'd listen to the recording and go, 'This is the guy I believe.' He'd ask me, 'Are you this guy right now?' And I was like, 'No.' And he'd say, 'Well, when are you this guy?' I'd go, 'In about an hour.'

"So I went down to this store, and this part of Nashville was kind of a predominantly black area, and I bought this framed picture of the black Last Supper in this liquor store, and a bottle of Southern Comfort, and commenced to getting trashed as hell walkin' down the strip, with a bottle of liquor in a brown bag, drinkin' Southern Comfort. So I got back there, and walked in, and I was the guy.

"Not that drinking pertains to that; I was lost, I had nothing to do, I needed to go walk down the street, I needed to feel something, feel alive. Because I'd been confined in the studio. So I come back, and I had been in the shit. And now I knew where I was."

You think that you have found a way
To ease your troubled mind
You fill a glass then drink it down
And fill it one more time
Well the wine will flow
And the pain will go
But the spell will never last
You'll never find the answer
In the bottom of a glass

    — "Bottom Of The Glass," Moon Mullican

One would be remiss not to address the significance of alcohol to the existence of a band that has whiskey in its name. "Down here, when somebody gets really fucked up, they put the word 'town' on the end of something," Adams explains. "You know, like, 'Goddamn, that guy's fuckin' coketown or something. Or you'd go like, 'God, I was so stoned, man, it was like fuckin' hallucinationtown.' And you'd go, 'God, man, we had so much liquor that night, we were fuckin' whiskeytown.'

"So, sort of metaphorically speaking, Whiskeytown pretty much means loaded. Means fucked up. I also liked the idea of a fictitional [*sic*] place where everybody was drunk. It's kind of this fictitional [*sic*] place, you know. Actually, not here, it isn't at all. Because just about everyone I know is drunk. Pretty much all the time."

Discussions of alcohol are scattered consistently throughout our interview—which, true to form, was conducted on a bar-hopping tour of the strip in Raleigh. At Sadlack's, Adams talked of how Gilmore would "play me Gram Parsons while I was getting early beers [i.e., before noon]. This is where you'd come if you were that bad. Which isn't that bad for down here. Because everybody drinks, all the time. This is what we do."

Of course, that's not exactly true. You can visit Raleigh, North Carolina, and find plenty of people who don't spend the majority of their time drinking. On the other hand, if you spend even a couple nights in the company of a certain crowd along The Strip, it's plain to see how easily alcohol becomes you.

Hang around with the people that I used to be
hang around on a corner waiting to go have a see
Now that I'm in town
I feel fine for now
    —"Inn Town"

"Almost all the songs on the record are about loss," Adams is quoted as saying in the press bio for *Strangers Almanac,* and a close listen to the lyrics verifies that confession. In the past year, Adams endured the loss of his old friend Jere McIlwean; a breakup with his girlfriend of three years; the departure of a couple bandmates; and an intangible loss of innocence as music became a full-time job. "It ultimately changed us—as a band, and as individuals," Adams admits.

But Raleigh remains a small town, and along The Strip, most everyone knows everybody else. Adams talks to the lady behind the counter at the bowling alley as if she's a longtime neighbor. At the Rathskeller, where he once worked, he runs into Brian Walsby, the drummer for his old band, Patty Duke Syndrome. Later, a Rathskeller waitress chides Wandscher and drummer Steve Terry as they scrounge through their wallets to pay the bill: "Shit, you guys *oughtta* have some money!"

"Half the people that we know hate us now," Adams says. "But at the end of the night, even the people that are disgusted that Whiskeytown got a great record deal are the guys that sit next to you at the bar and go, 'Hey, did you see that game,' or, 'I heard you went bowling, how'd you do.' No one cares at the end of the day."

Well the greatest love could be
At the end of every day
What is left for you and me
At the end of every day
    —"End Of The Day," The Reivers

It's four in the morning, and my flight back to Seattle leaves at 6:20 A.M., meaning

I've got only an hour or two more to kill without falling asleep. But those are the hardest hours. Ryan Adams really didn't have to oblige when I call up to ask if he's still awake and would it be okay if I stopped by—but he does.

Not much adorns the apartment he recently moved into. It's the first time in months he's actually had a place to live, after an extended stretch of recording and touring and living in hotels and sleeping on friends' floors. He still has no bed, apparently content to keep sleeping on the floor; on the walls hang album covers of Fleetwood Mac's *Mirage* and Gram Parsons' *Grievous Angel.* (Coincidentally or not, Adams was born one year to the day after Parsons died.)

From a small collection of videocassettes, he pulls out a couple tapes of early Whiskeytown gigs, even one of Patty Duke Syndrome, and offers to loan them to me—perhaps a long-delayed substitute for that tape of new songs he'd promised to send me when we met in Austin more than a year ago. (As fate would have it, I end up forgetting to take the tapes with me when I head out the door a little later.)

Sitting on a table is an envelope that just came in the mail the day before, which he proudly shows to me. It's his first-ever check for publishing royalties from BMI. The amount: Two dollars and seventy-four cents. Welcome to the big time.

Finally, he's ready to call it a night; there's still a couple beers in the fridge, but it seems Adams does know how to forgo one more drink after all. Instead, he brews up a pot of coffee to keep me awake on the road to the airport. In the final, waning moments of darkness before the dawn, it's a warm gesture, an affirmation of the Southern hospitality and human kindness at the heart of a North Carolina country boy.

You could see it in his eyes.

"Falling Down, Standing Up" first appeared in *No Depression* #10 (July–August 1997).

Selected Discography:
Whiskeytown, *Rural Free Delivery* (Mood Food) 1996.
Whiskeytown, *Strangers Almanac* (Outpost/Mood Food) 1997.

Backsliders

by David Menconi

The music scene around Raleigh and Chapel Hill, North Carolina, is about as balkanized as…well, the former Yugoslavia. You've got your punk rock kids, technique fetishists, frat-party bands, heavy metal bands, pop bands. Most all of them keep to themselves in their respective, mutually exclusive corners, which goes for the bands as well as audiences.

But if there's a single consensus band that cuts across the scene's different strata, it's the Backsliders, who rule the roost when it comes to Tar Heel country-rock. Locally, they're regarded with something akin to awe. They have the air of grizzled-yet-hip older brothers, partly because they're old enough to have been around the block a few times (all five are at least within shouting distance of forty).

All of them are also bordering-on-virtuoso players who wound up playing in this classic hard-core honky-tonk band after logging time in other far-flung quadrants of the scene. Guitarist Brad Rice and drummer Jeff Dennis played in hard rock bands; guitarist Steve Howell played blues and bluegrass; bassist Danny Kurtz played pop and country; singer-guitarist Chip Robinson did a little of everything.

"That's why the band sounds like it does," Robinson says. "Everybody came from different, almost fringe elements and ended up in this band. Everybody brought their own thing to this big stewpot, and that's the soup we got out of it."

The Soup du Backsliders includes plenty of *No Depression* verities —Buck Owens,

Lefty Frizzell, the Beat Farmers ("Gun Sale at the Church" is one of their live-set staples), Jason & the Scorchers, Neil Young and, of course, Gram Parsons. Had Parsons lived another ten years, his voice probably would have aged into something like Robinson's likable ragamuffin twang.

Parsons probably would have wound up with a band as rocking as the Backsliders, too. Their triple-guitar lineup brings to mind the mid-'80s glory days of the True Believers, another band with three guitars that sounded nothing at all like Lynyrd Skynyrd. Except the Backsliders *do* have one song that sort of sounds like Skynyrd: "Hey Sheriff," a spooky redneck tale of a standoff with The Law gone horribly awry.

"Hey Sheriff" is the one song that appears on both the 1996 live EP *From Raleigh, North Carolina* and the full-length *Throwin' Rocks at the Moon.* The live record captures the Backsliders in their natural element—a hot summer night last July at their hometown nightclub the Brewery, a club that is to the Backsliders what the Armadillo World Headquarters was to Commander Cody's Lost Planet Airmen.

The Backsliders were always a great honky-tonk band, going back to their early days five years ago with local guitar ace Larry Hutcherson on lap steel. But it was the punkier leanings of Brad Rice, who joined in 1995 after Hutcherson departed to concentrate on his own blues band, that kicked the Backsliders into a higher gear.

There's plenty of octane on *Live From Raleigh,* especially Rice's withering guitar flipout at the apex of "Hey Sheriff." The record also captures lots of the irrepressible Robinson's priceless between-song banter, although nothing as colorful as his usual intro for the song "King of the World": "This one goes out to every woman who's ever let me put my face in that special place."

Actually, Robinson says he's been advised to pursue a more, shall we say, low-key direction. "I'd like to figure that people would be pretty open-minded and get that it's just a joke," he says sheepishly. "We don't thrive on making people mad at us, so we're trying to tone it down a little —and I've gone a lot farther than that on intros before, believe me. But I kept kinda…you know, hearing about it afterward."

Throwin' Rocks at the Moon, produced with a minimum of fuss by Dwight Yoakam guitarist Pete Anderson, is as expert and elegantly simple as the live EP. From the first note of the driving shuffle "My Baby's Gone," the songs, the playing and Robinson's voice intersect perfectly. Each element enhances the other without getting in the way, building on the solid rhythms of drummer Jeff Dennis and bassist Danny

Kurtz. While Robinson is better known for his singing, his warm acoustic strumming adds texture to the exceptional electric guitar tandem of Rice and Howell. Rice typically plays loud and Howell pretty, but each does a lot of both, and it fits together seamlessly.

Anderson's production is simple and no-frills, as it should be. The Backsliders are nothing if not professional, and this ain't the sort of project where anybody needed to fog up the synthesizers. Getting Anderson to produce the album was a lucky break, one the band didn't think they'd get. While they were negotiating terms with Mammoth, the label told the Backsliders to come up with a list of "dream producers."

"Pete was probably the most longshot name on our list, but we figured, what the hell," Robinson said. "We hadn't even signed the deal yet and Pete was on the phone the day he got the tape in the mail: 'C'mon, man, I want you guys out here tomorrow! Let's make a record!' He was a great guy, real laid-back, didn't mess with anything too much. He basically tightened up the rhythm section and let Brad and Steve do what they do.

"As far as arrangements, we had them really together. We've been playing these songs a long time —and we'll have to play them a long time some more, once we start touring. Good thing none of us mind playing them. We still like 'em."

It would be nice if the album did well enough to allow Robinson to give up fixing guitar amps for a living. The best part of the rise of "insurgent country" is that bands like the Backsliders —veterans who have been playing music like this for years in relative obscurity —have suddenly found popular tastes tilting more their way than ever before.

Really, things aren't so different today from decades past. Whether Bakersfield in the '60s, Austin in the '70s or North Carolina today, as often as not, the best country music is coming from acts on the margins in places other than Nashville.

"We've seen this all before," Robinson notes. "There's been fringe country all along. Hell, Johnny Cash was fringe country. Those early Sun Records, Hank Williams, Buck and Merle and Bakersfield, Emmylou. Way before anybody appreciated all these people for being the American treasures they are, they started out on the fringes.

"It's kinda cool that it's come back, though. We had heard rumblings from various pockets, that this same kinda thing was happening in other cities for whatever reasons.

I think people just got tired of doing something they didn't want to do in order to make it in the business, and decided to go back to trying to write good songs and figuring out where their real roots are. We've been gettin' crowds the whole time, so maybe it's just something people missed hearing."

"Backsliders Slip Right Up To The Front" first appeared in *No Depression* #7 (January–February 1997).

Selected Discography:

The Backsliders, *Hard Core Honky Tonk From Raleigh, North Carolina* (Mammoth) 1996.
The Backsliders, *Throwin' Rocks at the Moon* (Mammoth) 1997.

6 String Drag

by Ross Grady

"Hey, we're 6 String Drag, and we don't know nothing 'bout playing no songs for y'all." Singer Kenny Roby shambles up to the mike and addresses the audience with his denim locomotive engineer's cap pulled low over his eyes. It's midnight on a sticky July Friday in Durham, North Carolina. 6 String Drag are minus their lead guitarist for the evening, and nobody in the band is too optimistic about their chances of surviving the show in one piece.

The crowd—a weird mixture of hardcore local country fans, aging singles-bar veterans, and a cluster of ballroom dancers out looking for a good 3/4 beat—is scattered at a handful of tables on the perimeter of an enormous, utterly empty dance floor. When I caught Kenny standing at the back of the room before the show, about all he could do was shake his head and say, "Get ready to laugh."

Now, onstage, Kenny shoots a couple of sidelong glances at his bandmates—bassist Rob Keller, drummer Ray Duffey, and part-time trombonist/pianist David "Pops" Wright. A few deep breaths later, Roby kicks his heel in the air, brings his right arm down hard on his Telecaster, and launches into "Bottle of Blues," the opening cut from *High Hat*, the band's second album and their first for Steve Earle and Jack Emerson's E-Squared Records.

Wright leans into his electric piano, remembering a song he hasn't played in the year since he quit being a full-time member of the band. And he's pulling it off, too.

The high notes come swirling out of the revolving speaker of his Leslie cabinet. They ricochet around the half-empty club, blending up near the rafters with Kenny and Rob's voices as they carry each other through the chorus:

Take me back, take me back, bottle of blues

Poor heart's crying, she's done trying to keep me away from you

By the time they make it to the bridge, and Roby is shouting "I ain't got no home no more," at least one thing is obvious to just about everybody in the room: Roby's home, at least for tonight, is right there in the middle of that stage.

Ten years ago, home was Clemson, South Carolina, and Kenny Roby was a sixteen-year-old punk, dressed like Madonna in a gold-nippled teddy and combat boots, heckling the audience, quoting Minor Threat lyrics and, with his band the Lubricators, opening for such '80s punk-rock luminaries as Suicidal Tendencies.

You couldn't grow up punk in Clemson without knowing Ed Campbell—and you couldn't know Ed Campbell without learning a good bit about country music. Ed was big and round-headed and bald, and his punk band, Next Generation, played the first version of George Jones' "White Lightning" that most of the teenage punks had ever heard. It was fast and fiery and rip-roaring and, when you finally got around to hearing the original, not all that different in spirit from Ol' Possum's rendition, hiccups and all.

It's no surprise, then, that Roby quickly outgrew the confines of punk. He took the Lubricators as far as they would go—which turned out to be about 270 miles northeast, up Interstate 85, to Raleigh, North Carolina. But the songs he was hearing in his head kept veering further and further away from the music he was playing with the band, and by 1992 he'd had enough. After six years, he broke up the Lubricators, and began thinking about what was going to come next.

Feeling a little homesick—personally, musically, or both—Roby packed up and returned to Clemson, moving in with Keller. For the next two years they woodshedded, nourished on a steady stream of country and bluegrass from Keller's parents' record store.

Says Roby, "We listened to a lot of Louvin Brothers, a lot of '30s to '60s stuff, country and bluegrass. Every night we were singing, and writing, and we were learning covers—just doing it for fun. We had a little side band that just did country covers, bluegrass and honky-tonk; Ed Campbell played mandolin, and acoustic, and slide, lap steel, that kind of stuff. We were called the Welfare Liners."

Out of those months of learning songs, and writing a whole lot of new ones, 6 String Drag emerged. But the self-titled album that documents those first two years is hardly some kind of pure bluegrass-and-old-time festival. Its songs run the gamut, from the full-on rock of the aptly titled "She's a Hurricane" to the near-perfect honky-tonk tear-jerker "The Hand That Knocks Me Down," with a chorus that performs the country-music equivalent of a hat trick: "And I would gladly take you dancing on the darker side of town/If I could only win the hand that knocks me down."

Although much of the bluegrass and traditional influence was reduced to accents—a mandolin here, a fiddle there—one traditional element remained firmly at the foreground: those old-time brother-style harmonies. Keller says, "I love the brother harmony, oh yeah. The Louvin Brothers had a lot to do with it. That brother-type style in general, it's great fun singing that stuff."

All those months of singing together every night taught Roby and Keller how to work out those harmonies almost without thinking. Kenny's rich, sweet voice sang the melodies; Keller's high, almost womanly tenor handled the harmonies. It's an unearthly effect, intensified by the fact that they're apt to use it at any point in a song—verses, choruses, anywhere it'll fit. "We probably use it a lot of places where we shouldn't," Roby suggests, but you'd be hard-pressed to find anybody to agree with him.

"We're gonna play an old camp meeting song we learned off Ralph and Carter Stanley." Back in Durham, Roby and Keller are standing together on one side of the stage, Keller leaning on his standup bass, as Roby undertakes to introduce their first cover of the night. "You know, my nine-week-old son's middle name is Carter, and that's no coincidence," Kenny tells the crowd, grinning. (Neither is the name 6 String Drag, a variation on the Stanleys' song "Five String Drag".)

Roby and Keller begin to sing, a cappella, a traditional gospel song named "Jacob's Vision"—scruffy, lanky Roby with his low voice, broad Keller with his high, clear tenor. The ballroom dancers stand frozen in place. The fortyish singles at the bar quit swapping notes about the thirtyish singles across the room. Every single person just plain stops, stands, and listens. When the song ends, two or three minutes later, they applaud, slowly at first, as if temporarily unsure where they are and how they got there. This is no isolated phenomenon, either. After ten or fifteen minutes of 6 String Drag, even a confirmed country maverick like Steve Earle confesses to feeling a little bewitched.

"Somebody wanted me to see Whiskeytown," Earle recalls, "so I went down to Bubbapalooza [Memorial Day '96] in Atlanta. I walked in, and 6 String Drag were playing before Whiskeytown. I'd never heard 'em before; I think I had a tape, but hadn't ever gotten around to playing it. Three songs into their set, I turned to my partner and said 'Let some neurotic co-dependent A&R chick sign Whiskeytown— I want to make a record with these guys.'

"We went to breakfast the next morning, and basically offered them the deal right there."

Back in 1995, Roby and Keller packed up and moved back up the highway to Raleigh, where prospects for playing and getting noticed were a little brighter. For over a year, guitarist Glenn Cannon had made the five-hour drive to Raleigh whenever they needed him to play. Now, however, things were getting serious, and Cannon opted to stay behind in Clemson. Taking his place was guitarist Scott Miller—not to be confused with the identically named leader of the V-Roys, a Knoxville, Tennessee, band also on E-Squared.

6 String Drag then went to Nashville to record their second album, *High Hat*, with Earle and his co-producer, Ray Kennedy. (Miller, too, has since left the band to spend time with his own newborn baby; he has been replaced by William Tonks of Athens, Georgia.)

If their first album was their own spin on the age-old collision between country and rock, then *High Hat* augments that already messy pileup with a healthy dose of Stax/Volt R&B and Dixieland. It's the direct result of what Earle half-jokingly refers to as the band's "obsessive musicology"—their persistent need to unravel musical threads, to trace styles and influences back as far as they can go.

Roby explains: "It's just a natural progression; it's just genuine interest. You'll go, 'Oh yeah, this is killer, where'd he get that from? Oh yeah, he got it from this guy. Yeah, Ray Charles, he was influenced by Charles Brown. Okay, listen to Charles Brown. Well, who's he influenced by?' And you go back, and split off, and before you know it, it's like 1920, and you're saying, 'What the hell am I doing here?'

"We're not freaks; we don't know everything about music, but we're interested in it. That's why I don't mind too much people saying stuff about us being influenced by bands, like The Band, who are obviously an influence on us. Because if we just say that, and it gets written somewhere, then some kid might pick up our record in twenty years and go, 'Well, I like this a lot; what did they listen to?' And then they go back and all of a sudden they're back at the turn of the century—or the turn of the century before that one."

And what a happily convoluted pursuit *High Hat* would give them. The record's identifiable influences are almost uncountable. There's the distinctive, Elvis Costello-style vocal phrasing of "Driven Man," which also provides the best single line of the album: "When your grandpa died they took his farm with a pen/I heard your new man used a pen like them."

There's Dixieland ("Over and Over"), rockabilly-gospel ("Top of the Mountain"), and anthemic, Springsteen-esque rock ("Cold Steel Brace"). And then there's "Gasoline Maybelline," with its familiar laid-back, walloping roll and punchy horns. "'Gasoline Maybelline' definitely came from watching *The Last Waltz* too much and then discovering Lee Dorsey shortly thereafter," Roby says. "Then all of a sudden I was listening to a bunch of New Orleans stuff, and within a period of a year it all sort of came pouring into the picture."

Despite the range of styles, Roby insists the band didn't set out to create a patchwork album. "None of the songs on the record were put on there because 'it's a horn song,' or 'it's not a horn song,' or 'it's a guitar song and we need a guitar song,'" he said. "We just picked which ones we liked the most, and then went, 'Okay, this is that kind of arrangement; that works together.' Whatever comes into our heads, you know—a horn, or a guy screaming falling down a hole—if it works with the song, it works with the song.

"Doug Sahm was a huge influence on us in terms of that—just having the courage to do a country song, into a horn song, into a hard-as-hell song. He just didn't give a damn. He just loved different kinds of music, and he said, 'Well, if I can get away with it, and I don't think it sounds too bad, then I want to try it. Fuck it.'"

6 String Drag repay the favor on *High Hat* with "Elaine," a loping, mournful song that openly evokes the spirit of Sir Doug:

Please don't mention New Mexico
Please don't even mention her name
I'd have gone anywhere she said go
I can still see the old Rio Grande
And the Pontchartrain
Why do I miss Elaine?

Back in Durham, their set nearly over, 6 String Drag choose to invoke the spirit of Sahm a bit more directly, with a spirited rendition of "Mendocino." The song is a staple of the band's live set, and it only missed being on *High Hat* because, as Earle puts it, "Kenny's too good a songwriter for us to take up any space on the album with covers."

Nevertheless, covers were an integral part of the band's genesis, and they're still an integral part of their live set, particularly when they're close to home. See, when 6 String Drag plays their Carolina home turf, they do so with the assistance of their part-time horn section, including trombonist David "Pops" Wright and sax player Steve Grothman (whom careful readers will recognize as Whiskeytown's former bassist).

And when Pops and Steve are on that stage, swinging the band through a cover of James Brown's "Night Train," or extending the band's own "Top of the Mountain" out through a few choruses of "When the Saints Go Marching In"—that's when the common thread running through all of 6 String Drag's disparate material becomes most obvious.

It's the one thing they've taken from every influence: Ray Charles. Elvis Costello. Doug Sahm. James Brown. Ralph and Carter Stanley. The Band.

Soul.

"Carolina, In The Pines" first appeared in *No Depression* #11 (September–October 1997).

Selected Discography:
6 String Drag, *6 String Drag* (Fundamental) 1994.
6 String Drag, *High Hat* (E-Squared) 1997.

Joe Henry

by Eric Babcock

It's a recurring dream, one you've had so many times that you no longer think of it as a dream; when it plays in your head, you feel like you're watching a favorite old movie. It's a movie of you and your former love, and you've seen it so many times that every scene, every cut, every rhythm and every detail is expected, anticipated, longed for…and you get so caught up in that familiar ache, that flood of emotion, you actually forget each time the dream/movie starts that it ends with the cataclysmic shock of a plane crash at the air show you and your love are attending. It's like watching the Zapruder film in slow motion, and as each frame crawls by, you can't think of anything but how beautiful Jackie is, until….

The soundtrack to this mental movie is a song from the latest Joe Henry record, *Trampoline*. OK, so the song title "Ohio Air Show Plane Crash" is a bit of a giveaway, but the fact is that I get so drawn in by the loping rhythms, the building up of layers of sound as the song intensifies, I get completely sucked in by the meticulous construction of the dreamy groove, which stretches out into a profound representation of the sound of a heart lost in longing. Moving, evocative songcraft is something I've learned to expect from Henry, but this all-powerful groove is something new. It turns out this is Henry's new modus operandi.

"I've grown less interested in my own limitations as an acoustic guitar-playing songwriter," Henry says in his characteristic self-effacing tone. "I'm writing songs to drum loops rather than picking them out on the guitar. It's liberating, as a singer and a lyricist, when vocal phrasing doesn't have to articulate the rhythm. You can stop singing and the rhythm keeps going."

But the rhythms here go far beyond a basic groove, fleshing out some remarkably hard-edged funk; as such, it comes as no surprise that Carla Azar, one of the principal players on the record, made her bones drumming behind Wendy & Lisa. And what really extends the groove is the record's use of unconventional sounds, from the zither that opens the record, to the gorgeous pedal steel on the closing song—each distinctively bent, often through the process of looping, to serve the song. Throughout the record you'll hear strings, a trombone, harshly metallic drum sounds, an operatic descant, and some ripping guitar (courtesy of Helmet's Page Hamilton). It's a wild ride, and not remotely what you'd expect from an artist whose last two records owed much of their well-grounded roots/country sound to the extensive use of the Jayhawks as a backing band.

"I'm not a purist in any way," Henry says. "Any sound is fair game, anything that can be made musical, made engaging. These days I work more like a collage artist, adding different elements, taking them away again....It's building a better song. I have no use for music that's delicate or fragile, music that you have to protect or explain. That kind of music is like fragile dishware—it just doesn't age very well."

His literate, imagistic songs have stood on their own since his first recordings. 1989's *Murder of Crows* and 1990's *Shuffletown*, both on A&M, had the benefit of the involvement of top-shelf player-producers: Anton Fier producing a cast of studio vets on the first, T Bone Burnett leading a more homey, eclectic gang on the second. Both reveal an obviously talented songwriter casting around in search of a more defined personal musical style, classic examples of the talented but tiny fish lost in the ocean of major-label projects.

But with *Short Man's Room*, Henry's 1992 release on Mammoth, he hit a distinctive groove, in part because he had begun working with an up-and-coming young band known as the Jayhawks. "After I was dropped by A&M, it was kind of refreshing to be starting over," he recalls. "I had met the Jayhawks before, and we all shared a vague understanding of what each other were up to musically, so we decided to pool our resources and play shows together." The Jayhawks would open the shows with their own set, then remain onstage to back Henry as he did his songs.

He came to like the dynamic. "I would have these brooding, claustrophobic songs, but their delivery was more like three-chord rock, all loose and splashy and great. So I recruited them to be my band for the next record, and built it around their sound." They recorded some demos over the course of a weekend in the empty offices of the Rykodisc label; Mammoth heard the tapes and issued them just as they were. "The beginning of a relationship I've since bastardized in any number of ways," smiles Henry.

The follow-up, 1993's *Kindness of the World*, also on Mammoth, was less fully realized. It was designed along similar lines, but had different players shuffled in and out; there was no palpable vibe of musicians inhabiting the material, as on the previous record. Henry began to move away from the idea of recording live tracks in the studio.

"It's not that I don't have a reverence for that magical idea, the idea of a song developing from the energy of five or six players in a room, but it's not the only way to get work done," he explained. "A song recorded that way has a tendency to reduce itself to the lowest risk factor at each pass. Making records like that is like doing live theater; I'd rather make a movie."

Enter producer Patrick McCarthy, known for his work with R.E.M., Patti Smith and Counting Crows. Originally signed on as an engineer, he slipped into the role of producer as he nudged Henry toward a new way of creating songs, compelling him to set up his own studio in his garage and experiment with new sounds, and to write songs to drum loops rather than to an acoustic guitar. "Plane Crash," one of the first songs completed for the record, became a model for much of what followed.

"The original nucleus of that song isn't even a part of the record anymore. I didn't know how it was going to work, just these same chords over and over for seven minutes. Then other parts were added on, more guitars, more percussion, and it became this bubbling, rolling thing. When I heard how good that whole process made it sound, I just sent the rest of the band home for the day—I had found a new way to make records. And it worked with the way the story within the song unfolds, one measured piece at a time, with this small, personal event in the foreground and this huge, tragic crash relegated to a backdrop." Cinematic, you might say.

As is "Flower Girl," a grim little vignette of a prospecting expedition gone very wrong. It reads like an old folk song, a tale you might expect to be told to the accompaniment of a fiddle and mandolin. Indeed, Henry confirms that. "We cut a live version of it, a country version, but I wasn't satisfied. So Pat instinctively worked in the pump organ, the rattle drum for texture, and that vocal…." The song features the disembodied operatic voice of soloist Miranda Dade-Lurie. "It's so ghostly, so detached—just completely appropriate to the song."

Appropriate, yes—and deeply affecting. Perhaps also confusing to an unsuspecting or less adventurous listener, as are funky drums and corrosive guitars. These aren't the kinds of sounds permeating your Americana-approved radio playlists. Individuals who relished the Jayhawks collaboration may not follow Henry down this path. "I know," he says. "It wouldn't be the first time I've heard that. Various people in my camp have suggested that it was foolish of me to jump off the bandwagon just as it gained corporate sponsorship."

But if Henry has forgone his opportunity to dominate a radio chart, he has gained something far greater. He is actively pushing his music's limits, taking real chances, opening up the boundaries of not only what people hear in his records, but the way those records get made. Short-sighted speculators and profiteers hope to cash in on the popularity of a musical "movement" by narrowing its scope; true artists are busy creating new forms beyond a movement's apparent limitations.

His next move may range even farther still: Henry would like to score music for films. He has had songs appear on soundtracks here and there, most recently in *Feeling Minnesota*. "I like the role that music plays in a movie," he says. "It may be a song, or a fragment of a song, or just noise, doing whatever it needs to do to work within the scene. Films can make you think of music in a completely different way."

So can Joe Henry.

"This Time He's Not Coming Down" first appeared in *No Depression* #6 (September–October 1996).

Selected Discography:

Joe Henry, *Murder of Crows* (Coyote/A&M) 1989, reissued (Coyote/Mammoth/A&M) 1993.
Joe Henry, *Shuffletown* (Coyote/A&M) 1990, reissued (Coyote/Mammoth/A&M) 1993.
Joe Henry, *Short Man's Room* (Mammoth) 1992.
Joe Henry, *Kindness Of The World* (Mammoth) 1993.
Joe Henry, *Trampoline* (Mammoth/Atlantic) 1996.

Golden Smog

by Peter Blackstock

The rumor's been goin' 'round town for a while now: Those happy-go-lucky Golden Smog dudes are gettin' *serious* on us, fer chrissakes. I guess being a comedic cover band on a lil' ol' indie label just wasn't good enough for 'em; they're movin' on up to a big ol' indie label, and they even *wrote their own songs* for the new record. And they might even go on tour.

One wonders what kind of effect all these changes have had on their music, a question guitarist Dan Murphy is happy to answer.

"It sounds more like Hootie & the Blowfish," he deadpans. "But don't print that." Oops.

Murphy's remark is the kind of crack that epitomized the spirit of the olden Smog days, back when the members of this loosely-defined Minneapolis stuporgroup first began doing one-off shows every six months or so at local hangouts such as the Uptown. Murphy, who moonlights with the Smog when he has time off from his day job at Soul Asylum Incorporated, remembers those days well.

"This was like the late '80s, and everybody was really big on punk rock and hardcore in Minneapolis. We went to this place and we brought, like, driftwood lamps, and wore ponchos, and we did all these Eagles covers real quietly, and we sang harmonies. And people just flipped. They didn't know what to think. That was the whole spirit of the thing—I mean, fucking with people for amusement."

It was also about old friends. Golden Smog's ever-devolving lineup has, at some point or another, included Minneapolitan members of Soul Asylum, the Jayhawks, Run Westy Run, Son Volt, the Replacements and the Honeydogs. Some of those bands have gone on to bigger, perhaps better, things; in any case, the increasingly demanding commitments of their respective bands has meant that they spend less time hanging around in clubs together playing shows and going to see bands. The Smog became a sort of reunion device to help revisit and renew the ties that bind in a tightly-knit musical community.

What began as a lark—an evening of Eagles covers here, an evening of Stones covers there (under the banner of "Her Satanic Majesty's Paycheck")—became slightly more serious when a small local label, Crackpot Records, released *On Golden Smog*, a five-song EP of cover songs, in 1992. The recording project was as off-the-cuff as the shows—except that the final product came out sounding not like a throwaway souvenir, but rather a really good record.

Sure, the closing cover of Thin Lizzy's "Cowboy Song," featuring Soul Asylum road manager Bill Sullivan on lead vocals, was predictably trashy. But the rest of the disc was a minor revelation. Murphy unearthed a remarkable tune called "Son," a lost '60s gem from a band called Michelangelo; it's precisely the kind of long-forgotten tune more bands should seek to dig up when they're looking for cover material. Soul Asylum singer Dave Pirner made a guest appearance on Bad Company's "Shooting Star," giving it a soaring vocal boost that puts it up there with the best tracks Soul Asylum has recorded in the '90s. And Jayhawks conspirator Gary Louris turned in perhaps his best vocal performance ever to make Three Dog Night's "Easy To Be Hard" the highlight of an already surprisingly strong EP.

Even so, Golden Smog remained primarily a sideshow curiosity, especially as the profiles of both Soul Asylum and the Jayhawks became increasingly conspicuous. There was talk of doing another Smog record if everyone ever got around to it, but no definite plans—until finally Run Westy Run's Kraig Johnson brought in a couple songs he had recorded at the tail end of a Westy recording session. Surprise, surprise— they were originals.

"He said, 'I want the Smog to record these,' and I was like, 'Wow, Kraig just upped the ante,'" Murphy remembers. "And they were great songs. So then I thought, 'Well we need a songwriter,' so I called up Jeff Tweedy, the guy from Wilco," Murphy continues. He and the other Smog members had known Tweedy for years, dating back not only to the days when Tweedy was in Uncle Tupelo, but to an interview Tweedy had done with Soul Asylum for a St. Louis zine years earlier.

Tweedy gladly accepted the key to the kingdom of Smog and headed to Minneapolis. "I had him come by my house—I have a little recording studio in my basement—and we spent about four days together writing songs," Murphy continued. "He wrote some stuff [on his own] and we wrote some stuff [together], and Gary Louris had some stuff. And then we did the record in five days."

"A lot of the songs we didn't play together until we were down in the studio," Johnson said. "We practiced the day before we went down there, but Jeff wasn't here to practice with us, so that made it more interesting. We hadn't heard at all what Jeff had. On a couple of songs, I just said, 'Well, let's try recording this.' And that's kind of what made it fun, was that it was a spontaneous thing."

Spontaneous, yes—but it's clear that *Down By The Old Mainstream* was given more careful consideration than the *On Golden Smog* EP. The Smogsters realize that may rub some fans the wrong way, but they don't seem to mind. "It's taken more seriously, and if people don't like it, then that's tough, if they want us to be a joke band," Louris says. "We're still pretty funny because when we play, we're not very good. But I think the songs are good."

Good enough to elevate Golden Smog to the level of a going concern? After all, the Jayhawks' situation is up in the air now, given the recent departure of Mark Olson. As the Minneapolis music community mutates, will the Smog rise again?

"It'll definitely give us a little more time to do things," Johnson said in early November, just a few days after Olson's departure from the Jayhawks became public knowledge. "We were kind of worried about not being able to get together and do a tour. But now those guys have a little more time on their hands, obviously.

"But everybody else is kind of busy doing other things too. I don't think we'll ever step up-front, but we'll be able to do more than we thought, probably. We really wanna do a tour, so that looks like a good possibility. And there's probably a chance that we could do another record. Because the songs are there."

And if the well of original songs runs dry, they could always become a Hootie & the Blowfish cover band.

"Hawks & Dogs Run West And Wilconvert Your Soul" first appeared in *No Depression* #2 (Winter 1996).

Selected Discography:

Golden Smog, *On Golden Smog* (Crackpot) 1992, reissued (Rykodisc) 1996.

Golden Smog, *Down By the Old Mainstream* (Rykodisc) 1995.

The Jayhawks

by Jim Walsh

In the wake of the departure of co-founder Mark Olson, Minneapolis band the Jayhawks invited a couple of musicians to the recording sessions for *Sound Of Lies*, released in April, 1997 on American Recordings. Guitarist Kraig Johnson, best known in the Twin Cities as a member of Run Westy Run, had worked with Jayhawks Gary Louris and Marc Perlman in the roots-rock stuporgroup Golden Smog. The Smog was also indirectly responsible for hooking the Jayhawks up with violinist Jessy Greene of the Geraldine Fibbers, who opened a tour for Golden Smog last year.

The new band's official live debut came at the South by Southwest Music and Media Conference in Austin. After running through a mitten-clad soundcheck before the big showcase, Greene—who recently quit the Fibbers to become a full-fledged member of the Jayhawks—and Louris sat down at Stubb's Barbecue to discuss their musical origins, the myth of cool and more.

No Depression: Had you listened to the Jayhawks before you started playing with them?

Jessy Greene: I loved the Jayhawks. I was very excited about doing the Golden Smog thing, specifically because of the Jayhawks. I first heard them on the radio, and I liked them right away. Because I play violin, it was really my kind of music. I listen to all different kinds of music, but I love the Jayhawks.

ND: When did you first start playing the violin?

Greene: I was four years old. I didn't have a choice. My parents handed me the violin and said, "This is what you're gonna do for the next fifteen years." My parents are very into classical music. I'm twenty-eight now; I stopped [playing] when I was in high school and kind of rebelled for a few years, and when I started again, I played contemporary music. And then I really started to love it. When I was playing just classically, I liked it for the first four or five years, but then I started thinking it was really tedious. Everybody else was having fun, and I was practicing six hours a day. I went to music camp, music school, everything you can imagine. It was torture.

Gary Louris: And we're glad you did it.

Greene: So am I, but at the time it was torture.

ND: When you were in classical training, were you listening to any pop music on the side?

Greene: I started listening to the Rolling Stones, and my parents would say, "That's not music! You have to listen to classical music only." So of course, it resulted in a huge gap in my musical knowledge. I mean, I had a real resentment toward classical music for a long time.

ND: Do you still have any of that?

Greene: No, because it's not what I do, so therefore, I got over it. If I was still a classical musician, I might have those feelings, because there's not a lot going on in that field as far as opportunities. It's very difficult. My brother is a classical pianist, and it's really tough to make it. To actually be a performer and make a living is a luxury. Most classical musicians become teachers and performers.

ND: Gary, what about you growing up? Can you relate to Jessy's experience of being pushed by parents?

Louris: I was slightly pushed. My first instrument was the piano, and I took seven years of piano lessons. And I liked it. I can't really remember sacrificing that much, because I wasn't really that involved with sports. I was really a pretty shy kid, so I wasn't involved in a lot of school activities.

ND: Where was this?

Louris: Toledo, Ohio.

ND: And where did you grow up?

Greene: Sheffield, Massachusetts.

Louris: When I was fourteen, I picked up a classical guitar, because my mom said I'd be more popular if I could take a guitar to a party.

Greene: Your mom said that? That's great.

Louris: And look. Here I am today. Thanks, Mom. So I played classical, and I started listening to the radio and writing songs, and I found that I had a good ear, and I found something I wanted. I've really found that I'm not that good at a lot of things, but I am good at music. I feel confident about music. I don't feel confident about anything else in my life, probably. But again, I was pretty shy. I was never in a band until after I graduated from college. I didn't pick up an electric guitar until I was about 22 or so. And I played Beatles stuff and things on my classical guitar, and one day I smashed it at a party. Which I thought was kind of cool—until I realized a couple girls got splinters, and I was afraid they were going to take me to court. But I started writing songs with my roommate at the time, and it was a big revelation: "Wow, my voice doesn't sound so bad." And we wrote a song the first time we tried.

ND: What was the song?

Louris: "Weekend Girls." I didn't write the lyrics. John wrote the lyrics: "Weekend girls from a weekday world/On a two-day whirl/Wearing plastic pearls/What a pretty sight/With their pants so tight/Wanna cringe tonight/Wanna take a bite." I didn't write the lyrics, okay? Every line rhymed.

ND: What year was that?

Louris: '78.

ND: So it was very new wave.

Louris: Yeah. Very pop. Very British. I was a total Kinks-Beatles-Stones-Who freak. And we used to write songs, and that's the first time I started playing electric lead guitar. That's when I started practicing a lot.

ND: Who were some of your first guitar heroes?

Louris: Cliff Gallup, the original Gene Vincent guitar player. And then Scotty Moore, and Link Wray, and a lot of the early rockabilly guys. And then from there, I was always a big Jimmy Page fan—more than Keith [Richards], even. I like Keith, but I like Jimmy even better.

ND: What was the first record you bought?

Greene: Pink Floyd, *The Wall*.

Louris: The Monkees' first album, on Colgems.

ND: What's your most memorable concert going experience?

Louris: The first time Elvis Costello played Minneapolis, at the Longhorn. Or the Buzzcocks, or the Stranglers. And I have to say, seeing Nirvana at First Avenue was a great one. I saw the James Gang blow Chicago off the stage when I was a teenager in Toledo.

Greene: I just saw Hadda Brooks, this eighty-year-old piano player, at Goldfingers in Los Angeles. She plays at the Viper Room a lot. She was around in the '50s, and she's this amazing jazz singer and she comes down off the stage and makes you sing with her. Really amazing.

ND: Jessy, you said earlier that there was an immediate musical connection between you and Gary. What do you mean by that?

Greene: With every instrument, you approach music from a different direction. If you're a singer-songwriter, you're very much in control; you have a certain role. Whereas if you're playing keyboards, guitar, or violin, you're more ornamental. And for me, as a violinist, with music that I like, I love to make it sound better. And with Gary, it's just very easy. With different people, it's kind of like a communication thing without words, but with instruments. I try to figure out not only how to make the music sound better, but what the person singing wants from the violin....I love when people have an idea. I'm not the kind of violin player who will just say, "This is how I want to play it. This is how I hear it." I love it when people say, "This is how I hear it, and how about this line here?" So he had great string parts, and great string ideas. He's a great string arranger.

Louris: (Laughing) I'd like to be. It was really fun, because whenever I'd suggest something, she'd always agree and get excited. And then she'd play something, and I'd get excited. Our minds were always in the same place. It was never a struggle. I just liked her choices: They were somewhat odd, sometimes, and kind of dark, and weird. She's definitely a violin player, and not like a fiddle player. She'll get into kind of John Cale-y, Velvets screeching things. She likes to get out there. And then she can play very beautiful, classical stuff, or make it sound like "Walk Away Renee" or something.

Greene: Yeah, I like to make things sound a little twisted—but within the realm of what I'm doing. Not to go too far out there, but not to always be so pretty.

Louris: I tend to write real pretty stuff, and I can be a little rigid in my own writing and playing. So I like to get people involved who will kind of fuck it up a little bit, because if it's too pretty, then it's sugary sweet.

ND: To you, what is the distinction between a fiddle player and a violin player?

Greene: Well, the fiddle has traditionally been a folk instrument, exclusively. The fiddle came way before the violin; it was used by many different cultures, and in different ways. The music was more of the people. And violin came along as an elite form of music. The idea was taken from the country folk, and they made it into this perfect instrument that was perfectly designed and had to be played perfectly. So a violin player has more of a grasp on scales, chops, and being in complete pitch with tuning. And you have to be really disciplined to play the violin. You have to practice a lot. Even though I practiced all those years, I still have to practice to be able to play right, and in tune. And the fiddle is a little easier, because you're playing more choppy, and you're playing open strings. You don't have to play as well. But then again, there are amazing fiddle players. It's just different styles. Basically, a violin player can play the fiddle; a fiddle player can't always play the violin. But that's not always true, either, because there's some violin players who can't break out of their classical thing.

ND: Do you ever see someone like classical violinist Naja Salerno-Sonnenberg and go, "Ooh, I wish I'd pursued this a little more"?

Greene: No, because I see my brother. He's an amazing classical player. When I was born, he was fourteen years old and he was already playing at Carnegie Hall. He went to Yale, Juilliard, and Stony Brook. He's an amazing classical pianist. His name's Arthur Greene, and he's really amazing. But the fact that I'm making a living at what I do is really amazing. I also love to write music, and if I were a classical player, I would never have time to write. And that's so important—to be able to create parts, even to create parts for other people's music. And if you're classically trained, you have to play what's been written already. I've never understood that concept of perfecting something that's already been perfected. I love classical music, I listen to it a lot; I think it's beautiful and I appreciate it greatly. I'm very happy that it's part of my style, but I don't regret at all that I'm not there. I'm actually quite happy.

Louris: In the grand scheme of things, music may have been more powerful and more beautiful back then than it is now, but I still don't understand how you can just devote your life to covering other people's music. Especially since they've all been recorded a million times.... [Although] it's fun to do covers; that's why we have Golden Smog, though that's not so much a cover band anymore.

ND: Where is the new Golden Smog album?

Louris: We recorded it; we spent ten days on it. It's not done yet. We decided to be a little more adventurous with it, and run the risk of taking ourselves a little more seriously. We kind of said, "We have the opportunity to record some music, let's try to make it great." And that wasn't the attitude we had when we last played. Some of those last Smog shows toward the end, the money was there, so we did it. And we were doing the same songs, and a lot of covers, and we got back, and the first day in the studio, Jeff [Tweedy] and I just sat up all night talking about how excited we were about making a new record.

ND: Gary, what was your introduction to the Fibbers?

Louris: It was through Ann, my ex-wife-to-be. A wonderful girl who has great musical taste, and she had the records. And then I think I read something about them in *Option* or something. So I started listening to their record, and I have to say it was my idea—it was Ann's idea, and then it was my idea— to have the Fibbers tour with Golden Smog. And because of that, a lot of wonderful things have happened. And when the tour was done, I decided to start lifting things from them. Ideas. Violin players. And by the end, they were all getting up and singing and playing with us. I thought they'd just think we were a bunch of squares. Like Jessy knows, I have a little bit of a complex of coolness. I always feel like we're really square, and not hip.

ND: I think that's a common malady. Because there's so much music, people don't have a handle on what is perceived as cool, or even what they really think is cool.

Louris: Well, I know we're not considered Atari Teenage Riot right now. But you know what? That's okay.

Greene: Yeah, but you should never say things like that. I don't think you should ever say things about perceived cool, because I think so much is perception. And it's all how you feel about yourself. I have the same problem. Like you said before, you have all confidence in your music, where you don't have that in other areas of your life. For me, I have confidence to a certain extent in all areas of my life, but none of them too much. I have a certain amount of confidence in music, but to have complete confidence, I know I need to practice, and I have to make sure I do my absolute best. But at the same time, I'm doing it for myself. So if it's cool to me, then that's all that matters.

ND: I have the same theory about "guilty pleasures," because I simply do not believe in the concept. You can hear a dumb pop song on the radio and be absolutely taken by it, and that's a legitimate reaction. And if you dismiss it from your scope of listening, you deprive yourself of experiences and emotions. If all you're doing is watching out for what's "cool," all you'll be listening to is the Velvet Underground.

Louris: Yeah, that's the only thing that's safe—among everybody.

Greene: I think that "cool" is a very bizarre word. What's more important is: Does the music relay something that matters? Is there passion? Is there truth? Do you believe what somebody's trying to tell you? And those kinds of things are what you get from classical music. There's definitely a passion and a truth there. I don't think music today is any less powerful than it was. I think there's a lot of music that is less powerful, but in general, there is good music; you just have to dig for it. But you can't base things on the cool factor at all, because then you're just misleading yourself, because money and all that stuff has so much to do with what defines something to be cool. And it's usually wrong.

Louris: I don't know how we got started on that question.

Greene: Inevitably, you knew we'd get there.

Louris: Yeah, it always comes back to that.

Greene: That's a very nice shirt, by the way.

Louris: Thank you. Long Beach style.

ND: What about fashion? Is it important?

Louris: It's very important.

Greene: It's about coming into your own, I think. I mean, I went through some very strange years. I grew up in a country town with all the country bumpkins and New Yorkers. And I kind of resented…When I quit the violin, I also quit the whole cultural thing. My parents were very into the cultural life. I got kicked out of private school. I was a nerd, kind of. But I was like a dropout version. And I listened to Lynyrd Skynyrd, and very Southern rock kind of stuff. I loved Aerosmith. And then when I went to college, I moved to L.A. and I had no concept of being a musician, or anything. It was just to get away from that whole scene.

ND: Did you bring your violin?

Greene: No. I didn't even bring my violin. When I moved to L.A., I started going to Santa Monica College, and there would be people sitting around the mall jamming.

And I thought, "God, I have to have my violin." So I had it sent out, and my biggest aspiration was to play with the Grateful Dead. That's where I was at.

Louris: And now you're stuck with us.

Greene: See? That's exactly the attitude I'm talking about.

Louris: It's a joke. I guess. Jessy's not only my violin player, but my psychologist.

Greene: But it's not about the fashion magazines, or anything like that. It's just about wearing what makes you feel good. And feeling good about yourself.

Louris: I'm a clothes freak. It's hard to figure out what to wear, so it's not a clichéd rock deal. I'm just one of those people who steps back and looks at things from a distance, and goes, "What are people going to think about this period of music and fashion?" You know, what are people going to think in fifty years? (Laughs) See, I not only worry about what people think now, I'm worried about what they're going to think in fifty years. No wonder I'm so fucked up.

Greene: God. And I thought I was bad.

"Tomorrow's Grass Is Green-r" first appeared in *No Depression* #10 (July–August 1997).

Selected Discography:

The Jayhawks, *Blue Earth* (Twin/Tone) 1989.

The Jayhawks, *Hollywood Town Hall* (American) 1993.

The Jayhawks, *Tomorrow the Green Grass* (American) 1995.

The Jayhawks, *Sound of Lies* (American) 1997.

Victoria Williams and Mark Olson

by Grant Alden

And while we spoke of many things,

Fools and kings,

This he said to me:

The greatest thing you'll ever learn

Is just to love and be loved in return.

    — "Nature Boy," Victoria Williams

The Original Harmony Ridge Creek Dippers live simply in a refurbished late-1950s cabin, tucked amid the high desert and surrounded by sand and sky, hearty herbs and huge, shy, loving dogs.

Mark Olson is in the kitchen, heating an early November lunch of leftover turkey, fresh-plucked arugula salad and squaw tea. Victoria Williams is in the bathroom, taking a quick bath before an afternoon encounter with the camera.

Out on the front porch an ex-Navy sonar man named Dave Royer is converting surplus ammo boxes into preamps for his handmade studio microphones, and one of the three dogs is sprawled the length of a shady couch. Royer is sundried, shirtless, more skittish than the dogs of strangers.

A recording console is cloaked and tucked into one corner of the living room, next to the stone hearth Mark and Victoria built, on the other side of the small concrete fault—a reminder of frequent earthquakes—which separates that room from the kitchen and the small, four-burner electric stove Victoria found in a junk shop. An upright piano next to the front door is the only instrument visible.

Born here, then, are the songs of Victoria's latest Atlantic release, *Musings Of A Creek Dipper*, and the full flowering of Mark's first post-Jayhawks outing, *The Original Harmony Ridge Creek Dippers* (available only from his P.O. box here in the California desert town of Joshua Tree). And if it sounds like Victoria sang her parts in the kitchen while doing dishes, she probably was.

Highway 10 east from Los Angeles, that long drive Hunter S. Thompson roared across twenty-five years ago toward the ruination of fame and the gaudy conflagration of Las Vegas, forks a few miles past the last outlet mall just before darting through the unflinching Mojave. A well-tended spur to the right winds into Palm Springs, where the streets are enclosed by lavishly irrigated lawns and named for prominent Republicans. To the left, rising toward the high desert where wind and rock and patient Joshua trees remind of a peace and endurance that politics can never fashion, up that road, not far from where Gram Parsons' ashes were once spread, is where Victoria and Mark live.

Damp-haired Victoria offers a short prayer before lunch, a reminder to their secular guest that religion need not be a caricature of itself. She speaks and laughs and sings in such a way that her surroundings are decorated with exquisite grace. Though she is thirty-eight now, Victoria's voice, her eyes, her smile, they all retain a gloriously childlike charm. She sings high and sometimes uncertain ("wobbly," she's called it) in a register that links her to occasional duet partner Julie Miller; mostly, though, it's an exceptional mix of innocence and wisdom that radiates through her songs: Peace.

Those sounds, and the spirit behind them, are Victoria Williams' blessing. It is a small curse that she is still, perhaps, better known for having multiple sclerosis, the disease she has battled since 1992, than for the rare joy of her songs.

Victoria Williams was nineteen when she came to Los Angeles in the early '80s, a hippie chick from Shreveport, Louisiana, probably a wild child—striking enough a weed even then that Mark well remembers watching her open for punk rock bands, just a gal and that voice and her guitar. She was married to somebody else part of that time (singer-songwriter Peter Case), but things have a way of working out.

"The not shady part of Victoria's past," Mark says with a warm glance, gently cutting her off before she reveals too much about leaving Louisiana to the tape recorder, "is that she learned…she has a unique rhythm style. She can play many different instruments, and she learned that in Louisiana, playing with a lot of different people. When I first saw her, that's one of the things that I just went, 'Wow, she can really play rhythm guitar, lead guitar, piano, in her own style, that kind of harks back to that part of the country.' On this *Creek Dippers* thing, I've always wanted her to be playing, not just singing, and that's why we did it that way, just her, Mike [Russell], and me."

The name that connects their two albums links Victoria to Mark as well. "I was out opening for the Jayhawks years ago," Victoria says. "Mark left the tour bus and rode with us and we'd go creek dipping every day. We came to this one place, it was called Harmony Ridge, and we creek dipped there." (They also adopted a revised version of the name, Rollin' Creek Dippers, for a European tour last year with Buddy and Julie Miller and Jim Lauderdale.)

Victoria was touring with Neil Young in 1992 when her hands became unexpectedly reluctant partners in the playing of her guitar and piano. A handful of doctors later, she had that unhappy diagnosis—MS is a non-lethal disease that attacks the body's immune system and damages the myelin sheath which surrounds nerves in the brain and spinal cord—and $20,000 in unpaid medical bills.

At the time, Victoria had no record label. 1987's *Happy Come Home* began and ended a relationship with Geffen; 1990's *Swing the Statue!* appeared on the ill-fated Rough Trade, a label/distributor whose bankruptcy all but destroyed indie rock that season. The response to her plight by friends and fellow artists sparked creation of the Sweet Relief organization.

Williams remains on the steering committee of Sweet Relief, which by her count has raised and disbursed some $350,000 to uninsured musicians, most of that funding coming from all-star tribute albums saluting her songs, and those of Vic Chesnutt.

"It's not going exactly like I would like it to go," she says, almost a parent speaking patiently of a wayward child. "We're broke right now. We gave away $350,000, which was good, but there's still people waiting. They've cooked up some sort of fund-raiser, and they want me to come play. So I'll do that. I'll do anything I can, you know. But my dream for the original, the original dream for Sweet Relief, was that people in every town would do at least one concert a year and give the proceeds to this fund."

Sweet Relief has been her principal concession to the disease. Her artistic response was 1994's *Loose,* a thoroughly engaging celebration of life and death. City living insulates us from that cycle, detaches death behind walls and hospital gowns, and thereby devalues life. Both city and country, gripping one with each hand, Victoria spun songs as direct and honest as anything the Carter Family mined from their hills.

This Moment in Toronto With Victoria Williams and the Loose Band followed a year later. Though she was careful to pace her touring schedule (fatigue and stress are contributing factors with MS) in support of those releases, *Musings of a Creek Dipper,* the first new material in four years, bears as few traces of that battle as she can manage.

Well. The cabin on the desert is hardly a concession, for it seems a place where Mark and Victoria are truly and happily at home. And yet she moved from Laurel Canyon out to the desert in part to escape the city's pollution and its impact on her health, the kitchen table is filled with pill bottles from health food stores, and, later, walking around the property, she notices that the bees—one experimental therapy for MS is to be stung many times each day—have abandoned their hive.

"Ever since I've been given the opportunity to record, since the very first record, I always prayed, 'Lord, let me do something that will be good for people,'" Victoria says. "And that's probably one of the reasons I haven't put out some of my more dour moments. Maybe I just don't want to shower people with that, too much. I suppose I could just put out a really black album," but even at the thought she begins to laugh that laugh.

Later, Mark digs up a tape and plays one of those songs, but they won't release it because the story's true and the names haven't been changed. A notebook in the living room holds another ninety-odd unrecorded songs, much of that the archiving work of her frequent bandmate Andrew Williams, who came out to the desert and sifted through work tapes and put them in some order.

"She has a lot of wonderful songs," Mark begins.

"Oh, I do not," but her eyes dart shyly toward his anyway. "There's some songs that I haven't recorded that I…you really have to be in the right place to record a song, where you can really share the song the way it was given to you. And sometimes…maybe I don't want to go to some song's place. And sometimes I'd rather write something new."

Victoria's records and concerts are like one imagines church should be. They are open and honest and celebratory, full of delight and respect, able to sweep black clouds to the side with a soft breath. In this way, in occasional gospel flavorings, and in her singular word choices (the first new song is called "Periwinkle Sky"), Victoria Williams' music retains the unique character of her Southern upbringing.

A lot of wonderful songs, and yet, if *Loose* was in part a meditation on the endless cycles of life and death—from "Harry Went To Heaven" to "Happy To Have Known Pappy" even to the unexpected cover of Spirit's "Nature's Way"—*Musings of a Creek Dipper* is just a trace sadder. Weary, in spots, but no less wise.

"I wonder…" Victoria says, squinting. "It's not as perky as some of my records are."

Well, as we head into middle age we probably aren't going to be all that perky.

"Exactly. Exactly! That is what Danny said, my manager said. This record is mature, it's mature. It looks at a lot of life-death issues."

But *Loose* kind of did, too.

"Yeah, it did, didn't it? I'm sort of prepared, I suppose. God's been good to me. I was prepared, I think. To deal with this, whatever. You know. The shortest prayer: Whatever." And then she breaks into a vintage Victoria Williams laugh.

Still, there is a pervasive sense of looking backward throughout *Musings*. The prayer is implicit within "Let It Be So": "Rejoice in this moment/And any hereafter/Sweet and holy/Be the sounds of your laughter." Early in "Last Word" she sings, "Who's going to bury the last man when he dies? All the money in the world can't help you if the world's on fire." The penultimate "Grandpa In The Cornpatch" plays almost as a prayer to her own life, with its elegant refrain: "Chores, chores, chores," during which Victoria's voice manages to age twenty years each time the word is repeated.

"In a way," she chuckles, perhaps delighted with that assessment, "it's a life. It's about a life. You know? There's a lot of chores in life."

"And I know that she was singing that song around here a lot," Mark adds. "And I got accustomed to hearing that. The song has been put into practice, definitely."

Musings was cut during June and August, first in the calm of the desert night at a local studio ("Fred's place"), then down in Oxnard, California, at a theater. In between, Victoria and Mark joined the Lilith tour, and found other reasons to hide from the excruciating heat of the desert; that heat, too, is a problem for people with MS.

"I had a lot of health problems the last year," Victoria says, earlier on and without prompting. "Even when we started on this, my hands had gotten weird, and I was like, I can't stop this. People were coming [to play] and everything, and I just had to have faith that it would come back and there were a lot of great musicians anyway, and they're such great players that it all worked out. Later on I could put stuff on, but it was backwards from the way I did *Loose* because *Loose* started with just my vocal and guitar. But this one, I had to play my own stuff later when my hands would work."

Are they better now?

"Uh, yeah, they're better, but…"

"She's moving a hell of a lot more," Mark says. "She went into the record—MS goes up and down—she went into it on a little bit of a down swing, but she just did it, you know? She just went ahead and did it."

"It's funny, though," she says, "because a lot of the pictures taken from the session at Fred's, I'm always sitting on the floor. Surprise, I'm sitting on the floor!"

And her smile is still radiant; so are the looks she and Mark exchange, and the tenderness with which they prod and protect each other.

Mark Olson is somewhat more circumspect about his record, but *The Original Harmony Ridge Creek Dippers* initially wasn't meant for the public. It is tempting to ask Mark about the Jayhawks, and his leaving, but one need simply compare the rough-hewn glory of his solo debut to the pop sheen of the Jayhawks' new *Sound Of Lies* for the only answer that matters.

It's just the three of them—Mark, Victoria (er, "Mabel Allbright," as she's listed on the liner notes), and Mike "Razz" Russell—recording through Dave Royer's microphones in that wood-paneled living room. It is a rare, beautiful, utterly genuine set of songs, everything Will Oldham has tried so hard to manifest throughout Palace's many incarnations and, in that hard trying, failed.

Indeed, there are several phone calls later as husband and wife try to decide exactly who produced the album, each deferring to the other. It is that seamless and organic a work, and unmistakably anchored to that place.

"For me, this place is a place where I really get into a project, or doing something like I've never experienced before, for some reason," Mark says. "I don't think either of us even thought we were going to put it out. We were just trying to record some songs and stuff. We both were kind of scared of even what we were doing."

Later, Mark admits, laughing softly, that it's all Victoria's doing. "Vic initiated the home studio," he says. "I dragged my heels for quite a while, saying, 'Oh, my goodness, here we are musicians and we're going to be in studios enough, why do we want to come home to work?' And then, boy, once we got going on it, I realized that she was right. It was a real good thing. Generally, if I listen to her, things work out pretty good."

Mark's first impulse was simply to hand out tapes to friends and fans. "I called two people that I knew, that I've known for years, and checked out what I thought their interest would be," he says. "And I had the idea of doing it ourselves. When I talked to them and played it for them I became sure that, yes, this is the right thing to do with it, try to establish our own little thing from the house.

"And then we went on the Lilith tour, and that was eye-opening to me in a lot of ways because we talked to people after we played, and we mentioned, 'Oh, well, we've recorded some stuff at home,' and they seemed very genuinely excited about that. I kinda realized I'm going to have to make a CD if I'm going to do this, because the cassettes really didn't sound that good, compared to the DAT."

Both releases share the co-written "Hummingbird," a lilting, glorious song, almost a hoedown. Mark's take is soft and gentle, barely brushing against the still night air, while Victoria's more fully orchestrated version darts confident into the world, but without once disturbing the fragility of the song.

Much of the constancy between the two discs is not simply the unspoken, unintended collaboration of husband and wife, but the presence of John Convertino and Joey Burns (Giant Sand, Calexico; they know a thing or two about desert rhythms) at the core of several songs on Victoria's record. They bestow a gentle, rhythmic grace to everything they touch. It is the same grace with which Olson proceeds, just framed differently by production.

Therein lies the salient difference between the two records. Mark seems to have pulled back from the glossy production of a major-label career like a child recovering from his first encounter with a hot stove. (Incidentally, he is not to be confused with

Marc Olsen, late of Seattle band Sage, who has also embarked upon a solo career.) Victoria, more certain for the moment, and long accustomed to being the center of her songs, is bent on trying as many new things as possible.

This will explain "Train Song (Demise Of The Caboose)," Wendy & Lisa (ex-Prince Wendy & Lisa; really), and the presence of a drum loop.

"It's the oddest thing I've ever…have you ever heard that song without the drum beat?" Victoria asks, fishing for a book on herbs to explain the chemical properties that make squaw tea such an engaging caffeine-free stimulant. "We'll probably put it out from our home-baked records, the way it goes without that. But it was Brian's idea, and I was really game to try this," she explains, referring to Brian Blade, who played drums on several of the album's tracks. "The first run-through, I felt very… pestered by it. I, um, basically just ruined the song. And so when I got to Oxnard, I completely went in there, took everything off but the loop and started over again. And rewrote the song so it would go with it. It's different for me. I kinda like it. I can dance to it."

Mark, sitting next to her at the table, seems to be holding his tongue. "No, I'm not at all," he says, innocent as a child on an illicit sugar rush, and then they both laugh. "No, nope, nope, I'm not. I'm glad that it's on the record like that. Because the thing is that she expressed an interest to work with some kind of patterns and loops, and she was able to do that."

"Well, with that particular song, it's not 4/4 all the way through it," Victoria says. "It goes to 6/4 a lot, and so when you've got a loop going around in 4/4 and all the sudden it's turning on me, it's wanting me to do this but I can't, 'cause the song doesn't go there yet."

"I had my old-fashioned whatever," admits Mark. "But she can write really great songs; she doesn't need to use that kind of thing that people who maybe don't write songs have to use to build them up. It's a different way of doing it. She's a step ahead of them by being able to write these…"

"Ahhh," Victoria says, head down, hair hiding everything but her smile, shushing her husband.

He comes back to it a few minutes later. "I think recording your record in Oxnard, that was pretty neat. They did it in an old theater. I think that recording at home's real great, too, but when she has the opportunity to record in some very nice studios with some real good people, and she's taking that opportunity, and that's great."

"Trina [Shoemaker, co-producer] was great," Victoria adds. "Years ago, I had started to make *Loose* with Trina, actually, down there in New Orleans, and it didn't work out. We'd always wanted to work with each other, and so she called…I said I'd love to work with a gal. She's great."

It's all great, and yet time is almost certainly not on Victoria Williams' side. Multiple sclerosis charts an uncertain path through each patient's life, and it is as possible that she will go into remission as it is that she will have another prolonged attack, or that she will lose the fine motor skills which help make her such a gifted musician.

One has the sense, seeing Mark and Victoria together, that he is less certain of his own muse than he is of hers, and that he has made—or has been tempted to make—a conscious choice to facilitate her work, rather than to pursue his own.

And that could all be nothing more than a visitor's misconception.

Still, the home studio, Royer's microphones, and the desert, they all make it possible for Victoria to work at home when and as she wishes. Should it come to that.

Meanwhile, she's got better things to contemplate. New projects. "I'd like to do a children's record. I think that would be really fun," she says. "And then I'd like to do a musical. Yes, I'd like to do a musical. I've thought about doing a musical; I actually started writing a musical, which is 'Blackbirds Rise' [from *Musings*], just from when I first started writing this musical, so it's an older song. It's on *This Moment in Toronto,* but it's called 'Graveyard'."

Neither of those notions can be a surprise. Children, she notes, instantly respond to her music. And there's a great deal of Tin Pan Alley in some of her songs, not to mention that she covered "What A Wonderful World" on *Loose.*

But mostly it comes to this: "I like playing shows. I like playing for people, so I can't work out of the home then. And I like traveling; I like meeting people and traveling around, seeing different locations, springs, hot springs, just I like to see places."

"Desert Bloom" first appeared in *No Depression* #13 (January–February 1998).

<u>Selected Discography:</u>

Victoria Williams, *Happy Come Home* (Geffen) 1987.

Victoria Williams, *Swing the Statue!* (Rough Trade) 1990, reissued (Mammoth) 1994.

Victoria Williams, *Loose* (Mammoth) 1994.

Victoria Williams, *This Moment: Live in Toronto* (Mammoth) 1995.

The Original Harmony Ridge Creek Dippers, *The Original Harmony Ridge Creek Dippers* (self-released) 1997.

Victoria Williams, *Musings of a Creekdipper* (Atlantic) 1998.

Palace

by Allison Stewart

Question: *Why have you started doing interviews after years of not doing them?*

Answer: *I don't care for the question "Why," because I think it's lazy on the part of the asker.*

Question: *Would you prefer "How come?"*

Answer: *No, I'd prefer meeting halfway because there's probably a point behind the question "Why." The questioner probably has enough information to steer the question into a direction that they would want to pursue. I could answer it one way, but it might not have anything to do with what you're interested in.*

Question: *You're being awfully obtuse. Are you doing it on purpose?*

Answer: *Obtuse? You know, I'm not an angle.*

Will Oldham, the lead singer, songwriter and brain trust behind Palace, hates being interviewed, and almost never is. When he does do interviews, he doesn't reveal much, but this is what an hour-long interview says about him: He used to like show tunes as a child, and even had the soundtracks to *Showboat* and *Carousel*. He loves Gene Kelly and Johnny Cash. He likes Patty Loveless, but not Emmylou Harris. His loathing for Winona Ryder is so abiding and deep, it's best not to get him started. He doesn't know where he lives, but he doesn't think it's Chicago, where his record company, Drag City, lives, and where this interview took place. He recently went to visit a friend in Africa, where they went into the wild using pygmy trackers as jungle guides. He loves the Mekons so much he wrote the first-ever Palace song for them, "For The Mekons, et al" ("Your tiredness and sadness/ Keep my spirits up"), which appears on the *Hey Drag City* compilation. He's friends with Steve Albini, who has worked on almost all Palace projects, although it's hard to imagine an actual conversation between the two. He once played the lead of the father in *The Baby Jessica Story*, a made-for-TV movie about the tot that fell down the well, in which he stands around a lot wearing an expression of brow-furrowing woe, and lots of flannel.

There's something about him that seems vaguely alien. Take him to a Starbucks and he'll keep craning his head around curiously, as if he'd never seen a coffee bar before, and has to take notes so he can report back to his home planet. It's impossible to picture him doing something normal, like, say, shopping, but then seemingly out of nowhere he'll say, "Hey, I was in a Best Buy the other day, looking for videos of *The Rifleman*. Did you ever watch that show?" and for a minute he'll seem almost jaw-droppingly normal. Then the veil drops again.

He has an ethereal sort of dippiness that makes him seem strange, even though it's mostly a put-on. With anyone else, such strenuously cultivated wackiness could be seen as a substitute for genuine talent, but, whatever else you can say about Oldham, he is fulsomely, awesomely talented. Maybe he's doing it simply because he can, because the public tolerates and even expects a certain amount of unbecoming behavior from its celebrities, and because he knows that the world is full of rock musicians that behave well, and who notices them?

Question: *There's an awful lot of religious symbolism in your work, enough so that any number of psychiatrists could have a field day. Where does it come from?*
Answer: *I don't know.*
Question: *Were you raised religiously?*
Answer: *Religious? What does that mean? I don't know what that means.*
Question: *Were you raised in a religious household?*
Answer: *I don't know how to put a perspective on it. I don't fully understand my relationship with God.*
Question: *Well, at least you have one. That makes you sort of religious.*
Answer: *Does it? I wonder.*

Oldham grew up in Louisville, Kentucky, actively pursued acting until well into his twenties, and was quite successful at it. Music was something that he never really considered doing, he says, until he was hanging out with a musician friend and picked up a guitar to pass the time one afternoon. When did he realize he was good? "I don't know. When I got a paycheck?" A Drag City seven-inch, "Ohio River Boat Song," led to Palace's debut, the seminal, haunting *There Is No One What Will Take Care Of You.*

Countless seven-inches followed, and several more records. Each time, the lineup was different; Oldham's brother Ned was almost always a player; other members of Palace have included members of Sebadoh and Slint, as well as several session musicians Oldham had never seen before or since. The sound veered from eerie, plaintive mountain folk to rock and, with his latest, *Arise Therefore*, back again.

He has aggressively shaped his image as a hillbilly *auteur*, turning out lyrics such as, "Then we mingle our limbs/O hear her all calling/When we swim and we buckle and I emote/It is the only time to catch it so," with their distinctly Old Testament vibe, and all the while emoting like crazy.

He denies feeling any pressure to make each Palace record different, although given the fact that each Palace project has a different band name, different players, and a different sound, each record must be like erasing your life and starting over. "It's not an overhaul," says Oldham. "It's just a continuous change. It's not a conscious effort, I guess it's a natural progression." Sometimes called Palace, sometimes called Palace Songs, Palace Brothers, or Palace Music, on *Arise Therefore*, Oldham won't be called anything. The record is being issued with only the record's title on the jacket ("It'll be in the Palace section of the record store," explains Oldham. "That's how they'll know.")

Oldham insists that "the music is not very country. It's pop," although he must know it isn't. Critics have accused Oldham of appropriating old folk constructs—the high, mournful vocals, the awkward lyrical formations, the preoccupation with grimly Biblical, fire and brimstone subject matter—for his own purposes, that a twenty-six-year-old former actor knows as much about traditional folk as Kathie Lee Gifford, even if he is from Alabama.

"Then it's a good thing I don't play folk music," says Oldham. "I don't live on a farm, or anything like that. I don't ride the rails. My parents didn't play the fiddle, or make me sing in a country choir. To me, that's folk music. I hate Pete Seeger, and I hate Arlo Guthrie. I like Woody Guthrie; he's all right. But if anything, [what I do is] more like folk-pop music. More like Judy Collins."

Question: *It seems like you have an awfully contentious relationship with the critics. You don't send them review copies of your records, you'll pull them off your guest list at shows. Why—or for what reason—do you do this?*
Answer: *Well, from reading their reviews, it seems most that most writers...well, that people feel good when they have some complication to deal with, a complication that they feel they have the strength to pull themselves through.*
Question: *What?*
Answer: *I guess most jobs are just tedious and boring, and I would hate for my job listening to music and writing about it to be continually as tedious and boring as any other job. If all I had to do was sift through all the stuff on my desk, and to be paid a ridiculous amount of money—*
Question: *A ridiculous amount of money? Are you kidding?*
Answer: *No. You'd be surprised what [people like you] make. Maybe critics get paid a lot just for the shame of having to put their name under such a trite piece of writing such as what's in most magazines. We're presenting a challenge to you.*
Question: *But it's not like you're Aerosmith or something. Most critics are pretty kind to you.*
Answer: *Well, I'm kind to the critics.*
Question: *Are you? Am I understanding you properly? Even though we give you plenty of free exposure that you wouldn't otherwise get, you don't send records to us because our having to go out and buy them will give us something to do, some meaning in our lives?*
Answer: *Exactly.*

He keeps answers to one or two words; questions he sees as out of bounds receive only reproving looks. He's either completely humorless, or really funny and everyone else just doesn't get it. His hubris is breathtaking, and extends to insisting upon photo approval for features (including this one), saying, "We don't do interviews without it. It doesn't seem right not to do it that way."

In conversation, he seems as elusive as air, though he'll happily spend hours talking about movies once the tape recorder is turned off. On the record, though, the conversation goes so awkwardly, so poorly, that after twenty minutes an interviewer has to resort to asking things like, "In one interview you did, you said you had an imaginary dog. Do you still? Is he, um, here now?"

"I don't remember saying that, but I might have," says Oldham. "That sounds like me. But that was a long time ago, and I don't do that sort of thing anymore."

When he was an actor, Oldham, who had a co-starring role in John Sayles' *Matewan*, used to get recognized all the time. "I'd walk around New York City, and it would be rare that I wouldn't be recognized at some point in a day." It would be nice to know what turned a Hollywood-ish actor, one who clearly wanted to be a major player, if not a star, into a semi-evangelical, pseudo-mystical folkie with a craving for anonymity, but if Oldham knows, he isn't saying.

Oldham, so proudly anonymous that a reviewer for *The New York Times* could only refer to him as "the singer" in a live review, prefers recording studios to playing the frontman every night on the road. He doesn't know if he'll tour for *Arise Therefore*, and what he would bill himself as if he did?

"To me, the live situation doesn't approach the significance of the recorded work, so I don't really care what I go as," he says. "It might as well just be [billed as] my name, because I'm just totally a fraction of what's going on on the record. I wouldn't be doing anything that tangible, as far as I'm concerned."

Oldham, frequently given to imprecise utterings like, "It's something that just occurs, and when things come together, they come together that way," is voluble only on the subject of the press, whom he doesn't send records to, or admit to his shows, but who, like spurned but hopeful suitors, continue to love him anyway. Oldham says that since writers have to go out and buy his records themselves, they'll like them more, presumably out of gratitude for the exercise. Doesn't this show a lack of confidence on his part that the records aren't good enough to stand on their own merits?

"No, because the energy is on our side," says Oldham. "I have total confidence, enough to say, 'I could give a shit whether or not you buy our records.' It's either confidence or recklessness, to say, 'If you don't buy it, you don't review it.' I've lasted without it. I keep making records, and I'm not going to stop, no matter what."

"The Prince of Palace" first appeared in *No Depression* #4 (Summer 1996).

Selected Discography:

Palace Brothers, *There Is No-One What Will Take Care Of You* (Drag City) 1993.

Palace Brothers, *Palace Brothers* EP (Drag City) 1994.

Palace Brothers, *Viva Last Blues* (Drag City) 1995.

Palace, *Mountain* (Drag City) 1995.

Palace Songs, *Hope* EP (Drag City) 1995.

Palace Music, *Arise Therefore* (Drag City) 1996.

Palace Songs, *Lost Blues & Other Songs* (Drag City) 1997.

Will Oldham, *Joya* (Drag City) 1997.

16 Horsepower

by Linda Ray

"The seed is the word of God."
   —Luke 8:11

David Eugene Edwards composes alone, picking out brooding and intense melodies on his accordion, on his banjo. "I play until I find something that strikes me and then I bring it to the group at practice and we arrange it." With the addition last year of Jeffrey-Paul, a multi-instrumentalist from Edwards' former band, the Denver Gentlemen, 16 Horsepower has substantially enriched the resources from which it fleshes out the skeleton Edwards provides. Jeffrey-Paul adds fiddle, guitar, cello and organ to Edwards' banjo, accordion and hurdy gurdy. Jean-Yves Tola contributes drums, percussion and piano, and Pascal Humbert adds double bass.

Music press around the world has characterized the band's output as "American music." If so, it's first-generation American: Appalachian jigs and flatland reels laced with remnants of Old Country polkas and cabaret adagios. Electrified, amplified and vocalized as if by Jim Morrison & the Walkabouts, the music is unbelievably, unmistakably the devil's own music, rock 'n' roll.

Then, however, comes the Word. "Lyrically, I usually wait until the song is pretty much done before I put lyrics to it," Edwards says. "I have a book where I write down what comes to me—one word or a sentence. When I have the music, I go into this book and I pick out things that maybe have the same feeling to me as the music does. One sentence to the next in a song, they could be written months apart. Sometimes it seems to me like an incoherent mess."

But: "He who has ears to hear—let 'em hear it." This line, echoing countless gospel references to Jesus' parables, is one of the phrases from Edwards' book that surfaced in "Golden Rope" on 16 Horsepower's new *Low Estate*. It seems to sum up best what David Eugene Edwards has to say about the droning, magnetic, minor mode summons that pervade his music. "I have a duty, an obligation to do what I do. The music I'm making is for the people who need that."

While all his secular work is stitched with catch-phrases instantly recognizable to churchgoing Christians (indeed, Edwards has written hymns for the nondenominational Christian church he attends in Denver), "Golden Rope" is the purest proselytizing he has yet recorded with 16 Horsepower. In it he contrasts the lightness of a faithful person's burden with the "lovely chains that bind" the listener "'neath their deadly weight…Warm is the breath of his holy spirit…May you know his name and fear it."

"Golden Rope" is unique in its explicitness and in the linearity of its message. In the main, Edwards is content for his songs to be a vessel from which people take whatever messages are meaningful to them. He is surprised that people find his music dark. "I'm not that way as a person," he says. "I'm just like everyone else—happy most of the time. I have more hope than I could ever hope for. I have a lot of faith in the power of God and the love of God and the joy of God." He adds, "I'm a New Testament kinda guy."

Of contemporary Christian music, he says, "I don't listen to any of it. I don't think it's bad, really; I think it's good for the people who need it. But I make music for people who would never want to listen to that. Christian music is just like any other business. There's a formula to it just like pop music. If you say the right joyful things you'll be on the radio. I agree with everything they say pretty much. I just feel like it's kind of vacant. I know there are a lot of good people in that; most of the best ones probably don't get heard."

If *Low Estate* delivers 16 Horsepower's first explicit Christian message, it also gives us the band's first recorded love song—"Hang My Teeth On Your Door," which Edwards and Jeffrey-Paul wrote during their days in the Denver Gentlemen. The song relates an almost giddy joy in mutual love and lust, the fun and comfort of it.

It's hard to say whether the message is more underscored or undermined by the woozy, beer-garden-waltz feel of the music, but it's a standout track on *Low Estate*. "I think it's pretty obvious that the songs on this record are much more varied," Edwards observes, "which has a lot to do probably with the different textures of it. Just the changes that we've gone through since we made the first record, and the different people that have also added different textures."

The moody, almost gothic sense of most of 16 Horsepower's sound arises less from the music itself, the rich instrumentation and weird tunings, as from the songs Edwards crafts to sing over all that. Influenced in part by Hassidic chants, the melodies link tense lyric images of guilt, longing and threats of retribution with exhortations to fear God. Even when the message contains no reference to religion, it seems intended to lay bare the moral bankruptcy of contemporary life played out in idolatry and lust, usually with respect to material things but also pertaining to the exploitation of others to one's own ends. Comfort is offered only by the Lord…and Ruthie Lingle.

Lingle first appeared on 16 Horsepower's A&M debut, *Sackcloth 'n' Ashes,* which includes a song that bears her name. She surfaces again atop a roof on *Low Estate*, light as a good conscience. "She's one of my first memories of being in church," Edwards says. "She was someone my mother would put in charge of me in church. She was twelve or thirteen. She was really beautiful and I loved her. She was really good to me and a good person. I use her as a symbol for a lot of things."

Ignore the lyrics, or listen in another language, and 16 Horsepower's music is still disturbing. Like it or not, it insists on a response. Its drama and depth were sufficient to lure PJ Harvey's producer/collaborator John Parrish to record *Low Estate* with the band in the spring of '97 in an antique studio in a bayou-side barn on an aging plantation in map-speck Maurice, Louisiana.

"Their sound is very defined…that's what, for me, makes it a successful band in my mind," Parrish said. "It doesn't matter basically what instrumentation you're doing, whether it's a song that we spend three days on constructing and doing a lot of overdubs and dropping in parts, or whether it's one that we recorded live with one microphone on the porch or in the big room or whatever. Every piece sounds like [them] because [16 Horsepower] has a very, very definite sound…a very difficult thing to create if it's not there in the first place."

Parrish's contributions to 16 Horsepower's development extend beyond what's evident on *Low Estate.* Says Edwards, "I've learned a ton, really; a lot in structure of songs, because I really have no structure when I write a song. It could go on for an hour and a half, the same part, and I'd be totally happy…It's not a formula or something like that, it's just a really, really healthy thing for me to be exposed to."

Tola adds, "Be patient with a song. If it doesn't happen when you've played it twice, it doesn't mean it's not going to happen. I've seen some of the urgency in it. Some of his songs were composed in half an hour, you know? You go to the studio and you want to record 'em and it doesn't work, then it'd be, 'Forget it, let's do something else.' John was good at telling us to keep trying, changing around a little bit."

"All those little details add up to make a huge difference," Pascal says. "Personally, what I've learned from working with John was to rethink and reconsider the placement, the range, the drive, when it needs to be there and when it needs not to be there, which is just as important."

How has all this translated to live performances? The band has put it to the test on several trips to Europe, where *Low Estate* was released some months before its U.S. debut.

"If we get people's attention—and it doesn't necessarily have to be in a positive way—then I feel that our point is gotten across in one way or another," Edwards said. "I mean, if people are just talking and disinterested about it, I would be frustrated, maybe, but we've been blessed with being able to play a show and everybody pays attention. Whether they understand it, what I'm trying to say—because I don't even know necessarily what I'm trying to say a lot of times. Maybe they understand it better than I do."

Tola adds, "When we're playing places where you know, for a fact, that people don't understand what you're saying, in countries where they don't speak English, we get at least the same kind of response that we get in America….People get a lot through just seeing it and hearing it live."

"The emotion behind the music and the atmosphere would be difficult to mistake in a live show," Parrish says, "and I think there's certain visual things that obviously enhance the atmosphere. There's a huge amount of energy coming from this fairly static, odd looking bunch of people with a bunch of even odder looking instruments. That's probably the first thing that strikes you. I think you get a feeling for what the songs are about, even though you probably know you're just hearing twenty percent of the actual lyrics the first time you see a show."

"I think the instruments that we use, the reason that we probably use them is because they help get across what we're trying to say," Edwards explains. "The actual sound of each instrument coincides with an emotion or something that I feel or want to get across, or I think that has a lot to do with it. When we're playing in Germany…they get the presence of it, they get the feeling of it just from the sound of the instrument, and the look of it as well."

The internal struggles Edwards' songs declaim seem depicted allegorically in the effort demanded by his bandoneon, an antique, wheezing Mexican accordion. Nearly as visually engrossing is his new hurdy gurdy.

Where do you get a new hurdy gurdy anyway? Edwards says they're now made only in France and Hungary. "I was listening to a lot of Hungarian music, which is some of my favorite music, just like traditional Hungarian folk music, and they use that a lot," he says. "I love anything that drones, pretty much. I love droning; all the tunings that I use are very droning, and the banjo is a very droning instrument."

So as not to leave interpretation entirely to chance, accompanying *Low Estate* will be a document somewhat more substantial than the customary liner notes, similar in character to the booklet that came with *Sackcloth 'n' Ashes*. Edwards contrasts this practice with Bob Dylan's tendency not to include lyrics, *Blood On The Tracks* being the lone exception. "To me, his words are what is important about his music, but you can understand what he's saying, and the way he puts it across is very self-evident," Edwards says. "I feel my words are harder to decipher, and it's important to me that people do decipher them, whether they do it the way I would want them to or whatever way they do.

"I think it's nice for people to have something to read when they're listening to the record," he adds. "They put it on and they open it up; it's like a little booklet….I like to sit and listen to it and read it like you are reading a newspaper."

Says Jeffrey-Paul, "It's like a cereal box."

Parrish quips, "You're not going to put any little plastic toys in it?"

"Not plastic," says Edwards. Of course not.

This article includes excerpts from an in-studio interview with 16 Horsepower conducted by No Depression *co-editor Grant Alden.*

"Sinners In The Hands Of A Twangry God" first appeared in *No Depression* #13 (January–February 1998).

Selected Discography:

Sixteen Horsepower, *Sackcloth 'n' Ashes* (A&M) 1995.

Sixteen Horsepower, *Low Estate* (A&M) 1998.

Richard Buckner

by Debbie Dodd

There's a fine line between intimate expression and melodrama, and Richard Buckner toes that line. His songs gracefully walk the tightrope between beauty and tragedy, leaving a lot to the imagination. They're full of personal references and insider information, but it doesn't seem to matter. People identify in their own way.

"Everyone's interested in somebody else's situation," Buckner says. "People want to know what the situation was and how we reacted to it. You're curious. You want to know, 'How did that guy deal with it? What happened to him in what way?'"

Often the situation in Buckner's songs is a moment of personal crisis and/or rapture. Like his favorite movies such as *Last Exit To Brooklyn* and *Leaving Las Vegas,* which he mentions he recently saw for the second time, Buckner often aims to "capture the characters at this point, right before they go over. They're just teetering and you get their experiences right before they fuckin' go over the edge....People want to know, when you're at the edge, what are you going to do?"

These days Richard Buckner finds himself at the edge—of breaking through to a wider audience with his music. His debut album *Bloomed,* which came out in 1994 on Germany's Glitterhouse label and last year on Dejadisc, turned up on *Spin* magazine's list of the top twenty albums of 1995, awkwardly sandwiched between the Red Hot Chili Peppers and the Foo Fighters. The new year finds him being seriously courted by a major label, even though *Bloomed* racked up significantly more critical acclaim than sales figures. Not that Buckner seems to care much about selling records or moving up to the big-label ranks: "All I want to do is get back to my obsessiveness," he says.

To Buckner, songwriting is like keeping a journal; it's how he puts the world in perspective. "It's worse than any drug. You keep doing it out of necessity, especially if you're any kind of a journal keeper at all, or you've still got any desire to keep reinventing your own language and keep your own spirits intact. For me anyway. And that's where writing comes in. That's the only reason I write, so that I feel like I'm keeping myself together. There are images I have now in my songs and I know it's shit I would have forgotten, but now I have this permanent record of what went on."

In "22," a song on *Bloomed*, Buckner set out to write a one-chord mountain tragedy song about the Marysville, California flood of '55. He found that without personal interest or experience, he couldn't get into it. "I ended up writing about a semi-autobiographical point in my life where I thought I wanted to die," Buckner says. "I created a character and a situation that had this very deep center that had a lot to do with me. I've had people come up to me and talk to me about their very personal experiences. I love when songs like that make people feel better about what they went through. Not only that somebody else went through it, but also that it's cool, it's fine to go through that, because if you live through it, then there you are. And you're a lot brighter than somebody who hasn't lived through it, or hasn't experienced it even."

In both music and life, Buckner never seems settled or content. When he was growing up, his father was a '60s golden boy salesman, so his family moved constantly from one small town in Central California to another. For years, as a pattern, his father got transferred, his parents broke up, his parents reunited. To this day, Buckner remains rootless. "I'm really happy when I'm not somewhere for long periods of time." As an adult, his longest stint was in San Francisco, but most recently, he lived on the Lummi Indian Reservation near Bellingham, Washington, a town he discovered while on tour.

Now, he's playing a series of mini-tours, and when he's done he'll be homeless once again. "I don't feel like I'm going to move back to San Francisco. I could move anywhere. I might just find some place when I'm on the road and take a liking to it. If I hadn't been married at the time when I was down in Lubbock, Texas (where he recorded *Bloomed* a couple years ago), I would have moved there right then and there. I thought it was a really beautiful little tiny little weird town."

He also spent some time in Atlanta, where, he says, he finally came alive. "I just kind of exploded. I just kind of fell apart in a really great way and I'm still suffering from it. I just fucking fired off a launch pad in Atlanta," he says. "Song Of 27," a spine-tingling elegy scheduled to be included on his new album, is about Buckner driving back from Atlanta to California, and saying, "Please let me keep this up. Please let me keep this."

Originally, Buckner intended his next release to be a concept album based around his family, a la Terry Allen's *Juarez or* Willie Nelson's *Red Headed Stranger*. He ended up scrapping the idea, however; some of the songs were too close to home, and some of the family members still alive. "I haven't seen my family in a couple of years, actually. I'm really distant from them. But if I wanted to say it to them, I'd just say it to them. I don't want to do it in the form of a record. I think that's really pansy."

If all goes according to the current plan, his upcoming album will have some of the less-injurious of these songs, as well as a batch of newer ones. "I have about twenty songs that are totally ready to go. I'll really get to pick the cream for the sophomore slump record...trying to keep it from being a slumper at all." Some of it will be recorded with his band the Doubters; much of it will be similar to *Bloomed*. And of course, there will be pedal steel. "Steel is my sucker instrument. Anything with slide on it, I fall apart. I'm always going to have any kind of steel at all on all my records. Always. It's going to be the rule."

Besides obvious influences such as Lucinda Williams, Steve Earle, Peter Case and Townes Van Zandt, Buckner cites Giant Sand, the Dirty Three and Pavement as inspirations who have taught him "about deconstructing a song and putting it together in a more perfect way." Buckner even covers a Pavement tune, "Here," in some of his live performances.

Not surprisingly, Buckner often is inspired by authors as much as by musicians. One of his favorite Raymond Carver collections is the series of poems written when Carver knew he was dying of cancer. "With each poem he wrote, they included a portion of each story he was reading at the time—as a reference point—also knowing the whole time that he was dying of cancer and that he was totally in love with his wife. There's one line where Carver says, 'Just when he thought he'd never write another poem, she began brushing her hair.' I just break down at that. At the very edge. You're capturing somebody that's right on the brink and there's some amazing beauty in that."

For a writer, finding the right words can turn a cliché into something completely singular, a feat at which Richard Buckner is expert. "I don't want to say anything anyone's ever said," he explains. "It's my own experience. I only want to say it in my own way."

So now he makes up his own words. "I have a song called 'Fater'—F-A-T-E-R. It's about somebody who believes in fate too much, and I call her a 'fater' in the song. Vic Chesnutt talks about ghosties. Nobody says the word ghosties ever, but he says it and you know exactly what he's talking about.

"It's the only way to express yourself sometimes because the English language is so stupid and ridiculous. Of course you have to break those rules."

"Home Is Where The Brink Is" first appeared in *No Depression* #3 (Spring 1996).

Selected Discography:
Richard Buckner, *Bloomed* (Dejadisc) 1995.
Richard Buckner, *Devotion & Doubt* (MCA) 1997.

Robbie Fulks

by Linda Ray

A wry smile crept almost imperceptibly across his face as the casually imposing figure stood onstage—head bowed, his acoustic guitar poised for a solo performance. Over a room crowded with fans of headliner Guy Clark, the club's announcer had just introduced this lanky opener as "Chicago's latest contribution to alternative country music, Robbie Fulks."

Few artists invite the alternative country brand, but Fulks could as justly smirk at the 'latest' label. As he later made plain to the crowd in an irony tinged aside, he's singing country music, hence the name of his debut CD, *Country Love Songs*. And while he may be Geffen's latest find, at thirty-four Fulks has been around a long time.

He was seven years old when his folk-singing dad handed him a banjo, back home in Creedmoor, North Carolina, and the music grabbed him by the throat. His musical path led him through his own folk career and to collaborations with members of Five Chinese Brothers, an East Coast band he met while attending Columbia University in New York City.

By the time he left New York, Fulks was chasing a slot in Chicago's relentlessly touring Special Consensus Bluegrass Band, but it was a long time coming. He was already almost a fixture at two prominent Chicago folk venues and was teaching at the venerable Old Town School of Folk Music when the opportunity finally came in 1987.

Two and a half years on the road with Special Consensus taught him a lot about restaurant food along America's interstates, but "the best thing I got out of that," he says, "was learning how to break the code, how to play well and consistently in front of people." Calling it a grueling way to live, Fulks quit, figuring, "There weren't other more famous bluegrass bands asking me to come play guitar for them."

Soon homesick for the stage, but pretty sick of bluegrass too, Fulks mustered a monthly rock 'n' roll review at the Chicago watering hole, Deja Vu. "It was three hours of screaming and jumping around—roadhouse rock 'n' roll and honky tonk music….The band never rehearsed. I'd start a song and…a lot of times it was a song we'd never played before. The pace was real fast. There were scantily clad dancers onstage kind of moving along with it. My future wife was one of them."

When this "Trailer Trash Revue" had run its course, Fulks stayed on the stage with a regular Sunday night slot at one of Chicago's favorite neighborhood joints, Augenblich. For the next four years, he and fellow Old Town School faculty member Jim DeWan would split an hour performing their own material, then share an hour of audience participation, musical gags, and romps through obscure subgenres of music. It was DeWan, then under contract to Acuff-Rose, who urged Fulks to try picking some money from the Nashville songwriting trees.

Meanwhile, back at the Double R Ranch (a storied Chicago bar that was home base for the legendary Sundowners), and uptown at the protopunk Crash Palace, events conspired to make Fulks Chicago's latest contribution to insurgent country. Nan Warshaw and Rob Miller had found a common obsession spinning traditional country tunes Wednesday nights at Crash Palace. Together they plotted to turn out a compilation of country-inspired songs by Chicago artists. As the last great country and western band in Chicago, the Sundowners headed the pair's list of desired contributors. The two also drew from *Chicago Country*, the Sundowners' CD of songs by Chicago musicians, which included "Cigarette State" by one R. Fulks. Figuring it might be worth finding out if he could sing it himself, Warshaw found Fulks in the phone book and called for a tape.

The tape he had handy was a four-song demo produced by Steve Albini. Fulks had become friendly with the indie rock icon through a member of Albini's old band, Big Black. The Albini-produced "Cigarette State" wound up on Bloodshot Records' opening volley, the compilation *For A Life Of Sin.* "I like working with Steve a lot," Fulks said. "He's invisible when I work with him except that he's a lot of fun to talk to. He's a really bright and really funny guy."

Fulks does credit Albini with the naked sound and bare bones instrumentation of the *Country Love Songs* track "Barely Human," a convincingly delivered ballad in which a drunk details with heart-searing self-contempt the effects of his drinking on his loved ones. "It's the most 'his' song on there," says Fulks. "[Albini] said, 'Give me twenty minutes with this and let me show you what I have in mind.' I wasn't sold on it at first, but now I think he did a really good job."

Although Miller and Warshaw had heard of the Trailer Trash Revue, the first time they saw Fulks perform was at the *For A Life Of Sin* release party at the Lounge Ax. "In that set," Miller recalled, "Robbie sang 'She Took A Lot Of Pills And Died.' You could hear the room's collective jaw drop. I mean, it was *the song*. That led to *Hell-Bent* [Bloodshot's second compilation, which featured "Pills"], which led to us sitting around going, 'You know, this guy's really talented but...what's the world going to do with a Robbie Fulks record?' We thought, 'Why not?'"

Warshaw and Miller banked on the cachet of Albini's production credits to help attract new fans. Fulks fleshed out the disc with cuts he'd made with esteemed Missouri bar band the Skeletons, another draw. "It was the Skeletons album with Jonathan Richman [*Jonathan Richman Goes Country*] that really tipped me off that they could do a good country album," Fulks said. "It's probably my favorite Jonathan Richman album.

"We shared a lawyer and I just bothered my lawyer till I got their phone number, and I called them up and said 'Man, I'm a big fan of you guys and I heard you have a studio and let's just go down and demo.' For a long time I was just casting about in the wind, trying to do anything with anybody, and just trying to network like in the Nashville years...just trying to get to meet people and upgrade my associations a little bit. So for no reason in the world I went down there and spent a lot of money to demo a couple songs with the Skeletons 'cause it was a big band and I thought it would be cool to do."

Bloodshot's release of *Country Love Songs* inspired a *No Depression* "Town & Country" article (#4, Summer '96) that caught the eye of Brian Long, a Geffen A&R executive. Long bought the record in Los Angeles the first week it was released, then saw Fulks play in New York. "I was totally blown away," Long says. "He has this wonderful trill.

His voice is just so captivating and he's such a complete entertainer. Then I played 'The Buck Starts Here' at an A&R meeting and it was the hit of the meeting."

Another memorable track on *Country Love Songs* was "The Scrapple Song," a tune about that most mysterious of meats which included the lyric, "It's hearty as a T-bone, slippery as a tadpole/Any old part of the hog will do/Dick and the nipples and the toenails too." But "Scrapple" had no sooner been recorded than Fulks had another live hit to top it and "Pills" combined. The forthrightly named "Fuck This Town" was a summation of his Nashville experience that's a ready-made anthem for the overtalented, underemployed, broke and broken muses in the shadows of contemporary country's bright happy lights.

The frustrations it recounts may be specific, but its sentiment is universal. "Fuck This Town" could be the "Take This Job and Shove It" of the '90s. The infectious chorus dares you to partake of its release, and whether or not you'd care to quibble, most traditional country music fans would indulge Fulks' fundamental premise, cynically delivered with the line, "I like old Tim Carroll/and BR5-49/but Nashville don't need that noise/No, Nashville'll do just fine." But then—"As long as there's a moron market/And a faggot in a hat to sign." Wait. Did he say that?

"It seemed to fit," Fulks explains. "I needed a two-syllable derogatory word for a man....I don't think homosexuals would object to that as much as the cowboy singers themselves. So long as I'm offending the right people."

"We're gonna get a lot of shit for that," says Warshaw, sheepishly. "He does a lot of things that are not PC and I love him for it. He'll insult everyone, so I guess that's why I don't have a personal problem with it even if I don't agree with his insults."

"Obviously, we're not putting out that record," says Geffen's Long.

The record Long refers to is *South Mouth*, Fulks' parting release for Bloodshot. "Fuck This Town" is just one dimension of South Mouth, which Fulks says "covers more bases" than *Country Love Songs*. "[That] was kind of like a concept album, which puts a certain limit on it," he says.

His next release will be on Geffen, sometime in 1998. "It doesn't appear that he's going to be making the same kind of record that he's making for Bloodshot," Long says. "There's a lot more to his songwriting style. One of the reasons Rob was interested in us and we in him is that he wanted to explore other kinds of music." Long acknowledges favoring Fulks' twang, and expects the next record to be more of a maturation, "like Whiskeytown," referring to that band's recent release on Outpost/Geffen, but he also mentions possibilities in TV theme songs and movie scores.

His idiomatic range is, by all accounts, nearly comprehensive. If Fulks' grasp of songwriting styles evokes Britannica or Colliers, his own approach befits the Coen Brothers: Send up, subvert, stretch the limits—and make it graphic.

"Cold Statesville Cell," for instance, establishes the mood of an antique hill-country murder ballad before veering off alarmingly, a pattern no doubt followed by many an actual murder. A victim chances into the headlight gleam of a man who, apparently at that instant, recognizes himself as a sex-motivated killer. The murder itself continues for an unprecedented two verses as the victim's body sinks ever lower "with each hammer blow" and the "earth beneath her darkens with her heart's blood."

Then comes the really gory part: the guitar solo.

In the Louvin Brothers-like epic "South Richmond Girl," Fulks and duet partner DeWan purposefully treat a second murder entirely differently. The motivation is more than apparent, but the murder is merely implied by the guitars playing on under an absent verse. In the last verse, the singer looks into his own grown son's eyes and finds, if not forgiveness, at least newborn understanding.

"Jim plays all over the record," Fulks says, but on DeWan's greatest contribution, the song "You Wouldn't Do That to Me," Fulks plays and sings alone. It's a tune of the Cole Porter sort for which the mold might as well have been broken in 1949. Fulks revives it with intimacy and resignation you might be embarrassed to overhear through the windows of the heartbroken guy next door: "Must be some problem with the telephone/Sometimes when I answer, all I hear's the dial tone."

Fulks explains he remembered this song when, stuck for a ballad the week before song charts were due to the Skeletons, he had to abandon one of his own. "A lot of times when I get to about the halfway point in a song and it just isn't grabbin' me, I have to really bite my lip and just throw it away. The whole week's wasted, but I don't have to work on it anymore....You can't take a word out of [DeWan's song]; there's no improvable word in the song."

In the indelible, Paycheck-like "Forgotten But Not Gone," Fulks sings how it feels when your loved one is present but their heart isn't. The Everly Brothers could easily cover the flip side, "Heart, I Wish You Were Here," in which a lover wishes he hadn't left his heart elsewhere long ago. "May The Best Man Win" and "I Was Just

Leaving" bow to Bakersfield, colored in by Tom Brumley on steel. "I Told Her Lies" and "Dirty Mouth Flo" are easy pitches to the fratboy set. Mostly, however, the record just swings like the dickens, owing largely to the Skeletons' full-service rhythm section. Especially in "Goodbye Good Lookin'," beat-deficient dancers get a free ride from the Sumo-wrestler-on-a-pogo-stick punch of Lou Whitney's bass and Joe Terry's keyboard.

Also highly danceable is "Busy Not Crying," wherein lies a microcosm of Fulks' Nashville troubles. Line after sly line enumerates useful and humorous distractions that resolve in one of the song's cleverest turns of phrase: "Movin' each day at a mighty quick pace/My heart stays in the same sad place/Nothin' that heavy's gonna ever catch up to me." Remarks Fulks, "Some Nashville publisher corrected me on that line because of the word nothin'—because its antecedent is somewhere in the previous line that the listener has already forgotten." At least it's a great two-stepper.

Long after a January midnight, Fulks held 300 people at Chicago's Empty Bottle spellbound with Merle Haggard's "Sing a Sad Song," his delivery rich with subtly shaded emotion. He climbed the "sa-a-ad-ness" with the authority of an Irish tenor. Moments later, his 6'5" frame easily dominating the rock club's stage, he turned his sidemen loose on a rave-up swing jam on dobro and bass fiddle. Getting into the act, the club's lighting technician flooded the turning disco ball, and the dance floor surged.

Fulks took advantage of the climactic moment to stroll from the stage, across the room to the bar and back, allowing Tuey Connell, drummer Dan Massey and company to steal the show and the crowd for as long as it took him to refresh his drink. Picking up his guitar on cue, he then stole it right back with interest, and fearlessly. In the very next song, Connell's banjo solo wowed the crowd yet again, but Fulks gleefully took him on, dukin' it out for nearly five choruses. Indeed, the quality of his sidemen may the best testimony to just how much Fulks commands a show.

Albini says, "Robbie's just an amazing songwriter, idiomatic issues aside....If there's a classic mold for a guy who writes good songs, I guess he's one of them."

Skeletons bassist Whitney has the bottom line, though: "He's a triple threat. He can run, hit and throw. He flat-ass thrills me."

"It Drawled From The Mouth" first appeared in *No Depression* #11 (September–October 1997).

Selected Discography:

Robbie Fulks, *Country Love Songs* (Bloodshot) 1996.

Robbie Fulks, *South Mouth* (Bloodshot) 1997.

Iris DeMent

by David Cantwell

Iris DeMent is belting out a protest song called "Wasteland Of The Free" to a packed house in Lawrence, Kansas, and even though the song is downright radical in a way that's hardly heard in this country anymore, the response is decidedly enthusiastic. The focus of that enthusiasm, however, seems to bounce all over the hall like a hot potato. One section down front goes nuts over "We've got politicians runnin' races on corporate cash/Now don't tell me they don't turn around and kiss them people's ass." A group upstairs voices vigorous agreement to "We got C.E.O.'s makin' 200 times the workers' pay/But they'll fight like hell against raisin' the minimum wage." Over at stage left, some folks whoop it up at the line "Let's blame our troubles on the weak ones/Sounds like some kinda Hitler remedy." It seems the song has a view to rally almost everyone.

On the other hand, there's also something to piss a lot of people off. When she sings "We kill for oil and throw a party when we win/Some guy refuses to fight and we call that the sin," the room is all but stunned into silence. DeMent stands out there at the center of these shifting reactions, all by her lonesome. As always, she's just a little ol' country gal in a print dress, strumming her acoustic guitar and flat singing her heart out. The difference is that now she's speaking her piece, too. Loud and clear.

Several months after that April show, DeMent spoke with me by phone from her home in Kansas City North, Missouri, an older working-class community just north of Kansas

City, where she lives with her husband and tour manager, Elmer McCall. "You know, there's a couple of songs I almost took off the new record," DeMent reveals between loads of laundry. "I realized 'Wasteland Of The Free' could get me killed—and I ain't ready to go yet. People aren't used to hearing things like that [the 'We kill for oil' line] in public....I had to ask myself if I was up for hate mail....But you know, I think the odd thing is that a lot of people have thought those words. So I guess the main reason I had to put it on there is because that's around-the-kitchen-table talk, and if I have the courage to say it around the kitchen table, and I don't have the courage to say it out in public, then I'm not as much of a person as I like to think of myself as being."

Courage is a word DeMent uses over and over when she talks about her third album, *The Way I Should*—and for good reason. Besides criticizing giddy reactions to the Gulf War, DeMent uses the disc to confront everything from yuppie parents who value "nice big cars" more than they do their own kids to the tragedy of the Vietnam War and the specifics of her own faith. "Letter To Mom," about a woman who feels compelled to tell her mother about the sexual abuse she experienced as child— "[She's] not wanting to be cruel...[she's] just been walking 'round with secrets now too long"—is another controversial song that DeMent felt she had to have the guts to record. "I know some people are really going to be offended by that song, but I left it on there because some people are helped by it," she says. "I know that from the letters I've gotten from people who've heard me sing it at shows."

Still, she was also concerned about the reaction of one particular listener. "It sounds like a letter to my mom—and even though I do that a lot in my songs, I've never done it with a subject like this," she said. "And I was actually concerned for my mother that it might bother her, that people would think that this was something I experienced as a kid. And I didn't....But I felt like if I don't have the courage—when I think of what those people went through who have experienced that, and the courage it takes to face life and deal with that—if I don't have the courage to even just identify with it in a song, then that's a pretty terrible thing. So if it helps somebody, even if it makes my mother uncomfortable, or me, I've got to go through with it."

Although Iris DeMent spent most of her formative years growing up in California, she was born in 1961 in Paragould, Arkansas, a small town just to the west of the

Missouri bootheel, and it's in that edge-of-the-Ozarks land that she found her voice. Her mom and dad were church-going working people who made their own gospel music—dad played fiddle, mom sang—but eventually they came down out of the hills, as so many of their generation did, to find decent jobs in the fields and factories of southern California.

Appropriately, DeMent's first two albums pay sweet homage to these influences. The final two cuts on her debut, 1992's *Infamous Angel*, are "Mama's Opry," about her mother's dream of singing on the Grand Ole Opry stage, and "Higher Ground," a country gospel number that features the fine old-timey vocals of none other than Flora Mae DeMent herself. 1994's *My Life*, in addition to including a cover of Lefty Frizzell's "Mom And Dad's Waltz," contains an exquisitely painful number called "No Time To Cry" about the death of her father. Produced by friend Jim Rooney, both albums have a spare, country gospel feel, with arrangements that use nothing more than twangy fiddle and guitar, bass and piano, and DeMent's plaintive, old-school vocals—part Kitty Wells, part Sarah Carter.

And part Loretta, too. The first record DeMent remembers ever hearing was one of her mom's Loretta Lynn albums. "I loved that record," she recalled. "It's the first album I memorized from front to back....A number of the songs [Lynn] wrote, but it was all gospel hymns. I don't know the name of it; I think it was just like *Loretta Lynn Sings Gospel Hymns*. She's got long red hair on the cover and a yellow lacy dress. That's probably why I liked the album so much as a kid. She looked really, really pretty on there."

The sound and message of that old-time gospel music has stayed with DeMent into adulthood, making inestimable contributions not only to her singing but to her writing. Though some listeners may hear the religious content in many of her songs and automatically assume she's some sort of homespun Ned Flanders with a guitar, her religious beliefs are far more complex. DeMent songs such as "Let The Mystery Be," "The Shores Of Jordan" and "Keep Me God" are always questioning and often ambivalent, even as they testify to great faith.

Like many people raised in churches, DeMent eventually took herself out of the church, but, at least artistically, she has never been able to take the church out of herself. And she wouldn't want to. "Even though I don't go to those churches anymore, I don't think I can ever separate myself musically from those churches," she says. "I was three days old when I went to my first church service, and the churches we went to had a lot of really great music—really soulful, sincere singing.

"That's pretty much what I was submerged in most of my life, even though today I'm not a Christian....From what I remember from church, being a Christian means that you believe that people have to believe that Jesus is the only way to get to a better place. For a long time I did call myself a Christian, even though I didn't go to a church. But then I realized that that belief is really at the crux of Christianity—that the foundation of Christianity is to make everybody become like them, because if they don't become like them, they are doomed to burn in hell forever and ever and ever. That's basically what Christianity is all about. I simply do not believe that, and I can't believe that, and as hard as it is for me to say, I'm not a Christian."

Even so, DeMent stresses that gospel music still matters to her deeply, both personally and artistically. "The thing I picked up on as a kid, and that I still sense in those older gospel songs, is just a lot of sincerity. People had struggles; they had a lot of problems. Most of the people who wrote those songs came from poorer settings where they were really struggling with life, and you hear that in the songs. That's the quality in them I'm drawn to...not the religious dogma. It's just that sense you can get from them that they were written for the right reasons.

"Also, I have so many good memories wrapped up with singing with my family and at the church, and I'm not willing to leave those behind. I don't, however, sing gospel songs that have ideas I just flat out don't believe. I won't sing the more extreme ones about hell because I don't believe it. But there's a lot of them that have really comforting concepts in them, and encouraging concepts, and I like that, so I go ahead and sing them."

The earnest, stripped-down country gospel of DeMent's youth has become closely associated with her music since *Infamous Angel*, yet another reason why *The Way I Should* is such a brave record. Besides tackling taboos such as religion, sex and politics, DeMent's new disc has a bigger, more atmospheric sound that, on at least a couple of occasions, is nothing short of rock 'n' roll. Produced by Randy Scruggs, the album pairs DeMent's music for the first time with a full, plugged-in band (including sidemen Steuart Smith on guitar, Chuck Leavell on organ, and Dave Pomeroy on bass, in addition to special guests including Mark Knopfler and Earl Scruggs). The result is a record that sounds nothing like what people expect to hear from Iris DeMent, and nothing like what people expect out of Nashville.

"In the middle of my last record, I knew I was bored," DeMent recalled. "I remember saying to myself, 'Next time around I have to do something different.' And it really didn't stem from the desire for my records to change or anything. It was more that I just was bored. I wanted to be in a different environment, and I know that a lot of that difference comes with a different producer.

"So when Randy and I decided to work together, he asked me, 'Is there anything that you don't want to do on this record? Do you want it to be acoustic, are you against drums?' And my answer was, I'm not against anything. If it sounds right, if it works, I don't care if we have half a dozen horns on there. I just want the songs to be treated totally without limitations....I just want to have a good time and be free the same way I am when I'm in my room writing a song.

"We did the album in four days with the same group of players. Then we spent a couple of weeks bringing in special guests and mixing and overdubbing—the finishing touches did take a while. But most of it was live, a group of people in a room. We talked about the songs, and we played 'em."

One of the new songs recorded in this fashion, the delicate "This Kind Of Happy," was co-written with Merle Haggard, the man who, at least in part, inspired DeMent to try a bigger band in the first place. After contributing a version of Haggard's "Big City" to the 1994 HighTone Records album *Tulare Dust: A Songwriters' Tribute to Merle Haggard*, DeMent gathered in San Francisco with other artists on the record to perform before Merle himself took the stage.

"I got to get up and sing with the Strangers," DeMent beams, like she still can't believe it. "I did 'Big City' and 'Hobo Bill's Last Ride.' And that was the first time I'd been onstage with a full band behind me, and a really good band at that, and I *really* liked it. That was it for me. That experience probably had a lot to do with the sound of this record and the fact that I want to go out with a band now. It was just one of the most thrilling experiences of my life."

She also got to meet Merle that night, beginning a relationship that has now spawned a Haggard recording of DeMent's "No Time To Cry" [on his *1996* album] and a brief touring companionship. "I went out [with Haggard] for two weeks. I just had a little electric keyboard. You know, I'm not a Stranger-quality player. It was really just a thing that Merle offered me to do. I think he…just knew that it would be a great experience for me to follow him around. And I knew that it would be too."

DeMent's stylistic shift seems especially appropriate in light of her new album's sweeping, socially conscious vision. Buoyed by swelling organ fills and gospel imagery, the disc's opening track, "When My Morning Comes Around," is a prayer of healing from a narrator who yearns for a day when she "won't be thinkin' there's something wrong with me/And I'll wake up and find that my faults have been forgiven"—and she's not necessarily willing to wait for heaven to find that moment of grace. The electric ebo that frames "There's A Wall In Washington" recalls the eerie chop of a military helicopter, even as it seems to be comforting the pain of those left tracing names in "cold black granite." Behind a full band, "Wasteland Of The Free" is transformed from Woody Guthrie-esque folk to an all-out rock 'n' roll anthem of what America needs to heal, to change.

It's the connection between healing and change that ties the new album together thematically. Heard in isolation, the piano-driven "I'll Take My Sorrow Straight" simply sounds like a woman demanding the truth from a departing lover. But after making the pilgrimage to the Vietnam War Memorial and taking a tour of the "Wasteland Of The Free," and after the prayer for peace that opens the record, "I'll Take My Sorrow Straight" delivers a more significant message: The way to heal pain and to work for change is to toss out the rose-colored glasses and look ghosts straight in the eye.

"'The Wall In Washington' is trying to get people to ask questions," DeMent explains. "First of all, to actually talk about the pain and the huge loss, which often takes a back seat. And then to try to get the next generation to reflect and ask, 'Why did this happen?' 'Cause if you don't do that, then how are you going to make a good decision when your time comes? And the whole idea of 'Wasteland' is: Here's what I see as a problem; now let's fix it.

"I hope with this album that it will just cause people to think and to talk. I don't really care if they agree with what I say, but I think it's really important for people not to forget how important it is just to think, and to look at the other guy's side."

The album's closer, "Trouble," has DeMent trading vocals with Delbert McClinton in a bluesy, juke-joint workout ("Ain't that old-timey," Iris declares as the music fades) that predicts the offended reaction some will have to her new record. "They're building prisons for people like you and me," she sings with a newfound roughness that only adds to the lonesome and sweet quality her voice has always possessed.

Then she lets fly with a shouted "Yeaaaah!" It sounds like a healing that's been a long time coming, as if she knows what troubles lay ahead but won't let that keep her from speaking her piece. Like the conscientious objector in "Wasteland Of The Free," she's just standin' up for what she believes in. She's singing her heart out. Loud and clear.

"Homespun Of The Brave" first appeared in *No Depression* #6 (November–December 1996).

Selected Discography:

Iris DeMent, *Infamous Angel* (Philo, 1992), reissued (Warner Bros.) 1993.

Iris DeMent, *My Life* (Warner Bros.) 1994.

Iris DeMent, *The Way I Should* (Warner Bros.) 1996.

Steve Forbert

by Rick Cornell

I can't recall the year. Steve Forbert is playing a solo show at the ArtsCenter in Carrboro, North Carolina, and in the front row sits a man and his two sons. Dad's in a Beatles T-shirt, and the two boys are honoring Jimi Hendrix and Rage Against the Machine—kind of a 100 percent-cotton rock music timeline.

Forbert, always looking for an excuse to interact with the crowd, acknowledges the Rage shirt, and you can sense the wheels starting to turn. A minute or two later, Forbert stops mid-song to comment, "You know, I can't help but picture some woman in curlers running in from outside and just beatin' on the washing machine with a broom." He resumes playing, but when the song is over, he hands the kid one of his harmonicas, the youngster's reward for being made the center of attention for a second.

I'm thinking that story will make a great ice-breaker for my interview with the journeyman folk-rocker in Charleston, West Virginia, where Forbert has come to play the renowned "Mountain Stage" syndicated radio show in late September. It's almost midnight when I catch up with Forbert, a couple hours after he had joined Marshall Crenshaw, the Verve Pipe and J.J. Cale for a taping of the show in front of a live audience. He's clearly tired but quite gracious, and as we begin he shares a grin as warm as a coal stove, which instantly melts any ice that might have required breaking.

Take away the few laugh lines that have bought up a little real estate around his eyes, and Forbert's still the spitting image of the guitar-toting Mississippian by birth/

New Yorker by the grace of Greyhound who released the aptly titled *Alive on Arrival* in 1978. His music was quirky enough—or maybe just fresh enough—to earn him stage time at new wave haunts such as CBGBs, while at the same time singer-songwritery enough to draw the "New Dylan" tag. (That was him at No. 4 on Greil Marcus' notorious "New Dylans" list, between John Lennon and Elliott Murphy.) Eight albums (including the excellent nineteen-cut career retrospective *What Kinda Guy*), a label battle or two, and many thousands of bus miles later, Forbert has released *Rocking Horse Head*, his best album since '79's horn-spiked *Jackrabbit Slim*.

Recorded for Paladin Records mostly in a four-day whirlwind in Forbert's adopted home city of Nashville, the new album's rustic songs look at lost love and its constant companions, loneliness and longing. "Real commercial themes," he says with a laugh—but clearly not autobiographical themes for the happily married father of twin boys with the soulful names of Sam and Dave and a baby girl Catherine.

All of which makes his ability to create powerful images of loss and emptiness even more impressive. The plaintive plea "Dear Lord" depicts the search for a soul-mate in simple but instantly recognizable terms ("My bed's cold, the game's old/ I'm awfully bored and blue"). "Open House" compares the newly loveless protagonist's "fading heart" and "dusty mind" to a house ready for abandonment, fond memories now looking like so much junk: "With silver dollars from a rag doll's ear/And mercury dimes for buttons, too/And flutes and whistles only kids can hear/ And peacock feathers green and blue." Another line from that same song—"Deep depression in walnut grain"—is destined to haunt me for months. And the interplay between banjo and harmonica that leads into a tasty late-song guitar solo on "Don't Stop" is so entrancing that I haven't even started paying attention to the words yet.

It's fitting that this talk is taking place on the night of the century's last total lunar eclipse, because five of the twelve songs on *Rocking Horse Head* have some kind of moon reference, most notably the Stones-y "Shaky Ground" and "Moon Man (I'm Waiting on You)." (The latter song's chorus chant of "Call, fax, e-mail soon," by the way, represents the first reference to electronic mail that Forbert and I have heard in a song.) And following in that same night-sky vein, there's always been a certain in-the-wee-hours quality to Forbert's expressive vocals.

As if a batch of first-rate songs weren't enough, the band supporting Forbert on *Rocking Horse Head* will no doubt help gain him a few new fans. Joining producer/

bassist Brad Jones are three guys who Paladin A&R man Andy McLenon [ed. note: McLenon is an occasional *No Depression* contributor] had been urging Forbert to play with and who just happened to be available for four days of recording: two members of Wilco, guitarist/organist Jay Bennett and drummer Ken Coomer, and an ex-member, anything-with-strings ace Max Johnston.

What initially seems like a slightly unusual combination makes perfect sense exactly thirty-five seconds into the album-opening "If I Want You Now," when Forbert's sandpapered pipes (the paper moving from 80 grit to 36 grit over the years) wander in over a restrained blend of mandolin, acoustic guitar and fiddle. This matchup is reminiscent of other recent pairings of cult-fave singer-songwriters with bands that are both sympathetic and solid: Vic Chesnutt getting together with Widespread Panic for last year's Capricorn Records album under the band name Brute, and Syd Straw enlisting bar-band extraordinaire the Skeletons for this year's *War and Peace* (also on Capricorn).

Mention his new friends and Forbert's words all but glow. "I like every note Jay played. And I think Ken played really great, and the more I hear the record, the more sensitively he played, I realize." And what about Max Johnston, who accompanied him on the five-song "Mountain Stage" set? "[Max's] mandolin and fiddle are the first things you hear on the record. He's responsible for all the colors."

Despite Wilco's attempts to distance themselves from the alternative-country scene, their presence on *Rocking Horse Head* is bound to lead to Forbert getting scooped up in the net currently trolling all fresh water for anything remotely alt-country. "It's still folk-rock to me" is Forbert's take on it. "If it's got a lot of country in it, that's fine. I mean, Gram Parsons walked that path a long time ago and did some great music. And it's good to see that thing is still going—why not?"

Prodded for more of his feelings regarding this most recent roots-rock resurgence, he continues: "You know, it seems sometimes these days as if sincerity is a crime punishable almost by death....And at the risk of getting in trouble here a little bit, it just seems like there's a certain amount of sincerity in, let's say, okay, the obvious ones, Son Volt or Wilco. And Steve Earle is often mentioned, and Lucinda [Williams] is often mentioned. There you go. Jimmie Dale Gilmore might be mentioned, right? And we can use that."

Forbert goes on, and when he's finished, he jokes about his rambling: "In other words, in 300 words or less, I'm all for it." However, there's a feeling that something has gone unresolved, a sense that Forbert hasn'tquite been able to express the reason he appreciates folk-rock or roots-rock or whatever as much as he does, and why he still marvels at the Byrds' "Turn, Turn, Turn" and keeps going back to Robert Johnson and Carl Perkins.

Pushing 1:30 A.M., the phone rings in my room at the Holiday Inn. It's Steve Forbert calling from his hotel a few blocks down the road. "Do you know the album *Music From Big Pink*, and the song 'In a Station'? It's one Richard [Manuel] wrote. There's a line in it that's been echoing in my mind since our conversation: 'Isn't everybody dreaming?/Then the voice I hear is real./Out of all the idle scheming/ Can't we have something to feel?' That's it. See you."

"An Old Dylan Rocks His Horse Head To A New Sincerity" first appeared in *No Depression* #6 (November–December 1996).

Selected Discography:

Steve Forbert, *Alive On Arrival* (Nemperor) 1978, reissued (Sony) 1989.

Steve Forbert, *Jackrabbit Slim* (Nemperor) 1979, reissued (Sony) 1996.

Steve Forbert, *Streets Of This Town* (Geffen) 1988.

Steve Forbert, *The American In Me* (Geffen) 1992.

Steve Forbert, *Mission of the Crossroad Palms* (Giant) 1995.

Steve Forbert, *King Biscuit Flower Hour Presents* (BMG/King Biscuit Flower Hour) 1996.

Steve Forbert, *Rocking Horse Head* (Paladin/Revolution) 1996.

Steve Forbert and the Rough Squirrels, *Here's Your Pizza* (Paladin) 1997.

Kim Richey

by Jim Caligiuri

One day last December, a coffee house in Nashville called Bongo Java made national news. Someone who works there turned one of their freshly made cinnamon buns sideways and discovered that it bore a remarkable similarity to Mother Theresa. Bongo Java also happens to be Nashville resident Kim Richey's favorite hangout. The counter help calls her by her last name and she doesn't have to order; they know what she likes. And yes, the cinnamon bun enshrined below the counter does bear a striking resemblance to the blessed Mother.

Bongo Java is precisely the kind of slightly off-center kind of place you'd expect an artist like Richey to frequent. An engaging singer-songwriter with a forceful yet pleasing voice, she may be signed to a major label (Mercury) out of Nashville, but her music is not exactly what passes for country, at least according to commercial radio these days. The lanky blonde has just released her second record, *Bitter Sweet,* a fine collection of pop songs that tugs at the heart in refreshing ways and twangs in all the right places.

Richey moved to Nashville nine years ago at the urging of her old Western Kentucky University friend Bill Lloyd, formerly of Foster and Lloyd. "I moved around a lot after college and didn't have a lot to do with music," she explains. "I can't believe I've lived here that long, because it's the longest I've ever lived anywhere. Anyway, Bill said, 'Come on down here and try it.' He also sent me the first two Steve Earle albums. At that point I'd never heard of Steve before. I just flipped over them; I thought they were amazing. So there was a combination of things that got me down here.

"But after I moved down here, I started writing songs and started learning a lot about songwriting. I started writing with Radney [Foster] and we co-wrote 'Nobody Wins,' the song on his first record that went to No. 2 on the *Billboard* chart. I sang backup on a few cuts on that record, so that got me going."

Her first record was produced by Richard Bennett, who also has worked extensively with Earle. But Bennett was not available to make Richey's second album, which left her in a bit of a panic. "He told me over lunch that he decided to go out on tour with Mark Knopfler," she says, "which was a great thing for him. But I was really bummed out because I had never even thought about making a record with anyone else."

Here the story gets a little remarkable. Richey approached Luke Lewis, the president of Mercury Nashville, about the possibility of using Angelo, her band member and songwriting partner, as producer. "Angelo and I work really well together. We would make these demos up at Polygram Publishing, where he would play everything and they would end up sounding really great. We would go in there after Polygram closed and stay up all night and do what we wanted. When you have to book a studio to do demos, you only get to do one or two takes. There we could work on one song all night and make it sound really good. We actually got a cut or two from those demos.

"So, I think it was right after that lunch with Richard, I went up to Luke's office and I hemmed and hawed a little bit. Finally I just blurt out, 'What do you think about letting Angelo produce some sides?' He goes, 'Well, how much money do you need?' And I go, 'I don't know.' I didn't actually get that far in my thinking. I didn't figure that he was just gonna say yes."

Angelo's work on *Bitter Sweet* resulted in a natural follow-up to Richey's first record. There are no big changes in her style, just a little more maturity in her songwriting. "I just do the music that kinda comes naturally to me, with all the different influences that I have," Richey explains. "Being in this town for so long has been a huge influence, you know—just being part of this musical community. I'm really proud to be from here. It's been a great place for me to be."

Indeed, Richey has remained left-of-center enough to escape the cookie-cutter mold that all too often is applied to major-label country acts in Nashville. "You get in a lot of trouble if you try to pigeonhole something," she acknowledges. Prime examples of her not getting caught up in that game are two songs on *Bitter Sweet*: "Fallin'," which was co-written by John Crooke of North Carolina alternative country band Jolene and also features him on vocals, and "I Know," which was co-written and produced by John Leventhal (known for his work with Shawn Colvin, among others). Only a talent like Richey would be able to work with such disparate writers and make it seem natural.

Richey also appeared in a duet with Crooke on Jolene's 1996 debut, *Hell's Half Acre*. "I'm hoping that we can get it together and play some shows together sometime this year," she says. "I discovered Jolene by accident, really. I mastered my first record at Ardent Studios in Memphis. That was the label that Jolene was on [Ardent Records], and they made their record there. I was up in Boston checking my messages and one was from Matt who works over at Ardent. He says, 'I got a guy here who wants to know if you'll sing on his record. Will you call me back?' My reaction was, I don't know. Who is this guy? What does his music sound like? So they got me a tape and I loved it. So of course I agreed to sing with them. We've become good friends. I think they're really talented."

With *Bitter Sweet*, Richey has avoided the dreaded sophomore slump; she has created a second record that defies categorization and done it on her own terms without any pressure. "Most of the pressure comes from within myself," she says. "I feel a little bit more pressure to succeed now than with the first one, because with that one I didn't feel any pressure. I felt that no matter what happened, I won. I got to make a record exactly how I wanted to and with the people that I wanted to. But with all the good stuff that happened to after that record came out, and after all the things that I learned about the music business, I expect more from this record."

"Sweetness Follows" first appeared in *No Depression* #8 (March–April 1997).

Selected Discography:

Kim Richey, *Kim Richey* (Mercury) 1995.

Kim Richey, *Bitter Sweet* (Mercury) 1997.

Cheri Knight

by David Cantwell

"Everything in the world that I like doing is like knitting," Cheri Knight says, and she means it. "It involves time and blood and guts and sweat and all of your best energy—and that's *why* you do it." The first time you hear Knight sing, you know she means every word of that, too. Even spread among the Blood Oranges' great albums, Knight's songs always stood out as distinctive, gripping and emotionally ambitious. Filled with the straightforward soul of her voice, her slow and intense songs can make you feel as if she were fashioning the threads of her life into something that lives and breathes, leaving you spellbound.

She's been casting those spells for quite awhile now. In 1988, after realizing that the "raging girl guitar rock thing" she'd been playing for years wasn't doing it for her anymore, Knight answered an ad placed by Jimmy Ryan in a Boston newspaper and soon found herself in the Blood Oranges. (Guitarist Mark Spencer signed on the next month.) After two albums and an EP on East Side Digital—not to mention countless live dates, including many with fellow alternative country visionaries such as Uncle Tupelo and Bad Livers—the band had gained a scrapbook full of great clippings, but not much of an audience.

"I think we came along about six years too early," Knight says in retrospect. "We'd been at it for quite awhile, and we covered as much ground as we could....We tried to sort of make things happen, but we didn't ever get to the point where we could support ourselves by doing it. And I think that fact finally got to…Jimmy and Mark, who really wanted to be making a living playing music." Knight was fortunate enough to be able to pay the bills by farming when she wasn't playing music. As Ryan and Spencer began to get other paying gigs that took them away from the band, the status of Blood Oranges became increasingly hazy. Knight finally decided to do a solo project; *The Knitter* was released on East Side Digital.

She remains close to her old Blood Oranges mates: Mark Spencer plays B3 organ on two tracks from *The Knitter*, she provides harmonies on a track from Spencer and Ryan's new *Wooden Leg* disc, and Oranges drummer Keith Levreault has often joined her for live solo dates. And she seems proud of what the band accomplished musically, even if they never quite had the impact commercially they deserved. "I hope people remember Blood Oranges and the contribution we made," she said.

In all likelihood, they will, as the Oranges' legacy looms large among the current crop of alternative country bands. There was a dark quality to Knight's work with the Oranges that was also profoundly life-affirming. Her best songs—especially "Crying Tree," her masterpiece—leave the listener devastated by life's inevitable tragedies, yet somehow better for the encounter.

While death, or its threat, rarely looms far away in her songs, the effect is never morbid. Instead, it's clear that life is a cycle, filled with its fair share of both joy and heartache, which quite naturally moves from living to dying. "Which is the perspective that anyone would get if they'd done the farming thing," she explains, referring to the New England farm life she loves and which has filled her springs and summers for years. "I used to raise dairy goats for years, and every year, when one goat would die, I'd be bummed out, but then you just know that the next spring you're going to have kids again. There's totally a connection between that perspective and my songs."

It's fitting, then, with the Oranges now dead, that Knight has been reborn as a solo artist. Recorded live and in just two days, *The Knitter* builds upon this worldly-wise vision, but often weaves Knight's stories through decidedly different surroundings. Frequently, this is courtesy of Eric "Roscoe" Ambel, who not only produced the album (as well as the final two Oranges discs), but who plays guitar throughout. A virtual explosion of Ambel's menacing guitar on the title track opens the album. He continues blazing on the following track, a great bit of alternarock called "Megalith" that could show Veruca Salt or Belly a thing or two about pop hooks and crunchy guitars. Ambel's wickedly bluesy work helps the disc's closer, a cover of Bottle Rockets leader Brian Henneman's "Very Last Time," sound less like a sad realization than a deadly threat. And along the way, Ambel adds a gorgeous twelve-string shimmer to "That I Might See" and "Waiting For Sarah."

But don't think Knight has given up on the alternative country sounds that first brought her to our attention. As it should be with a writer of her talents, the songs are the thing here, and Knight's latest batch is usually highlighted by rootsy settings that flesh out her tales of murder and suicide, of hard work and missed opportunities, with haunting fiddle and sweet flecks of mandolin. The twangy "Down By The River" could've been lifted verbatim from a Blood Oranges disc. Meanwhile, the album's moving centerpiece, "Last Barn Dance" ("You know, I think that's my favorite," she confides), adds a dash of hope and vital community to the mix: The song's character moves from a kind of willed isolation to a point where she is able to proclaim to her lover and the world, "Here we are on a road bound together, you and I."

But despite the ground swell of popular awareness that may be building beneath the alternative country sound, Knight remains humble, and a bit skeptical, of her own chances for breakout success. "I know what Triple-A radio is all about, and there really isn't anything on *The Knitter* that would catch on Triple-A as far as I can see," she says. "[My music] is either too rock or too country....Around here, Triple-A is just Sting and Bruce Hornsby and Hootie.

"But I'm really happy when my friends have good fortune, like the Bottle Rockets and Jay [Farrar of Son Volt] and now the Scud Mountain Boys. So I want to see people do well, but I think it's always good to be a little bit leery of what the business can do to things—particularly music like this that's so based in a grassroots thing. It's going to really make me angry if it gets fucked up by the industry.

"I'm just going to keep doing what I'm doing, no matter what, because it's what I love," she says. Listen to her sing on *The Knitter*, and you can't help but know that she means it.

"The Knitter" first appeared in *No Depression* #4 (Summer 1996).

Selected Discography:
Cheri Knight, *The Northeast Kingdom* (E-Squared) 1998.

Chris Knight

by Grant Alden

This is how it happened: A stack of cassettes clattered onto whatever was between them and the floor, and so in the annoyance and the cleaning one finally slipped into the deck. Out of the speakers, then, came one of those shocks that happens… well, not often enough. Not very often at all. Almost never, in sad fact.

The song is titled "If I Were You." The voice is solitary, unsanded, and an acoustic guitar tags along for comfort, but you don't notice that much because it's the song and the story being told that grabs you hard and fast, and there's no solace in that. "If I Were You" is the elegantly rendered tale of a beggar with a gun, full of regret and resignation, honest and broken, innocent and unfed.

It is as striking as the night in 1989 when Lucinda Williams unleashed "Changed the Locks" to an indifferent crowd of Cowboy Junkies fans, and they all sat back down in their chairs and started looking to see what just hit them.

Nashville is overrun with cassettes, cracked plastic swapped at night among friends, the tacit understanding seeming to be: This is what we could do if things were different. And so one accumulates albums recorded in living rooms that no label will agree to release, or albums somebody paid for but lacks the courage or the interest or the faith to release, or albums recorded before the band broke up and so why bother? And songwriter's tapes, one stacks them up. It's a transitory kind of permanent record, the last refuge of music before it succumbs to memory and the musicians turn to fresher rainbows or minimum wage.

"If I Were You" is on a four-song demo, but it doesn't take long to find out there's more, and then a friend willing to dub a copy of the whole thing. Somebody's named it *The Trailer Tapes*, and the shorthand description is that it's what might have happened had Steve Earle cut *Nebraska*.

This, then, is how one stumbles upon a one-time strip mine reclamation inspector from Slaughters, Kentucky, named Chris Knight.

The elation of discovery is tempered by the logos on the tape and the dawning awareness that one has arrived late to a party that has been going for some time. That is, Knight has been driving down to songwriter nights in Nashville for most of this decade, has been signed first to a publishing deal, then to Decca, and his eponymous debut is scheduled for a February release.

And then there is this: "If I Were You" isn't on that debut.

Lunch is early and Knight chose the spot. Brown's Diner. Tables and cuisine from a family reunion, a big-screen TV in one corner, so much wear that the bar in back has accumulated character even if it still doesn't precisely amount to style. A mile or so down West End, closer to Music Row, things get more decorous, but Brown's is across from a 24-hour laundromat, next to an army surplus store, and by that accident (if not the accommodating price of beer) has become a musician's sanctuary.

Knight might pass for a better groomed Jay Farrar, perhaps a cousin. The geography almost works, for St. Louis is the nearest big city to where both grew up. Of average height, Knight carries the casual, stocky bulk of a working man, a physique tailored to labor all day and drink all night, if needed. And, like Farrar, Knight is miserly with his words; not unkindly so, just shy. Private.

Spooked, maybe, because the interview with another writer for his bio took eight hours and two days, and this is his first proper meeting with the press. Knight is so unaccustomed to the etiquette that he even picks up the check.

And remember, this is Nashville. Chris Knight is signed to a major label, and somehow is being allowed—encouraged, even—to release a debut album entirely of his own material. (Though, being Nashville, a fair number of the songs are co-writes, including cuts with Dean Miller and Fred Eaglesmith.)

"I've been writing songs for about ten years," he says, not before his plate is clean. "And most everything I write—not everything I write—but all the stuff I write is just for myself. Nobody's beating down my door to record my songs. So...I guess they just liked 'em anyway. They liked the songs for some reason or other, and wanted me to record them. So I didn't have to convince anybody."

Thus revealing a curious mixture of confidence and indifference, and almost nothing. Knight doesn't come from a particularly musical family, and yet knew somehow that he was good enough, that he should try. "I always had a job," he says. "I never really wanted to be a bum on the street trying to get in the music business. I always had a job, and there's always a side of me that was drawn to having a normal job. I got a day job and, you know, it wasn't a bad deal."

Not a bad deal, no, just not what he wanted to do. "Let's see, January '92 I came down here and auditioned at the Bluebird for the writer's night, and they put me on the show," he says. "I played like three songs. I have one song that still survives ["Framed"], and Frank Liddell really liked it a lot. I just talked to him a little bit. I came over and played some songs, and I just kinda started—it wasn't really defined— working with him and the people at Blue Water Music Corporation, that's my publishing company. And then Frank worked for Decca about the time I signed with Blue Water, and we kept working together."

One song from that night is on Knight's debut, and yet Frank Liddell, there by accident and only to see a friend from Austin, remembers this: "'If I Were You' is the first song I heard him play at the Bluebird. The reaction was amazing. When he sings that song people just react emotionally, they don't react with their head."

And so Liddell and Greg Droman, an engineer recently moved from Los Angeles, slowly began assembling what became Knight's debut. It all sounds so easy, commonplace, even if it has taken five years.

"My deal was I stayed at home and wrote songs," says Knight. "When I write songs, it's almost like the best thing about the song is sitting and writing it, if I'm really into it. It's kind of like the guys who write short stories or something; they sit around and drink whiskey and write short stories."

Do you write prose?

"No."

Who do you read?

"Cormac McCarthy, Larry McMurtry. I've read a lot of books, John Steinbeck...it's kind of like after I read Cormac McCarthy or Larry McMurtry or somebody like that I can't read anything else."

What is it you value about that writing?

"It's just real."

How much polishing do you do?

"I wouldn't know how to go about polishing a song. I might say isn't instead of ain't. I might do that, that's about all I know to do."

Real. Knight's best songs are short stories, plain, lyric glimpses into desperate lives, coiled violence, the cockroach-endurance of the stomped-upon and still hobbled working poor. Told honest, though a good writer is inevitably a great liar. That is, these characters are fully imagined, "You know, people that I've known, family 'n' friends and just people I grew up with." These are not, then, lives Knight has lived, but characters he is able to inhabit for the duration of the song.

And so, on "Bring The Harvest Home," he is able to write with disdain of Los Angeles, though he's never been that far west (presumably co-writer Craig Wiseman has been).

"No, I've just heard about it," he chuckles. "I heard about it enough to write that I didn't like it. I seen it on TV."

How much traveling have you done?

"Not much. I've been to Florida. I just came back from Wichita this morning; I was opening for Emmylou Harris last night, so I went to a motel, and got up at 4:30 this morning, flew back here. Oh, Little Rock, Arkansas. I drove there to open for Alison Krauss. Went to St. Louis to get a few ball games in."

Roots. In a rootless, relentless, postmodern world, so many centers spinning by all at once that there is no center and nothing to do but catch as catch can and hope, Chris Knight seems to know exactly who he is and precisely what he does.

And yet, "If I Were You" is not on his debut. Nor is a song written with Eaglesmith called "Blame Me," a brutal portrait of a single mother driven to armed robbery and her estranged husband returning too late to accept responsibility.

This is unfair. The writer has songs the reader will never hear, except perhaps in concert, or, maybe, on the next record, but too many of those tapes on the floor hold songs that were meant for the next record. The result being that Chris Knight's official debut is being compared to a demo recorded, as Knight says, "in two sessions up in Kentucky. Just guitar-vocals. We'd go for a couple of days, just drinking beer and running the tape machine."

We come here to the crux, for both the singer and the critic are also capitalists. It is at this point that the art of the song and the commerce of selling music diverge. Nobody—be clear about this, please—nobody is wrong, here. There are choices to be made, and they are not easy.

But here's the thing: Those *Trailer Tapes*? They really are as good as if Steve Earle had cut *Nebraska*. Decca could have chosen to release an album as striking, as powerful, and as enduring as the debut of John Prine, one of the songwriters whose work inescapably informs Knight's. It could have been a classic. Hell, it *is* a classic, except that nobody seems likely to hear it.

Decca nearly did take that plunge. After all, they paid for (and, thus, own) *The Trailer Tapes*. "I thought it would be cool if we got all of this stuff on tape before he was a star," Liddell explains, "before he was a major recording artist. So that we have it in its most basic and innocent form, as opposed to going back and revisiting and trying to do something contrived later on. And I thought it would be something we could use initially, maybe it would be even like a pre-release or something, or an original label. And I think…the label sort of vetoed that ultimately."

Pity.

In the end, "If I Were You" didn't make Knight's debut because the properly recorded versions didn't quite fit. "We cut a really cool track," Liddell explains, "but we felt like it was a little too heavy-handed and took away from the lyric of the song. When we started mixing the record and mixed 'If I Were You,' we felt like it didn't do the song justice. So we went back and booked another session. We sat there one night for three or four or five hours recording 'If I Were You' over and over again. Well, I think we finally got something, but in a weird way I think everybody's interpretation of that song might be a little bit different….We had spent so much money at that point that we figured we'd go back and get it for the next record."

In fairness, the producers, the label, the management company, the artist even—whoever makes these calls—haven't gussied up Knight's songs too conspicuously. They've added drums, some prominent session guitar players (David Grissom, Kenny Greenburg, Richard Bennett), that's about it. Recorded live, with very few overdubs.

"There's no lies in any of these songs," Liddell says. "None of the songs were rewritten or sugar-coated so that we could possibly get airplay. I mean, we cut what Chris Knight wanted to cut, for the most part. If somebody gets killed in a song, they're going to get killed in the song and that's it."

Still, Knight is a striking artist all on his own. The drums and the supporting players pin him to a tempo, and sometimes that's not how the cadence of the song naturally falls. And they drape the trappings of ordinariness around work which is not at all ordinary. Somehow the presence of these first-class players, whose sound and confidence is comfortingly familiar, works against the rough urgency (and uncertainty, even) of Knight's songs. Especially the drums, so cleanly and conventionally striking two and four.

Then there is the matter of song selection. The most gutty, gripping, challenging songs from *The Trailer Tapes* do not appear here. This may all be accident, fate, the logic of assembling a coherent opening work. But instead of his strikingly dark compositions, we are left Knight's more anthemic, ordinary tracks, paeans to small farmers and land, love and losers. The most conventional of his works (and this is still relative, mind you) are displayed here, songs that might brush up against Travis Tritt and not jump too far back into the shadows. Knight's best songs are of the present, and most of what's on his debut is like a memory painting, an idealized re-creation of the past.

And yet this, too, is inescapably the reality of producing country music for a major label: If radio won't play it, it's dead. One is mindful of what the daily papers here in Nashville remind, that most country singers don't recoup until their record has gone gold. These are not, then, casual choices.

"Are they going to play him?" Liddell asks, and remember that he has earlier said he believes Knight will become a major artist, while spending much of his last five years working toward that goal. "I doubt very seriously that [radio's] going to play him initially. I think Chris is country. Is Chris what some of these guys are playing right now?" Liddell works around the subject for a while. "Chris is country, and his lyrics are reflective of who he is and what he's seen and where he's grown up. And he lives in Slaughters, Kentucky, a town of 400 or so. Is that not country? I could say a whole lot but I'd probably get in trouble. There's a lot of things on country radio that are not country.

"Very few things I hear right now are real. There's people that want to be stars, not people that want to be artists. Chris Knight can take making this record or leave it. His artistry, if he sat out there on his front porch the rest of his life and went back to inspecting coal mines, he wouldn't leave himself short at all."

Maybe not. But if that's where Chris Knight ends up, sitting on his front porch picking, somebody best bring a tape recorder by every week or two.

"The River's Own" first appeared in *No Depression* #13 (January–February 1998).

Selected Discography:

Chris Knight, *Chris Knight* (Decca) 1998.

Johnny Rodriguez

by Kurt Wolff

The early 1970s was one of the most exciting eras in country music. The Nashville Sound was on the wane, thanks in part to singers such as Waylon Jennings, Kris Kristofferson, Bobby Bare and Tom T. Hall. But as individualistic as these singers were, they also recognized the importance of community. So when they pushed through the doors of Music Row, they didn't let them slam, but instead held them open. Thus, the world became aware of such talents as Mickey Newbury, Billy Joe Shaver, and a Texas kid barely in his twenties named Johnny Rodriguez.

Rodriguez's rise from obscurity to top-of-the-charts fame was about as quick as it comes. He hitched into Nashville with, as he puts it, "a guitar and $14, two pairs of pants and three shirts." The first thing he did was call Tom T. Hall, whom he'd met a year earlier, and ask him for a job. The next day he was playing guitar in Hall's band; less than a year later he was on the national charts with a hit of his own. It was a fantasy-come-true picture of every lonesome picker's American Dream.

"It was wild, man," said Rodriguez during a recent phone interview, laughing at the memory. "I guess it was one of those things that was meant to happen."

Rodriguez had a dazzling burst of hits during the first half of the '70s, including "Pass Me By," "Ridin' My Thumb to Mexico" and "Just Get Up and Close the Door." His debut album, *Introducing Johnny Rodriguez,* was also immensely popular. Ripe with the dusty good looks of a gold-hearted rebel, Rodriguez also became a country music sex symbol, fueling the fantasies of eager fans who, burning with Kristofferson fever, were desperate for another fantasy figure. Times had changed, and Roy Acuff's withered mug was long out of style.

A decade later, though, despite a steady stream of hit recordings, the sexy young boy had more or less dropped out of sight. The seemingly endless tour schedule—and all the accouterments that come with the territory—had gotten the better of him, Rodriguez says.

But his longtime fans got a big surprise this past summer when he resurfaced on HighTone Records with *You Can Say That Again*, his first album in close to ten years and his most down to earth, traditionally minded collection since his mid-'70s heyday. The record features a dozen covers by songwriters ranging from classic (Merle Haggard, Frank Dycus) to contemporary (Lucinda Williams, Robert Earl Keen).

Rodriguez has had a penchant for cover material since his earliest days in the business. The first two songs he played for Mercury Records executive Roy Dea, in fact, were by Haggard ("If I'd Left It Up to You," which is on the new album) and Don Gibson. "It was just me and a guitar," recalls Rodriguez of the office demo session. "I sang 'I Can't Stop Loving You' half in English and half in Spanish, and [Dea] stopped me and said, 'I want to sign you right now.' I thought, 'What?' I couldn't believe it, man. Here I'd gone from poverty to having a recording contract in one day."

Rodriguez co-wrote all but one song on his debut album with his mentor, Tom T. Hall. "When I was traveling with Tom T., I was sort of like his secretary when he was writing songs. He'd be saying them and I'd be writing them down. And then we started writing together."

The only song the pair didn't write for that album was by Billy Joe Shaver. Another up-and-coming songwriter, Shaver was one of the first guys Rodriguez met when he got to Nashville. "Bobby Bare introduced us. As a matter of fact, I was the very first person to record one of his songs, 'Ride Me Down Easy'—except on my first album I called it 'Easy Come Easy Go'. After that, Bobby Bare jumped on it, put it out as a single, and got himself some airplay. Then Tom T. recorded 'Old Five and Dimers,' and Billy Joe was off and writing."

Rodriguez agrees that the time he got started in the business was exciting and full of superb writers and singers. He brings up the name Bob McDill and then gets excited at the mention of another, Mickey Newbury. Rodriguez's knock-down mid-

'70s version of Newbury's sad, beautiful "Poison Red Berries" is just one example of his excellent sense for timeless material.

The idea for the new album, says Rodriguez, was initiated by HighTone's Larry Sloven. "Larry got ahold of Roy Dea saying he wanted to do a project with me. I suggested we talk to Jerry Kennedy [who produced Rodriguez's earliest records], and one thing led to another." Dea and Kennedy share production credits on *You Can Say That Again*.

The arrangements are far more traditional in melody and spirit than most of what comes out of Nashville these days—which is just the way Rodriguez likes it. "We didn't even have to work on it," he says proudly. "A lot of these musicians worked with me before. And Roy Dea and Jerry Kennedy were a perfect pairing, because Roy likes his music pretty raw, and so do I. With Kennedy, it's raw, but it's a little bit cleaner."

The mix of songs—from gems by Haggard and Whitey Shafer ("When It's Your Turn to Fall") to newer material such as Williams' "Big Red Sun Blues," Keen's "Corpus Christi Bay" and Dave Alvin's "Every Night About this Time"—gives *You Can Say That Again* an extra shot of courage. Don't be put off, though, if the album doesn't blow your mind the first time around: It's a slow-grow kind of affair. After several listens, songs such as "Your Turn to Fall," Michael Hearne's "Mexico Rain" and the title track suddenly are running like rabbits through your head, drawing you back for another spin. This album may just be the honky-tonk sleeper of the year.

Sloven, Kennedy and Dea each brought in songs for Rodriguez to choose from for the album, but one the Texas singer dug up himself was "Mexico Rain," a conjunto-flavored number with a gentle acoustic guitar melody. "He's a good singer himself," Rodriguez says of Hearne. "He used to have a little group called South By Southwest. But that song is about the only one he's had recorded."

Hearne first sang Rodriguez the song during a fishing trip to New Mexico, and he liked it immediately. "I recorded it when Billy Sherrill was producing me back on Epic [Rodriguez switched from Mercury to Epic in 1979 and stayed with the label through 1985], but it was never a single. But I'd go to these Texas dance halls, and they played that song a lot. A couple of DJs down in San Antonio asked me to record it again, so I did."

"The Best Thing Going," written by Mike Geiger, Woody Mullins and Michael Huffman, is another standout. Rodriguez's voice is long, tall and heartfelt, and it's perfectly mixed against a spare background that includes piano, guitar and pedal steel. "That's a new song," Rodriguez says. "It's one of those songs I'm more comfortable with—for some reason I can sing that shit-kicking stuff real easy."

In a way, says Rodriguez, the songs on *You Can Say That Again* are all different from each other. "That's what I like about 'em—and the fact that they all in a way say something about me."

Which gets us around to the grand prize winner of the bunch, Keen's "Corpus Christi Bay," which Rodriguez says reminds him of "something me and my brother would have done." Rodriguez had heard of Keen (whose "The Road Goes on Forever" has been covered by Joe Ely and the Highwaymen) but had never heard anything the fellow Texan had recorded himself until Sloven brought him a tape of "Corpus Christi Bay." Rodriguez's recording brings the song's bright, youthful spirit to life and makes it shine.

Rodriguez was born in Sabinal, Texas—about fifty miles west of San Antonio—and grew up listening to all kinds of music. There were originally ten kids in his family—all with different musical tastes. "Everybody was always fighting over the radio," he says.

His first experience playing music was in a high school rock band called the Spocks—though perhaps the most memorable aspect of that group was the set of clay Vulcan ears he wore when he performed. "I wanted to be something different," he says, cracking up as he tells the story.

The band's glory days were short-lived. "I was singing that song, 'Oh where oh where can my baby be?' and there were some chicks sitting around, and all of the sudden my damn ears fell off." Suddenly, show biz didn't seem so glamorous. "I said, 'Okay, boys, that's it with the ears.'"

Growing up in small-town Texas, hearing country music was unavoidable. Rodriguez's inspiration to start singing it himself came partly from Merle Haggard, who during the 1960s had a string of hits about fugitives on the run and the loneliness of prison life.

You see, Rodriguez himself is an ex-con of sorts. He spent a few months in jail for stealing a couple of goats one night when he and his friends were eager for a summer barbecue. It's a story that later—after he was a bona fide Nashville sensation—was picked up by the Associated Press wire service and was run by newspapers all over the country. David Allan Coe even mentions the incident in his song "Longhaired Redneck."

That goat rustling business, though, has dogged Rodriguez throughout much of his career. "I was embarrassed to damn death," he says. "Everyone thought it was funny, but I almost went to prison for a long time."

Rodriguez, who'd just turned eighteen, was sentenced to three to seven years, though he wound up only doing about three to four months thanks to a Texas Ranger named Joaquin Jackson. "He got me a job working at Alamo Village, where they made the movie *The Alamo*. When he took me there, he said, 'Don't run off or I'll find you,'" Rodriguez recounts with a laugh. "I cleaned my act up real fast."

Rodriguez did all sorts of odd jobs at that tourist park, from driving the stagecoach to staging gunfights to singing in the cantina. "That's where Tom T. Hall heard me," he continues. "He and Bobby Bare were on vacation visiting with Happy Shahan." Shahan—who eventually became Rodriguez's first manager, and who just recently passed away—owned the park. "Tom T. told me that he'd like to have me in his band someday. I just thought he was being nice."

"The next year, though, my dad died of cancer, and then a few months later my brother was killed in a car accident. I wasn't ready to go to college, so I just took off and came up here [to Nashville]."

Rodriguez played in Hall's band for six or eight months. "He ran me off. I had had a couple of hits, and it got to where he said, 'You son of a bitch, I can't follow you anymore. Get your ass out there on the road by yourself.'

"So I took his bus and his band, and played my first gig in San Antonio at a place called the Farmer's Daughter. The next morning, after I paid for the bus and the band, I think I was in the hole about $400. I told that damn Tom T., and he said, 'Welcome to show business.' Ha-ha! Thanks a lot."

"Ridin' Back On More Than Just His Thumb" first appeared in *No Depression* #5 (September–October 1996).

Selected Discography:
Johnny Rodriguez, *Run For the Border* (Intersound) 1993, reissued (Branson) 1996.
Johnny Rodriguez, *You Can Say That Again* (HighTone) 1996.

Chip Taylor

by Grant Alden

In the keen clarity of night, just before descending into dream's solace—a craving that can no longer be admitted into the busy hours of daylight—there is always time enough to suspect that one has not fulfilled the promises of youth. That moment when the fulcrum shifts and truth is more important than the rent, and the slippage of time is more troubling than the chattering clutch.

Truth. Which eventually cloaks itself in the same shades of gray that color our days, the same one as the other. Perhaps that's why, in the hunger of innocence, the best work is done by young physicists, painters, and poets, and the most elegant compromises are fashioned by the aged, who have grown accustomed to that enterprise.

Not always.

Not quite always, for we have the careers of Stephen Hawking, Pablo Picasso, Neil Young…others; not so many, but enough. Enough so that it is still possible to go willing and armed deep into the night, to remember that it's the going and the enduring that matters, and to accept whatever truths that may reveal.

One morning last year Chip Taylor woke up and picked up his guitar, instead of the *Daily Racing Form.* And he began writing songs again, a habit he'd mostly dropped back in 1979. That was when Capitol, like Columbia and Warner Brothers before them, dropped Taylor. This would be a matter of small consequence, except that

Mr. Taylor is one of those scattered few whose work has continued to endure the vagaries of radio programmers everywhere.

To wit: He wrote "Wild Thing."

And "Angel Of The Morning." And Anne Murray's "Son Of A Rotten Gambler," co-wrote the Janis Joplin epic "Try (Just A Little Bit Harder)," co-wrote the Hollies' "I Can't Let Go"…stuff like that. Maybe somebody else has had cuts by Jimi Hendrix, Frank Sinatra and Willie Nelson, but it's got to be a pretty elite club.

It is possible that he has just released his best song (and with it *The Living Room Tapes*, his finest album since 1973's *Last Chance*), though it's hard to imagine that "Grandma's White LaBaron" will become a radio staple. Nor that anybody else could sing it. It's about his mother, her living and her dying. And it has about it the unmistakable stain of truth, hard-won words sung gently into the good night.

Conventionally told, Chip Taylor's story should be a morality play of redemption: Talented writer succumbs to the temptations of gambling, abandons his muse for years, returns to his true calling only at his mother's deathbed, finds success, happiness, and the girl in the coda at the end. Oddly enough, it's the succumbing and temptation parts of that sentence that are inaccurate, though the gal was still up in the air at last report. See, Chip Taylor was as good a gambler as he was a songwriter, and there is an excess of discipline in his story, not dissipation.

Indeed, Taylor has walked away from a very successful career to play music to small audiences wherever he's welcome. That's the remarkable and almost inexplicable part of his story, but we rush ahead of ourselves.

"Ever since I was eighteen or nineteen years old," he says in a quiet, rich voice, sitting a few steps from his guitar in a Nashville songwriter's suite, "my drive was music and gambling. When I had my first hits, I allocated a certain amount of time to both. I never really slept much, so it was a lot of work and I loved both things."

Taylor is the middle son of Elmer and Barbara Voight, a remarkable upstate New York couple—Elmer was a teaching golf pro; his short stint on the PGA tour ended with a back injury at the Bahama Open—whose three sons became a volcano scientist, an actor, and a songwriter. (The actor is Jon Voight, known for his roles in *Deliverance, Midnight Cowboy* and more than a dozen other films. Chip Taylor, born James Wesley Voight, changed his name because he didn't think the original fit.)

Chip drifted through a couple colleges in the early '60s, worked for a short time as a golf pro and became a staff writer for April-Blackwood Music. In which capacity he dashed off a song for a group called Jordan Christopher & The Wild Ones. Their version of "Wild Thing" disappeared without a ripple, and only a quirk in April-Blackwood's English publishing deal placed the single in the Troggs' hands. He also produced a bit, notably the Flying Machine, in which James Taylor (no relation) was first found.

Like most songwriters, Chip hoped to sing his own work. In the late '60s he formed a duo with Al Georgoni (with whom he wrote "I Can't Let Go"); they recorded one LP for Buddah as Just Us, then added Trade Martin and cut two more LPs as Georgoni, Martin and Taylor. Chip went solo, first for Buddah, then three LPs for Warner Brothers, one for CBS, and one for Capitol.

All along the problem seems to have been that Chip Taylor's music didn't quite fit anywhere. His are deceptively simple structures, the words given plenty of room and space, attractive places for singers to let their voices, imagination and emotion take flight. Rather like Willie Nelson's songs. Like Nelson, Taylor half-sings, half-talks his way across melodies that do not require operatic range. In Chip's case, he's simply too self-effacing to attack the microphone.

"So I had this record out that I really believed in," he says, glancing out at the rain. "I don't think the album was really that good. I'd say my most inspired work was the *Last Chance* album that came out in '73. I loved that album. And after that I was trying to find a way to fit in to different places. But the single was called 'One Night Out With The Boys,' and I loved this single. It just felt good to me, I thought it sounded like a hit.

"I wouldn't let the record company release it until we had an understanding with the country division that they would promote it, because I didn't want to go through what I had gone through before with Columbia. Their country division just refused to promote my record. So the Capitol people promised me they would, the record came out, and sure enough within a couple of weeks the thing was the most requested record wherever it was played. A couple of easy listening stations and three country stations. I talked to distributors, [and they] said it's the hottest little jukebox single they had, and in a couple of weeks I was just really excited."

And then Taylor called one of the stations that was playing his single, only to be told by the program director that they'd been asked to stop playing it. By Capitol's country division. "In retrospect, I look back and I can understand this," he says, utterly without rancor. "Let's say if I was down in Nashville signing six or seven artists. I would say, 'Well, these are my artists. Who's this guy coming in from New York with a record that I now have to include as part of my package?'"

In the end, and to keep the corporate peace, his record was dropped. "I had some wonderful sentiment from the Capitol people," he says, "but it really killed me. I said, 'What am I gonna do now?' I had another album ready to make, and I had the budget for it, and I had even started working on the next project. I just stopped making records. Neil Diamond's manager took over Polygram Records and asked me if I would help him make some decisions, because they were in the hole $60 million."

He spent a few months helping with Polygram's reorganization before turning to his other love. "It wasn't like I totally said I wouldn't write a song again, or anything like that," Taylor says, but his schedule was a bit full. "In the middle '80s I got to be partners with probably the best handicapper in the world, the guy who's made more money at it, and a wonderful, wonderful guy. His name's Earnest Bahlman.

"So it wasn't like it wasn't lucrative; it was. But it certainly was an obsessive thing, because pretty much I'm obsessive no matter what the hell I do. Gambling was the thing I'd wake up at 8:30, work like crazy for like three hours, talk to my partner Ernie for about an hour and a half, go over every race, and every little possible thing you could think about. We each had hired people at the race track to look at the horses as they came out, to look at the shoes and stuff like that, and get back to us on cellular phones about any changes.

"I'd usually drive out to Long Island and spend my afternoons with him, betting, at an off-track betting satellite where he bet so much money that they gave him an office. And maybe at six o'clock I'd drive back to my apartment and shower and change my clothes and go down to the Soho Kitchen and lay my race track work out for the next day and start to work on that. And maybe at eleven o'clock I'd break for two hours and socialize and go out and have a few drinks.

"And my life was like that. I'd do the same thing the next day. Every once in a while I'd write a song. I had no calluses on my fingers. That went on until, I guess, '95, when my mom was real ill. I started to go down to her house and sing for her. And I would sing for her and remember the look in her eyes. And it just made me feel so good.

"Playing for her, seeing her response, I remembered when I used to do it. Not so much when I did it as a business in the '70s, when I was trying to break, trying to make these hits and whatever I was doing. But the way I did the *Last Chance* album, that spirit in a way, [the way] I did it when I was younger, when I was in high school. So I got that whole spirit back.

"[Gambling] was a very unsocial thing. I mean, yes, I had my social stuff with Ernie, because when you're working with a master and he's patting you on the back and saying great job and high fivin' all day long and you're winning all this money, it's great. Hit pick-sixes for hundreds of thousands of dollars. I remember one day hitting a pick-six for $32,000, and it was like nothing. In retrospect I look back and say, What, are you kidding? I could use that to pay for my shortfall for my touring this year."

In 1995, Taylor put his racing records to the side and began to make records of his own. Three all at once, more or less, beginning with a friend's suggestion that he record his most famous songs by way of reintroduction. "So I was doing the *Hit Man* album at the same time I was doing *The Living Room Tapes*. Actually, I was doing another album, too, like a folk-rock album." There was, of course, the matter of finding a label willing to release Taylor's music once again.

"I had lots of problems," he admits. "And then this one label was interested in Vermont. Peter Gallway, one of the artists on that label, had seen me do a show and suggested I call this guy. I did and sent him my records, this Mitch Cantor at Gadfly Records. And Mitch liked my stuff very much, he said, 'Yeah, I'll put your stuff out.' He did it with such a nice spirit that I didn't even want to look anymore."

Taylor toured some of the East Coast behind *Hit Man*, selling copies of *The Living Room Tapes* from the stage; it was finally released more formally in late March, complete with a party at Douglas Corner in Nashville. Guy Clark sang along for a few songs (including a reluctant "Wild Thing"); Lucinda Williams dropped by to say hello and ended up singing on Taylor's *next* record.

Something changed within Chip Taylor during all those years at the track, and if he knows how it happened—or even what it was—he isn't saying. But somehow, at fifty-something, he has at last come to believe in the worth of his work.

"I don't know. It just started with my mom," he says. "That spirit just spiraled. I don't know why the hell Jon [his brother] is working so hard now, but maybe it was the same kind of spirit that I've had since mom passed away. I think he did six movies in the last twelve years, and now all the sudden he's done seven in the last year, or something like that.

"I'm just loving what I'm doing, and I'm not afraid of it anymore," he adds, and there is the innocence of a child gazing at the blue ocean in his voice. "I'm not afraid like I used to be, years ago, when somebody from the Rolling Stones camp called my then-publisher and said, 'I think we can hook something up with Chip and Mick.'" He shakes his head and laughs softly.

"Right away it was like, 'No way I can do that.' I didn't even think about it. I was embarrassed. I didn't want to go over there and have them see how limited I was. Because I only played three or four chords, and I could lock myself in the studio and get out of me something that I wanted, but I thought I was doing it with mirrors."

Funny thing is, as hard as Taylor tried for stardom in the '70s, he never really toured. Sure, he played around New York (usually when he was hunting a new deal), and spent a month in Holland, where he had a No. 2 record one season. "I've done more touring since October than I did in my entire life. And I'm a singer-songwriter," he laughs, and stumbles on something as if for the first time. "I mean, *how do you expect to be successful if you don't play for people?* It's pretty simple, isn't it? You'd think I would know that."

Italo Svevo, an Italian industrialist, was forty-six years old in 1907 when he showed his second book to a young James Joyce, who was his English teacher. Joyce was quite taken with the novel and suggested its English title *As A Man Grows Older*. It is the story of an aging man's fascination with a young woman. It may also be a metaphor for the difficulty of pursuing one's art past the fire of youth, but I found the novel in my early twenties and never finished it.

Chip Taylor's new songs are compelling because, like Svevo, the circumstances of his life do not compel him to fashion art out of economic desperation. Instead, his work is the product of rigorous self-examination, discipline, and an almost Zen-like stripping away of ego. As simple as they are, they hide nothing. *The Living Room Tapes* includes songs to the four important women in Taylor's life: His mother, his ex-wife who is also the mother of his two children (later, he asks that I turn the tape back on so he can tell me how wonderful his grown kids are), the woman he nearly married during the gambling years, and the woman he met recently, to whom he has written his next CD.

He's still learning. One day he turned to Cody Melville, the singer-songwriter he has pressed into service as a manager. "I said, 'Boy I love Chrissie Hynde's version of "Angel Of The Morning."'" She sings with such passion, it's one of the best versions I've heard of that song. He says, 'What the hell are you telling me for? Tell her.'

"He sent a letter over to Chrissie, and within a couple of weeks got a response back from her manager of how excited Chrissie was to get my note, and then a couple weeks after that, another message, would I write a song for Chrissie? Which I did. I don't know if it'll ever be recorded, but she's holding it, and I think it's a real cool song, she just inspired me to do it. Garth Brooks is holding the same song."

Taylor also has spent time writing with Randy Travis, who is now in search of a new record label. "I liked his earlier things more, probably, but I love him as an artist, and I was so shocked that he's such a good songwriter. And we wrote great together."

Mostly, though, Taylor is enjoying himself, and the possibilities his life has offered up. "Wherever it goes, as long as it keeps going, will be fine with me," he says. "As long as I can continue to write my songs, make my records, record them with the spirit that I want to record them, and get them out for the public and still play for people…if I can break out even and make a little bit of money, then that'll be fine."

"As A Man Grows Older" first appeared in *No Depression* #10 (July–August 1997).

Selected Discography:

Chip Taylor, *Chip Taylor's Last Chance* (Warner Bros.) 1973, reissued (Train Wreck) 1996.
Chip Taylor, *Hit Man* (Gadfly) 1996.
Chip Taylor, *The Living Room Tapes* (Gadfly) 1997.

Charlie Louvin

by Peter Blackstock

Across the evening sky
All the birds are leaving
But how can they know
It's time for them to go?
Before the winter fire
I will still be dreaming
I have no thoughts of time
For who knows where the time goes
Who knows where the time goes?
　　—"Who Knows Where the Time Goes," Sandy Denny, 1967

Just twenty years old when she wrote those words, Sandy Denny seemed wise well beyond her days, as if the spirit of the ages had been channeled through someone who couldn't possibly have gathered the life experience to make such poignant observations about the Earth's never-ending rotation. Underscoring the irony is the fact that Denny died from a fall down a flight of stairs eleven years later, leaving this world long before it was time for her to go.

But the song lives on.

September brought a rare and unexpected treasure to the record racks in the form of *The Longest Train,* the first new album from Charlie Louvin in seven years. As a member of the Louvin Brothers, whose close harmonies and memorable song-writing during the 1950s and early '60s made them one of the most accomplished and influential duos of their era, Charlie has earned an esteemed place in country music history. His brother Ira died in a car wreck in 1965, shortly after the two had stopped performing together. Charlie, now sixty-nine, has remained active, recording occasional solo albums and still appearing regularly at the Grand Ole Opry.

The Longest Train is a welcome return to the recorded form for Louvin, and an interesting pairing of his talents with a younger generation of accompanists. Produced by English singer-songwriter Julian Dawson, the album features a backing band highlighted by renowned guitarists Steuart Smith and Barry Tashian, plus harmony vocals by the likes of Rosie Flores, Katy Moffatt and Jim Lauderdale. The contents include half a dozen songs from the Louvin Brothers' heyday, as well as three written by Dawson (perhaps a bit overly indulgent on the producer's part, as these are generally the disc's weakest tracks).

But the real highlight is a trio of songs—"I Wanna Die Young (At A Very Old Age)," "Turn Around," and Denny's "Who Knows Where The Time Goes"—that seem ideally suited to an artist who has seen the birds leaving and the seasons changing often enough to have no thoughts of time. (It seems particularly fitting that Denny's song answers the title of the Louvin Brothers' classic "When I Stop Dreaming" with the lyric, "I will still be dreaming.")

"I love what the song says," Louvin said in a telephone interview from his home in Wartrace, Tennessee, in early October. "I've often wondered how do the birds know when it's time to go. The fickle friends [another lyric in the song], I can understand that—when the food and booze is gone, they leave. But the birds is another story."

Ironically, Louvin wasn't familiar with the tune when Dawson first suggested they record it, despite the fact that it was the title track of one of Judy Collins' better-known albums in the late '60s (in addition to appearing on a Fairport Convention album during Denny's tenure with that band).

"Julian gave me a record, I think it was Judy Collins," Louvin recalled, "and I couldn't understand what she was sayin'. So three or four different times I faxed Julian in London and told him, 'Julian, I need the words on that song, I can't even figure out what she's sayin', and I need the words before I can learn the melody.' So the day that he came in [to Nashville], and we were going to record that evening, he brought the words with him. So I said, 'Well, I'll tell you what, it's an odd song, it don't lend itself to the kind of music I've been doing.' I said, 'Julian, you go ahead and put your voice on this rough soundtrack, and let me take it home, with the words, and tomorrow I'll see if I can record mine.' And that's kind of the way it happened. But it's like an easy-listening song; it's not a Charlie Louvin-style song."

Indeed—and that's one of the reasons it comes across as such a revelation, with Louvin's weathered-and-worn yet still special voice providing the soul and spirit that Denny's words seemed to call for in the first place, at last fully realized three decades hence. It's intriguing, however, to hear Louvin refer to it as "an easy-listening song," given that Denny is considered one of the primary figures in British folk-rock.

A similar situation surfaces later when we're discussing Texas country singer/ yodeler Don Walser, with whom Louvin was scheduled to play a show at the Broken Spoke in Austin later in October. "He sings a fine two-step song," Louvin said. "If I were to go out dancin', I'd like to go where Don was playing, but I'd have to set out three-fourths of the tunes because it was rock 'n' roll." Don Walser—rock 'n' roll? Well, there's an observation you don't hear every day.

Louvin's uncommon perspective in both of these instances simply reveals that he's from a different era, when "rock 'n' roll" or "easy listening" or "country" may have carried very different meanings than they do today. It also points out the shortcomings of genre tags as a way of describing or categorizing music; how else to explain a classic country artist such as Louvin being covered in a magazine devoted to "alternative country"?

Of course, much of the reason classic country artists are more likely to be discussed in alternative avenues nowadays is because the powers-that-be in modern-day Nashville no longer dance with those who brung 'em. "If I had a big truck, I could round up a truckload of good artists who have made the record companies millions, but do not have a label in this town today," Louvin says. He knows whereof he speaks, as he was in the same boat (er, truck) until Dawson convinced the folks at Watermelon, an Austin-based indie, to sign Louvin.

"I first met him [Dawson] in England, I think in '88," Louvin said. "He asked me what I was recording on, and I told him nothin', I'd just kinda got tired of playin' the game. Because about the time you think you've learned the rules, then all the players change, from the top again. So I just got tired of playing the games. I work all I want to, and I didn't feel that I had to shine boots to get a record deal. So I told him that, and he said, 'Well, that's sinful. If I find a label that would pay for a session and put it out and distribute it, would you do it and let me produce it?' And I agreed to do that."

It took a few years before Dawson was able to arrange the deal with Watermelon, which had worked with Dawson both as a solo artist and as a member of Plainsong, a reunited British ensemble that also includes Denny's old Fairport Convention bandmate Iain Matthews. Dawson was largely responsible for gathering the musicians who played on *The Longest Train*, most of whom Louvin had never met.

One exception was guitarist Barry Tashian, whose storied career includes opening the Beatles' 1966 U.S. tour as leader of the Remains as well as stretches playing in the bands of both Gram Parsons and Emmylou Harris. "I'd met him before; in fact, I'd worked in England on a show that he was on, and I knew that he was with Emmylou at one time," Louvin said.

Tashian's involvement with Parsons led us to the subject of Gram's love for the Louvin Brothers' catalog, expressed in his own rendition of "Cash on the Barrelhead" on *Grievous Angel* and in the Byrds' version of "The Christian Life" on *Sweetheart of the Rodeo*. As an artist who played a major role in bridging the gap between country and rock audiences, Parsons seems partly responsible for keeping the Louvins' music alive through a couple of generations.

Louvin knows one person, at least, to whom Parsons introduced the music Ira and Charlie recorded. "I would have to thank Gram Parsons for introducing the Louvin Brothers sound to Emmylou," he says. "Emmylou tells me that Gram said, 'I've got something here I want you to hear.' And he played it, and Emmylou said, 'Who is that girl singin' the high part?' And he said, 'That's not a girl, that's Ira Louvin.' And she has been very kind to the Louvin Brothers music catalog; she cut about four of five of our songs."

Of course, Harris and Parsons haven't been the only ones to carry on the Louvin Brothers' legacy. Both Southern Culture on the Skids and Uncle Tupelo have recorded "The Great Atomic Power," and several acts have recently revived "Knoxville Girl," a song the Louvins didn't write but were generally responsible for popularizing. Much of the Louvins' music has also recently been made available to the public again, thanks to a Razor & Tie compilation, *When I Stop Dreaming: The Best of the Louvin Brothers*, released last year, and Capitol's reissues this summer of the classic Louvins albums *Tragic Songs of Life, Satan Is Real* and *A Tribute to the Delmore Brothers*.

Asked if he's surprised to see songs he and Ira played four decades ago still surfacing on today's musical landscape, Louvin replies, "I don't think I'd use the word surprised. It pleases me. I mean, I think they've carried it as far as it can be carried. And so, when you go as far down a road as you can go, you either have to turn left or right and go out in the woods, or you gotta turn around and come back."

"Turn Around," in fact, is the title of the last song on *The Longest Train*, and it's a song Louvin himself turned around and came back to. "It goes way back. I heard a Harry Belafonte recording of it many years ago," he said. "I heard it about the same time I heard the song 'I Gave My Love A Cherry,' which was originally named 'The Riddle Song.' I guess it would've been forty years ago, or more, that I first heard those, so they're old tunes."

"Turn Around" appears on the record as a guitar-and-vocal-only number. While Louvin himself wasn't particularly pleased with the version—"I would've liked for it to have been better; other instruments could've been on it"—it seems a beautifully minimalist way to conclude the album, with only Steve Wilkerson's Spanish guitar backing Louvin's lonesome vocal as he sings the longing lines, "Turn around, you're two/Turn around, you're four/Turn around, you're a young man/Going out the door."

As with Louvin's version of "Who Knows Where The Time Goes," this song vividly demonstrates the emotional impact that an artist in the autumn of his years can deliver. "Just because you get forty or forty-five or fifty, or even as old as I am, that don't mean that you can't perform anymore," Louvin says. "But the major labels absolutely won't look at you…and I think that's tragic, because some of the best music is done by older artists. I think that basically the whole world is wasting all their youth on the young these days."

Louvin's careful distinction between the words "youth" and "young" in that comment mirrors the sentiment put forth in Helen Hudson's "I Wanna Die Young (At A Very Old Age)," the penultimate and perhaps most significant track on the new record. Ironically, it was also one of the last songs to be selected for the album.

"I first heard that song in April or May of this year, just like a month before we cut it," Louvin says. "I was up at the Opry one night, and there was a kid there, this kid's not older than twenty-one or twenty-two years old. He calls himself Dak; I think his name is David Alley. He's a very young writer, and we were just sittin' in there, me an the people workin' with me was running through a song, and he said, 'Would you listen to a song that I play?' And so I handed him the guitar and let him sing it. And I loved what it said. It just kind of floored me that a twenty-two-year-old man would be thinking like that."

Indeed, the song seems tailor-made for Charlie Louvin. With a spring in his voice that bounces along to the song's rollicking arrangement, he declares, quite simply, all that needs to be said:

Over the hill there lies old age
But I ain't a-gonna walk that way
If I lose a step or miss a beat
It won't knock me offa my feet
Life's too short to let it kill me.

"Magic Songs Of Life" first appeared in *No Depression* #6 (November–December 1996).

Selected Discography:

The Louvin Brothers, *Tragic Songs of Life* (Capitol) 1956, 1996.

The Louvin Brothers, *Satan Is Real* (Capitol) 1959, 1996.

The Louvin Brothers, *A Tribute to the Delmore Brothers* (Capitol) 1960, 1996.

The Louvin Brothers, *Songs That Tell A Story* (Rounder) 1978, reissued (Capitol) 1996.

The Louvin Brothers, *Live at New River Ranch* (Copper Creek) 1989.

The Louvin Brothers, *Radio Favorites* (Country Music Foundation) 1990.

Charlie Louvin, *Louvin Brothers Music Celebration* (Strictly Country) 1995.

Charlie Louvin, *The Longest Train* (Watermelon) 1996.

The Louvin Brothers, *Christmas With The Louvin Brothers* (Razor & Tie) 1997.

ND-101

The name *No Depression* was chosen for a magazine about alternative forms of country music in large part because it concisely mapped out the continuum of performers—from the Carter Family through Uncle Tupelo and beyond—who have provided us with such enormous pleasure. At our publisher's suggestion, and for your entertainment, we have created the more formal discographical primer which follows.

It wasn't easy. These 101 titles reflect the collective wisdom of seven of *No Depression*'s principal contributors. We imposed two rules: First, all titles on the final list had to be in print, and second, only one title per artist. David Cantwell, Bill Friskics-Warren, Roy Kasten, and Linda Ray did most of the work; Jon Weisberger served as our technical delegate for bluegrass affairs; Grant Alden and Peter Blackstock refereed and tossed out the odd hand grenade.

Unhappily, Music Row's disinterest in its own past made this task all the more difficult. That is, many titles we would have wished to include on (or consider for) this list are currently out of print. Some of the most egregious examples of that indifference are included as a separate list of "travesties" below.

Because country music traditionally has been far more concerned with singles than with albums, many of the titles we have chosen are greatest hits compilations of one form or another. In some instances, we felt this was the best reflection of an artist's career; in others, it was the only choice we had.

In any case, this list, like all human endeavors, is imperfect, and is intended only as a jumping-off point, as a reminder of a rich and rewarding heritage. Enjoy, and happy hunting.

1. **ROY ACUFF**, *The Essential Roy Acuff 1936-1949* (Columbia/Legacy) 1992.

2. **DAVE ALVIN**, *Blue Blvd.* (HighTone) 1991.

3. **BAD LIVERS**, *Delusions Of Banjer* (Quarterstick) 1992.

4. **CHUCK BERRY**, *The Great Twenty-Eight* (Chess) 1982.

5. **BLUE MOUNTAIN**, *Dog Days* (Roadrunner) 1995.

6. **DOCK BOGGS**, *Country Blues* (Revenant) 1998.

7. **BOTTLE ROCKETS**, *24 Hours A Day* (Atlantic) 1997.

8. **BR5-49**, *BR5-49* (Arista),1996.

9. **RICHARD BUCKNER**, *Devotion + Doubt* (MCA) 1997.

10. **BUFFALO SPRINGFIELD**, *Again* (Atco) 1967.

11. **T BONE BURNETT**, *T Bone Burnett* (Dot/MCA), 1986; reissued (MCA Special Products) 1994.

12. **BYRDS**, *Sweetheart Of The Rodeo* (Columbia/CBS), 1968; reissued (Columbia/ Legacy) 1997.

13. **CARTER FAMILY**, *Anchored In Love: Complete Victor Recordings 1927–1928* (Rounder) 1993.

14. **JOHNNY CASH**, *The Essential Johnny Cash 1955–1983* (Columbia/Legacy) 1992. Box set.

15. **ROSANNE CASH**, *King's Record Shop* (Sony) 1987.

16. **RAY CHARLES**, *Modern Sounds In Country & Western Music* (ABC-Paramount), 1962; reissued (Rhino) 1988.

17. **GUY CLARK**, *Keepers* (Sugar Hill) 1997.

18. **PATSY CLINE**, *The Patsy Cline Story* (MCA) 1989.

19. **COWBOY JUNKIES**, *The Trinity Session* (RCA) 1988.

20. **CREEDENCE CLEARWATER REVIVAL**, *Chronicle: The 20 Greatest Hits, Vol. 1* (Fantasy) 1988.

21. **J.D. CROWE & THE NEW SOUTH**, *J.D. Crowe & The New South* (Rounder) 1975.

22. **IRIS DEMENT**, *My Life* (Warner Bros.) 1994.

23. **HAZEL DICKENS & ALICE GERRARD**, *Hazel & Alice* (Rounder) 1973; reissued 1995.

24. **BOB DYLAN AND THE BAND**, *The Basement Tapes* (Columbia) 1975.

25. **STEVE EARLE**, *I Feel Alright* (Warner Bros./E-Squared) 1996.

26. **ALEJANDRO ESCOVEDO**, *Gravity* (Watermelon) 1992.

27. **EVERLY BROTHERS**, *Cadence Classics: Their 20 Greatest Hits* (Rhino) 1985.

28. **FLATLANDERS**, *More A Legend Than A Band* (Rounder) 1990.

29. **FLATT & SCRUGGS AND THE FOGGY MOUNTAIN BOYS**, *The Complete Mercury Sessions* (Polygram) 1994.

30. **FLYING BURRITO BROTHERS**, *Farther Along: The Best Of The Flying Burrito Brothers* (A&M) 1988.

31. **FREAKWATER**, *Feels Like The Third Time* (Thrill Jockey) 1993.

32. **LEFTY FRIZZELL**, *Look What Thoughts Will Do: The Essential Lefty Frizzell, 1950-1963* (Columbia/Legacy) 1997.

33. **JIMMIE DALE GILMORE**, *Spinning Around The Sun* (Elektra) 1993.

34. **GRATEFUL DEAD**, *Workingman's Dead* (Warner Bros.) 1970.

35. **WOODY GUTHRIE**, *Dust Bowl Ballads* (Victor) 1940; reissued (Rounder) 1988.

36. **MERLE HAGGARD**, *Down Every Road: 1962–1994* (Capitol) 1996. Box set.

37. **TOM T. HALL**, *Storyteller, Poet, Philosopher* (Mercury) 1995.

38. **EMMYLOU HARRIS**, *Pieces Of The Sky* (Reprise) 1975.

39. **BUDDY HOLLY**, *Greatest Hits* (MCA) 1996.

40. **JOHNNY HORTON**, *Honky Tonk Man: The Essential Johnny Horton 1956-1960* (Columbia/Legacy) 1996.

41. **WANDA JACKSON**, *Rockin' In The Country: Best Of Wanda Jackson* (Rhino) 1990.

42. **JASON & THE SCORCHERS**, *Fervor* EP (Praxis) 1983; reissued (EMI America), 1984; reissued (Mammoth) 1996.

43. **JAYHAWKS**, *Hollywood Town Hall* (Def American) 1992.

44. **GEORGE JONES**, *The Spirit Of Country: The Essential George Jones* (Epic/Legacy) 1994.

45. **DOYLE LAWSON & QUICKSILVER**, *Rock My Soul* (Sugar Hill) 1981.

46. **LEAD BELLY**, *Where Did You Sleep Last Night* (Smithsonian/Folkways) 1996.

47. **JERRY LEE LEWIS**, *Killer Country* (Mercury) 1995.

48. **LITTLE FEAT**, *Little Feat* (Warner Bros.) 1971.

49. **LOS LOBOS**, *How Will The Wolf Survive?* (Slash/Warner Bros.) 1984.

50. **LOUVIN BROTHERS**, *Satan Is Real* (Capitol) 1959; reissued 1996.

51. **LORETTA LYNN**, *Honky Tonk Girl* (MCA) 1994. Box set.

52. **LYNYRD SKYNYRD**, *Street Survivors* (MCA) 1977.

53. **MADDOX BROTHERS & ROSE**, *America's Most Colorful Hillbilly Band* (Arhoolie) 1993.

54. **JIMMY MARTIN**, *20 Greatest Hits* (Deluxe) 1994.

55. **DEL MCCOURY**, *Don't Stop The Music* (Rounder) 1988.

56. **MEAT PUPPETS**, *Meat Puppets II* (SST) 1983.

57. **MEKONS**, *Original Sin* (*Fear And Whiskey* plus extra tracks) (Twin/Tone) 1989.

58. **BUDDY MILLER**, *Your Love And Other Lies* (HighTone) 1995.

59. **EMMETT MILLER**, *The Minstrel Man From Georgia* (Columbia/Legacy) 1996.

60. **ROGER MILLER**, *King Of The Road: The Genius Of Roger Miller* (Mercury) 1995.

61. **BILL MONROE**, *The Music Of Bill Monroe: 1936 To 1994* (MCA) 1994.

62. **WILLIE NELSON**, *Red Headed Stranger* (Columbia) 1975.

63. **NITTY GRITTY DIRT BAND**, *Will The Circle Be Unbroken?* (United Artists), 1972; reissued (EMI America) 1994.

64. **ROY ORBISON**, *All Time Greatest Hits Of Roy Orbison* (Monument), 1972; reissued (Columbia/Legacy) 1989.

65. **BUCK OWENS**, *The Buck Owens Collection, 1959–1990* (Rhino) 1992.

66. **GRAM PARSONS**, *GP/Grievous Angel* (Reprise) 1973, 1974; reissued 1990.

67. **DOLLY PARTON**, *The Essential Dolly Parton, Volume Two* (RCA) 1997.

68. **JOHNNY PAYCHECK**, *The Real Mr. Heartache: The Little Darlin' Years* (Country Music Foundation) 1996.

69. **CARL PERKINS**, *Original Sun Greatest Hits* (Rhino) 1986.

70. **ELVIS PRESLEY**, *The Sun Sessions* (RCA) 1976.

71. **RAY PRICE**, *Night Life* (Columbia) 1963; reissued (Koch) 1996.

72. **CHARLEY PRIDE**, *In Person* (Koch) 1998.

73. **CHARLIE RICH**, *Feel Like Going Home: The Essential Charlie Rich* (Epic/Legacy) 1997.

74. **MARTY ROBBINS**, *The Essential Marty Robbins: 1951–82* (Columbia) 1991.

75. **JIMMIE RODGERS**, *First Sessions, 1927–1928* (Rounder) 1991.

76. **ROLLING STONES**, *Exile On Main Street* (Rolling Stones Records) 1972.

77. **BILLY JOE SHAVER**, *Old Five And Dimers Like Me* (Monument) 1973; reissued (Koch) 1996.

78. **JEAN SHEPARD**, *Honky Tonk Heroine: Classic Capitol Recordings, 1952–1964* (CMF/ CEMA Special Projects) 1995.

79. **SILOS**, *Cuba* (Record Collect) 1987; reissued (Watermelon) 1994.

80. **CONNIE SMITH**, *The Essential Connie Smith* (RCA) 1996.

81. **HANK SNOW**, *The Essential Hank Snow* (RCA) 1997.

82. **SON VOLT**, *Trace* (Warner Bros.) 1995.

83. **SONS OF THE PIONEERS**, *Country Music Hall Of Fame Series* (MCA) 1991.

84. **BRUCE SPRINGSTEEN**, *Nebraska* (Columbia) 1982.

85. **THE STANLEY BROTHERS**, *The Early Starday/King Years, 1958–1961* (Starday/ King) 1993. Box set.

86. **HANK THOMPSON & HIS BRAZOS VALLEY BOYS**, *Vintage Collections* (Capitol) 1996.

87. **ERNEST TUBB**, *Country Music Hall Of Fame Series* (MCA) 1991.

88. **UNCLE TUPELO**, *No Depression* (Rockville) 1990.

89. **TOWNES VAN ZANDT**, *High Low And In Between/The Late Great Townes Van Zandt* (Poppy) 1972, 1973; reissued (EMI) 1996.

90. **VARIOUS ARTISTS**, *Anthology of American Folk Music* (Folkways) 1952; reissued, 1997. Box set.

91. **VARIOUS ARTISTS**, *For A Life Of Sin: A Compilation Of Insurgent Chicago Country* (Bloodshot) 1994.

92. **VARIOUS ARTISTS**, *From Where I Stand: The Black Experience In Country Music* (CMF/Warner Bros.) 1998. Box set.

93. **GILLIAN WELCH**, *Revival* (Almo) 1996.

94. **KITTY WELLS**, *Country Music Hall Of Fame Series* (MCA) 1991.

95. **WILCO**, *Being There* (Reprise) 1996.

96. **HANK WILLIAMS**, *The Original Singles Collection…Plus* (Polydor) 1990. Box set.

97. **LUCINDA WILLIAMS**, *Sweet Old World* (Chameleon) 1992.

98. **BOB WILLS & HIS TEXAS PLAYBOYS**, *Anthology 1935-1973* (Rhino) 1991.

99. **WHISKEYTOWN**, *Strangers Almanac* (Outpost) 1997.

100. **TAMMY WYNETTE**, *D-I-V-O-R-C-E* (Epic) 1968; reissued (Koch) 1998.

101. **NEIL YOUNG**, *Rust Never Sleeps* (Reprise) 1979.

TRAVESTIES:
ALBUMS WHICH SHOULD NOT BE OUT OF PRINT
OR OTHERWISE MIGHT MAKE THE ND-101

BOBBY BARE, *Bobby Bare Sings Lullabys, Legends And Lies* (RCA) 1973.

BLASTERS, *Non-Fiction* (Slash/Warner Bros.) 1983.

BLOOD ORANGES, *The Crying Tree* (East Side Digital) 1994.

GLEN CAMPBELL, *Reunion: The Songs Of Jimmy Webb* (Capitol) 1974.

FLYING BURRITO BROTHERS, *Gilded Palace Of Sin* (A&M) 1968.

GREEN ON RED, *Gas Food Lodging* (Enigma) 1985.

WAYLON JENNINGS, *Honky Tonk Heroes* (RCA) 1973.

JIM & JESSE AND THE VIRGINIA BOYS, *Berry Pickin' In The Country: The Great Chuck Berry Songbook* (Epic) 1965.

JIMMY MARTIN, *You Don't Know My Mind (1956–1966)* (Rounder) 1990.

MOON MULLICAN, *Seven Nights To Rock: The King Years, 1946–1956* (Western) 1981.

O'KANES, *Tired Of The Runnin'* (Columbia) 1988.

THE OSBORNE BROTHERS, *Yesterday, Today And The Osborne Brothers* (Decca) 1968.

RANK & FILE, *Sundown* (Slash/Warner Bros.) 1982.

SILOS, *The Silos* (RCA) 1990.

SIR DOUGLAS QUINTET, *Together After Five* (Smash) 1970.

JOHN STEWART, *California Bloodlines* (Capitol) 1968.

JAMES TALLEY, *Got No Bread, No Milk, No Money* (Capitol) 1975.

HANK THOMPSON, *At The Golden Nugget* (Capitol) 1961.

TOWNES VAN ZANDT, *Live At The Old Quarter* (Tomato) 1977.

HANK WILLIAMS JR., *Hank Williams Jr. & Friends* (MGM) 1975.

LUCINDA WILLIAMS, *Lucinda Williams* (Rough Trade) 1988; reissued (Chameleon) 1992.

Contributors

No Depression co-editor **Grant Alden** lives in Nashville, Tennessee, where he writes about music, sports and art.

Eric Babcock resolutely avoided country music in his native rural Michigan until the day in his early teens when he was third-row witness to a Johnny Cash concert at the Allegan County Fair. He got right in a hurry.

Peter Blackstock, co-editor of *No Depression*, moved to Seattle in 1991 from Austin, Texas. He writes a weekly column for the *Seattle Post-Intelligencer* and has contributed to various publications including *The Rocket, Pulse, Request, Rolling Stone, The Bob*, and the Texas Chili Parlor men's restroom wall. He also served as archivist for the South by Southwest Music Festival from 1989–1997.

Brad Buchholz is a freelance writer based in Austin, Texas, who has written about sports, music and other interests for such publications as *The Dallas Morning News, Texas Monthly, Inside Sports* and *Sports Illustrated*.

David Cantwell is a college composition instructor and freelance music writer from Kansas City, Missouri. He is a contributing editor to *No Depression* and *Rock & Rap Confidential* and is the author of *Liner Notes—George Strait: An Illustrated Musical History*. His work has appeared in the *Houston Press*, Miami *New Times*, Phoenix *New Times, Trangin'!, Addicted To Noise* and the *Kansas City Star*.

Jim Caligiuri is a transplanted New Yorker currently living in Austin, Texas, with his two cats, Waylon and Willie. Besides *No Depression*, his writing has appeared in *CMJ, Pulse!, Newsday, Austin Chronicle, Houston Press* and *New Country*.

Rick Cornell fled upstate New York to central North Carolina eleven years ago, moving for the climate but staying for the Backsliders, 6 String Drag, Whiskeytown, *et. al.* In addition to contributing to *No Depression* and the power pop bimonthly *Amplifier*, he writes a local music column for *Record Exchange Music Monitor*.

Debbie Dodd moved from Seattle to San Francisco in 1989, escaping grunge by the skin of her teeth. She works for Rhino Records and lives in Oakland with her husband —also a *No Depression* contributor—whom she met on the No Depression music bulletin board on AOL.

Bill Friskics-Warren is a Nashville-based cigar-smoking distance runner, an ordained minister, a lapsed advocate for the homeless, and a full-time critic of music nobody listens to.

Phil Fuson is a Knoxville, Tennessee, guitar-twanger and *bon vivante*. This is his first (and only) published prose.

After seven years of writing about music, **Ross Grady** has finally come to his senses. He is now more or less content just to listen to the stuff. He's currently living in Chapel Hill, North Carolina, where he eagerly awaits the inevitable collapse of the entertainment industry.

Roy Kasten is a writer, teacher and songsmith in St. Louis, Missouri. He is a contributing editor at *No Depression*, and his work regularly appears in *The St. Louis Riverfront Times* and *Country Standard Time*.

Jon Maples is a Bay Area writer and editor.

David Menconi is the music critic at the Raleigh (North Carolina) *News & Observer*. A contributing editor for *No Depression*, he has also written for *Spin, Billboard, Request,* the Music-Hound record guides and a host of other publications that have since gone out of business.

Linda Ray started her grandson's record collection with the Replacements, Smokey Robinson and the Louvin Brothers. First published in *No Depression*, she has since inflicted prose on readers of *Option, Guitar World, RockrGrl* and the *San Francisco Bay Guardian* website. She also edited and published *The Original Alt.Country Community Cookbook* and adds that she has an MBA, an office job and a passport with only Communist countries on it.

Tom Skjeklesaether is a Texan trapped in a Norwegian's body, senior writer at Norwegian rock magazine *BEAT* and promoter of the annual alternative country (whatever that is) festival, Down On The Farm in Halden, Norway.

Allison Stewart is a freelance writer living in Chicago.

Jim Walsh is the pop music columnist for the *St. Paul Pioneer Press*. Before that, he was music editor at *City Pages* in Minneapolis. Before that, he was singer/songwriter/producer/booker for the late-great Minneapolis band Laughing Stock/REMs. He has written for lots and lots of music and non-music publications. He lives in Minneapolis with his wife, Jean and their son, Henry.

Kurt Wolff is a San Francisco-based freelance writer who pines for a cabin in the woods and feels country music is the next best thing to being there. He's currently writing *The Rough Guide to Country Music*.